THE PEOPLES OF KENYA

THE PEOPLES OF KENYA

by

JOY ADAMSON

Epilogue by

G. W. HUNTINGFORD

B.SC., D.LIT.

A HELEN and KURT WOLFF BOOK

HARCOURT, BRACE & WORLD, INC.

NEW YORK

To
the people of Kenya
and to
all those who love Kenya

CONTENTS

COLOR PLATES

NOTE BY THE AUTHOR

I have lived in Kenya since 1937, and I have been fortunate in being able to spend much of my time on safari, often using donkeys or camels as pack animals, camping in remote areas, and seeing no white people for months on end.

My life in Kenya has been closely associated with the Coryndon Museum,[1] because of my interest in botany, and with the Game Department in which my husband George served as Senior Game Warden of the Northern Frontier Province, an area of one hundred and twenty thousand square miles. Our home was at Isiolo, the headquarters of the province, but we spent most of our life in the bush. I became deeply interested in wild life and fascinated by the African people, and these safaris—which also took me into other parts of Africa—gave me a unique opportunity of collecting anything that I found of interest, and of making a considerable photographic record of what I saw.

I taught myself to paint and so was able to make a pictorial record. First I painted the indigenous flora, then the coral-fish along the coast, and eventually I made portraits of the people of Kenya. Some of my paintings were used for illustrating books, while many more were purchased for the Coryndon Museum in Nairobi and the Fort Jesus Museum at Mombasa, where they are now exhibited. In all these fields I am an amateur, with all the advantages and disadvantages that having no academic training entails.

Because my roots are in Europe, I have the greatest respect for all that man has achieved, but in those parts of Africa where Nature has not been tamed by man, I found a much bigger world than that we have created within our Western culture. This wild world, where the balance of Nature is still law, is fast disappearing and today men need to find a way of preserving it: some compromise which will save it without impeding the progress of their own development.

In my books about Elsa the lioness: *Born Free, Living Free,* and *Forever Free,* I wrote of my experiences with animals. In the present book I am writing about the people of Kenya and their traditional life as it is lived, where it has not been touched by foreign influence. I shall not attempt to cross the threshold of anthropology, or to comment on current developments; I shall simply describe the experiences I have had and mention the problems I have observed when different cultures and races meet and have to live together. The conflicts and difficulties involved are a challenge to all of us, and I hope that my narrative and the reproductions of my paintings and photographs may make a small contribution to a better understanding of the efforts which the Kenyans are making in order to play a constructive part in the family of man.[2]

[1] Now the National Museum.

[2] The years covered by this book are prior to the independence of Kenya; the political and administrative organization here described have, of course, no counterpart today and some of the areas referred to now bear other names.

Similarly the abbreviations used to denote various posts and regions belong to the same period.

CHAPTER I

HOW IT ALL BEGAN

On a glorious morning in September 1945 I was listening to the waves of the Indian Ocean washing against the beach. My husband George and I were at Malindi, a popular holiday resort on the Kenya coast. For the past month, the Mohammedan population here had been under the strain of the long fasting period of Ramadan, which had ended with the rising of the moon on the previous night. The final ceremonies *Id-el-Fitr* were to be held that morning in a large public hall facing the sea, and George and I had been invited to attend them. As I dressed for the occasion, I had no idea that this day would become one of special significance for me.

In general I seldom plan anything but, instead, find myself driven by my curiosity to find out about things which I see happening around me. Anything I have carefully planned has never worked out, while, on the other hand, I have often found myself deeply enslaved to something which started as a hobby.

As we mixed with the gay crowd approaching the hall, I was fascinated by the colorful setting. The white coral stone of the simple building, framed by scarlet clusters of flamboyant trees, was in striking contrast to the blue sky and the still deeper blue of the Indian Ocean. Inside the hall the scene was even more vivid. Along the whitewashed wall the dignitaries of the Arab community, their sharp features often framed by long beards, were seated. Their heads were either covered by bright turbans or crowned with a *sagal* (a quadrangular head-rope worn over a loose cloth) and they wore long robes of softly draped material.

Amongst them I recognized some of the shop-keepers who usually shuffled about the narrow streets of the bazaar in less ornate garments; today all looked like figures who might have stepped straight out of the Arabian Nights' palace.

The *Liwali*, the head of the Arabs in this district, presided over this picturesque assembly. Sheikh Azan was notable for his many years in Government service, which had earned him unrivaled popularity and distinction. He was a patriarch of the Hadramaut and with his sensitive features and long white beard he certainly embodied my idea of Arab nobility. He sat in a heavily carved chair, richly ornamented with inlaid ivory, next to the District Commissioner, who wore a stiffly starched white uniform which showed off the decorations he had put on for the occasion.

I was fascinated by the scene and, hardly listening to the official speeches, became more and more obsessed by the wish to paint one of these men. Although so far I had only painted flowers in water-color, I could not resist this challenge and ambitiously hoped that by experimenting I would learn how to paint portraits.

As soon as the addresses were over, I asked the District Clerk if he could arrange for one of the shop-keepers to sit for me in his festive garments. The Clerk promised to do his best and I could hardly wait for the next morning when I expected him to arrive with a model.

We were staying at the District Commissioner's guest-house, a small, two-roomed bungalow right on the beach. By hanging up a blanket to soften the bright glare and shelter us from the strong breeze, I improvised a studio in the open verandah. The next morning, as I sat waiting for my model, I saw to my surprise the tall figure of the *Liwali* himself approaching. He was dressed in the robe he had worn at the assembly which was made of deep-indigo cloth, richly embroidered along the edges with gold and scarlet thread. He carried a silver-hilted sword attached to a belt heavily embroidered with silver and his commanding face was crowned by a turban of fine silk interwoven with gold and scarlet thread.

My heart sank. Ought I to have the courage to confess that I had no right to waste his time by asking him to sit for a portrait that I had no idea how to make— or should I boldly pretend that I was a portrait painter? Looking at this superb Arab, I found I could not resist the temptation to pretend.

Then, torn between my bad conscience and my struggle to catch the likeness of my sitter, neither of which was eased when he told me that he had recently posed for a well-known French artist, I labored on for several hours. By this time the *Liwali* seemed as exhausted as I was, but at least something was in the sketchbook that looked vaguely like a head. I have kept this rather unsatisfactory painting more as a memento of the tolerance of a tactful model who had surely from the start seen through my pretence, than for any other reason.

Soon afterwards I planned to go to London as I was ill and needed treatment, and I began to wonder how I could occupy myself during evenings which would certainly be lonely in a city where I then had few friends. Suddenly I had an idea. Why shouldn't I carve a set of chess-men in ivory, of which each figure would represent tribesmen, animals or things that I had seen in the Northern Frontier District? The pawns might be African girls and boys, the knights giraffes, the castles phallic towers, such as we had found amongst ruins along the coast, and so on. We bought some ivory chips from the Game Department which I sawed into blocks of three different sizes.

16

I was not leaving for a few weeks and during this time George was called to deal with cases of game poaching in Marsabit; this seemed an ideal opportunity to make sketches which I could later use for carving my chess-men.

Mount Marsabit lies halfway up from Isiolo in the direction of the Ethiopian border; it is a beautifully forested range, of volcanic origin, which rises like a green island from the surrounding Kaisut Desert. Hidden in the dense forest lie several craters which fill up during the rains; to these elephants, buffaloes, greater-kudus and many other animals come to drink. Except for the craters, all life at Marsabit depends for water on two springs in the forest, and therefore few people can live in this area.

As Marsabit is of strategic importance, an Administration Post and Police Post are established there, and there is also a mission belonging to the Church Missionary Society. A few shops supply essential goods for the BORANA,[1] RENDILE and GABRA people, who come from the plains below to do their shopping or to visit friends.

Most of the inhabitants around Marsabit are Borana. To be in a good position to detect the poachers, we camped in a remote part of the forest. Here we came across some men wearing unusual garments. They were dressed in a white cloth resembling a toga, and wore a phallic emblem above their foreheads, and their hair was interlaced with fiber and shaped into a kind of halo. They kept away from us and we were told that they were Borana *Gadamoji* elders going through the final ritual stages of a circumcision cycle lasting eight years.

Our Borana Game Scouts acted as intermediaries and eventually succeeded in persuading one of the elders to pose for me. As soon as I started sketching, I found the flies attracted by his greased body so irritating that I put a mosquito net over both of us. This kept the flies away, but forced me to sit too close to my model for comfort, for his ointments exuded a very strong smell. When I felt I could bear it no longer, I suggested that he should have a rest and get himself some tea. But he was eager to oblige me and indeed ritual custom demanded that he should be particularly kind, so he asked me to continue and I was left with no choice but to live up to his good manners and go on painting.

During the next weeks I painted as many Africans as I could get to sit for me. I was still wrestling with the problem of how to do a portrait; with each sketch I tried a new technique, but my main ambition was to catch the expression and character of the sitter.

These first sketches were rather crudely executed water-colors, but the features of the people and the ornaments they wore were so arresting that when, on the boat to England, I showed them to a fellow-passenger, he advised me to offer them to Michael Huxley, then the editor of the *Geographical Magazine*. To my great surprise some were accepted and reproduced in color.

When I came to carve the chess-men for which these sketches had been made, I found the ivory extremely hard to work. I knew that when Africans carve ornaments out of ivory, they soak it for several weeks in cow manure to let the ammonia content soften the substance. But when I tried this out, in a more hygienic and concentrated form, I found that the ivory lost its characteristic texture and soon cracked into fine lines. Eventually I used an electric dental drill, but did not find this satisfactory and for the time being gave up carving.

While I was in London, I took the opportunity of studying for three months at the Slade School of Art, but this was too short a time for me to get beyond the very early stages, such as sketching the capitals of Greek columns, which I found difficult to relate to portrait painting.

After my return to Kenya I was surprised when Sir John Ramsden became interested in the sketches I had made for the chess-men and bought them for the Coryndon Museum in Nairobi.

A short time later I joined a Swedish expedition to Ruwenzori, the so-called 'Mountains of the Moon', because I wanted to paint the alpine flora near the glaciers. On our way home we met, to our surprise, a small group of Pygmies who were living temporarily at the foot of Ruwenzori. Two of them agreed to pose for a sketch and I was also able to buy from them a woman's necklace, a heavy iron ring as thick as my thumb with a few ornamentations engraved on it. It was just big enough when bent to the shape of a horseshoe, to fit around a person's neck. I couldn't find out how this iron ring was put on a woman's neck and removed again after her death. This was not the only puzzle that I met with: in my small collection of African ornaments I have two similar necklaces, but the material used was aluminium instead of the traditional iron ore which tribesmen found in dry riverbeds. One of these necklaces I had collected from the KAMBA, a BANTU tribe who live near Nairobi, and the other I found among the Gabra, who are HAMITES and live near the Ethiopian border in the Northern Frontier District. Was it only a coincidence that peoples so different and living so far apart wore the same type of necklace? Or could it give a clue to their origins and relations?

Although I had only a scanty knowledge of the migration of the Kenya people, I knew that the Bantu now living near Lake Victoria had come from the west and south; while those now living in Central Kenya had originally dispersed from the Teita Hills; from the Teita Hills many more had moved to the coast, but were later driven by the invading GALLA, most of them further south along the coast, and a few into the Meru country near Mount Kenya. I knew that the Hamites and the NILO-HAMITES had come from the north and that the LUO, the only

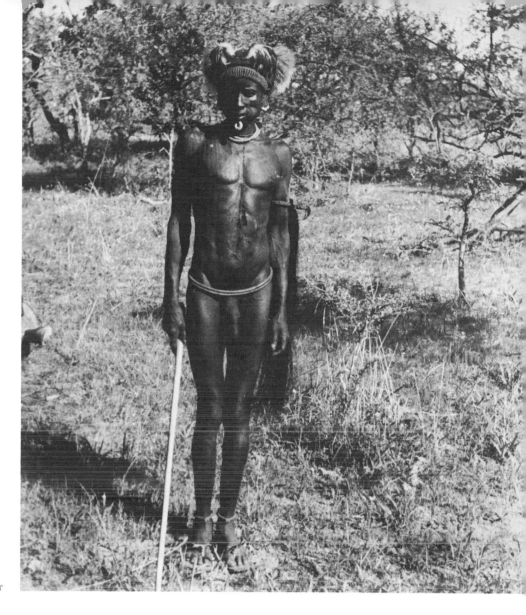

1. Kadam warrior

pure Nilotic tribe in Kenya, had moved from the Nile and Eastern Uganda to settle by Lake Victoria. Perhaps some of these people had met during their various migrations and exchanged customs and ornaments?

After our Ruwenzori expedition I joined my Swedish friends for another month up at Mount Elgon on the Uganda-Kenya border and continued to paint the alpine flora. We camped in the moorlands, close to the peak of this extinct volcano at an altitude of about fourteen thousand feet. Here we met the KONY, a small tribe of NANDI stock, who had remained on the forested slopes of this mountain at heights of up to ten thousand feet, while the rest of the Nandi had moved to various parts of the Rift Valley. They are also sometimes called the ELGON MASAI, probably owing to their habit of building huts similar to those of the MASAI and because they graze their cattle, wherever possible, in the forest. I was fortunate that I was able to add two paintings of these rather shy people to my collection.

19

After our stay at Elgon, we made a short safari to the north, camping in the plains near Kacheliba. One day two men walked into our camp wearing nothing but magnificent head-dresses, and carrying spears (1). These were KADAM, a small group related to the SUK. We could not understand each other's language, but after I had given them tobacco and sugar they agreed to sit for me. One had his hair moulded with mud into a large hood which extended to his shoulders and was ornamented with a few ostrich feathers (pl. I, p. 33). Both men were dignified and friendly.

2. Suk warrior

CHAPTER 2

THE NILO-HAMITES
OF THE RIFT VALLEY

All these experiences made me become more and more interested in painting Africans, so, as I had a few months at my disposal, I decided to paint some of the tribesmen of the Rift Valley Province. The Africans of this area had been very little exposed to European influences and wore their traditional garments. Most of the inhabitants of the valley were Nilo-Hamites, which accounted for their fine looks and great height. As many of the Administrative stations were in remote parts of the country, a pass was needed to enter the areas. I was lucky that the District Commissioner of Kitale near Elgon was a friend of mine, for he was very helpful when I asked him for introductions to the various District Commissioners of the province. As a result, I was invited first to Kapenguria, the Administrative Center of the West Suk

All I knew about the Suk was that they were divided into the pastoral or East Suk (also called the Plains Suk), and the agricultural or West Suk (also called Hill Suk), and that they were Nilo-Hamites (2).

Like the neighboring TURKANA, the men wear a chignon of shoulder length hair, moulded with a special bluish clay into a thick pad which hangs down the neck. At the bottom a flexible spiral is inserted; it is carved from the horn of an Oryx antelope, wrapped tightly around with hair from a giraffe's tail. It is very resilient and where its end touches the chignon again, the fur of a hare is attached like a pompom. To begin such a chignon, the short hair is twisted into tiny plaits away from the forehead in a particular pattern across the skull. As it gradually grows longer, it is mixed with clay and shaped into a small pad on top of the head, a process that is continued until the hair becomes long enough to be shaped into a proper chignon. Then a patch of hair, about two inches wide, at the edge of the forehead is separated and worked with clay into an oblong, shieldlike shape. While it and the chignon are still wet, little sockets made of gut or dried cow teats are inserted into the soft mixture of hair and clay and their ducts widened until they can be used to hold ostrich feathers. Their colors, as well as the painted lines along the edge of the chignon, indicate the stages of training through which a

3. Suk men

warrior is passing. Until recently it was the custom of the eldest son when his father died to cut off the chignon and add it to his own. After each successive death this was repeated, with the result that one sometimes saw chignons hanging down to the waist, the heritage of several generations. Sometimes a chignon was shaped into a thin hood extending to the tip of the shoulders and hanging in a triangular shape down the back. My Kadam friend had worn such a chignon.

To prevent these bulky head-dresses from getting damaged during sleep, the men carry a small, wooden two legged head-rest and so have a pillow handy whenever they want to rest. Although it might appear uncomfortable to sleep with the head bent almost at a right angle, this position is known to induce sleep. These head-rests are used by the Suk and Turkana; sometimes they also sit on them.

In Kapenguria the European population at this time numbered only the District Commissioner's family and an agricultural officer, and we enjoyed the peaceful life of this remote station which lies tucked away in a beautiful forest in the Cherangani Range. I had no difficulty in finding men to pose for me (3). All they wore were fur capes over their back and elaborate head-dresses (4).

I learned that here the women made the pottery and that no man, or uncircumcised person, was allowed to watch them at work. The married women were easily recognized not only by their ornaments, but also by a leather bracelet worn on their right wrist which must never be removed, and which is the equivalent of our

22

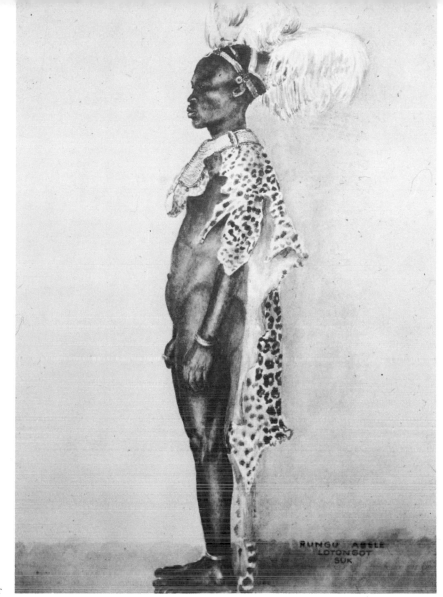

4. Suk warrior

wedding ring (5). A man may have as many wives as he can afford, but only a very rich Suk would have as many as ten wives. Should a woman be barren, her husband can divorce her, paying compensation in terms of goats and grain to her father.

The Plains Suk are a mixture of KARAMOJONG, Turkana, and Hill Suk. This can be recognized by their common use of the chignon, of shields which are oblong and very narrow, and of head-rest stools. All wear wrist and finger-knives, lip-plugs and nose-discs, and capes made of skins. The Hill Suk (6) share with the Nandi the circumcision rites and the custom of extracting the two lower middle incisors. Both Plains and Hill Suk speak a language very similar to Nandi.

After spending three weeks at this attractive place, I moved on to Tambach, another of the remote Administration outposts in the Rift Valley where I hoped to paint some of the ELGEYO people.

JEPTEROKWA LOTAEN
RIWUA
SUK

5. Suk married woman

The way led across windswept plains at an altitude of 8,000 feet, then I reached the Elgeyo escarpment. From here I overlooked part of the gigantic trough of the Rift, its wall breaking abruptly some 5,000 feet into the Kerio Valley, only to rise equally steeply immediately beyond the river of that name to the Kamasya escarpment; these two parallel mountain ranges ran north for some hundred miles, beyond them still another two ranges ran parallel towards Lake Rudolf. After having found my bearing in this magnificent scenery of desert and rock, I descended along precipitous cliffs to a narrow ledge where, at an altitude of 6,500 feet, is Tambach. Here are a D.C., a D.O. and an Education Officer who administer the Elgeyo and MARAKWET. Both people are often described as cliff-dwellers because the hilly country forces them to cultivate their crops of maize, millet,

24

6. Suk elder

beans and coffee on whatever ledge they can find. An irrigation system bringing water from a few mountain streams makes this escarpment—in spite of its steepness—into one of the best watered areas of Kenya. The Elgeyo and Marakwet are under an obligation to maintain the ditches, and anybody failing to turn up for duty after three days' notice, or not sending at least his sister, is fined one goat.

Nobody knows who originated this system of irrigation, since the present inhabitants found it when they arrived. It is generally believed, but wrongly, that the SIRIKWA, an extinct section of the Masai who were pushed out by other Masai, are responsible for its construction. Ruins just below Tambach, consisting of two or three parallel circular stone walls built around a central mound, are also attributed to these people. The District Commissioner, who was a friend of mine and interested in archaeology, kindly detailed some prisoners for excavation work which yielded pottery, tools and arrow-heads different from those used by the present inhabitants.

My studio was close to the District Commissioner's office so I could pick my models from the people crowding daily to it. My first choice was a local chief. In

7. Elgeyo chief

this district chiefs were elected by a council of elders and their status was not hereditary as in most other places. My model wore a magnificent coat of blue monkey fur and had a fly-switch made from the long white hair of a Colobus monkey. His head-dress was a large pompom of black ostrich fluff which almost covered his fat, friendly face. His good humor put everybody at ease, and he was very popular. He was proud of his beautiful carved ivory snuff box which he used frequently, and of a thick ivory bracelet, made from a large elephant tusk, obtained

26

no doubt before poaching was controlled (7). In those days the Colobus monkeys were also killed for their striking skins, and many people still carried little bags made from their fur in which they kept charms and pay-codes. Later I painted an elder wearing a coat of Colobus fur worked into an impressive black and white pattern.

One day my attention was drawn to a girl of about fourteen who wore an elaborate head-dress of beads and tiny metal chains and a necklace of bamboo sections (8). I was told that these indicated that she had recently undergone clitoridectomy and that she was in a state of seclusion which would last for three months. However, her state of seclusion did not prevent her from being painted by me. For the time being I was satisfied with painting the girl in her traditional ornaments and did not take any particular interest in the initiation rites she had undergone.

8. Elgeyo girl in seclusion

27

I did, however, learn various things about the Elgeyo including the fact that they practice, what might be called trial, marriage. If a young couple decide to marry, the girl lives with the man for about two months before the wedding, at which time he presents her father with beer. Should the girl become pregnant within the next twelve months, a beer party is held and the bride's mother is given two goats, and the ceremony seals the union; after the birth of a child, marriage becomes indissoluble, and there is no divorce. On the other hand, should the girl not become pregnant during the year, the couple is under no obligation to each other and the man can look for another wife.

Most men had their hair braided into pigtails and greased with ocher and fat, but once I noticed a young man wearing a head-ornament of blue beads of a distinctly Egyptian style (9). I was fortunate that this youth agreed to sit for me, as his set of blue beads was the only one of its kind I have ever seen. He was a Marakwet, whose people lived some distance to the north. The District Commissioner arranged for me to visit them and offered me a lift on a lorry he was sending there for the day, so that I would be able to bring back some models. During the drive through the magnificent cedar forest, I watched Colobus monkeys jumping from tree to tree with outstretched arms; when the sunlight caught their long hair, they looked more like fantastic flying dragons than leaping monkeys. I also saw many flowers that were unknown to me.

When we arrived we found a large crowd enjoying a market day. Among women selling sweet potatoes, bananas, gourds and pottery, and old men squatting by heaps of sandals made of old car tires, tobacco wrapped into small packages made of leaves, bars of soap, and beads, the young warriors strode about proudly. They were partly covered with an ocher-dyed hide, well impregnated with fat to make it soft, which was knotted over the right shoulder and hung loose to their knees. Each man carried a spear and a wooden club. Most of them had their hair twisted into tiny plaits, smeared with fat and ocher, which either fell to their shoulders or were tied into pigtails, though some wore it as a mop. This is the custom of all Nilo-Hamites in Kenya with the exception of the Turkana and Suk, who wear a chignon. I photographed as many young warriors striding around as I could before the sun set, at which time we were due to return to Tambach. After several punctures in the dark forest, we arrived exhausted at dawn.

I had found some splendid models among the Marakwet (10, 11) and it took me several days to paint them. The women dressed like the Suk (12). The men also used the Suk type of spear, although they hunted with bow and arrow—otherwise their customs, though not their garments, were akin to those of the Elgeyo.

After painting the Marakwet, I moved across the Kerio Valley to Kabarnet which is situated on top of the narrow Kamasya range; from here the Nilo-Hamitic

9.   Marakwet warrior wearing Egyptian style head-dress

10. Marakwet
warrior

KAMASYA or TUKEN, the NJEMPS and East Suk are administered. The Njemps
were originally Masai with whom they have most customs in common. After they
broke away and settled at Baringo, they took up agriculture. In this they have
been very successful. As early as 1880 they supplied fresh provisions to Joseph
Thomson and Count Teleki who explored in this area and ever since then they
have provided food for caravans.

By good luck my arrival coincided with preparations for a visit by the American
writer, Attilio Gatti, who wanted to film the tribes around Lake Baringo. The
District Commissioner and his family, who had invited me to stay with them,
suggested a drive to the lake so that I could select good models from among the
people who were being assembled for Gatti's visit.

30

11. Marakwet warrior

Winding our way down a very steep road, we soon left the cool forest and reached the Baringo plains. The heat here was in great contrast to the brisk highland climate of Kabarnet and was only bearable under the shade of a few acacias close to the lake, where there was a small rest-house. A European was camping there; he had been sent to improve the local fishing methods and thereby to increase the food supply. He was also teaching the Africans how to catch crocodiles in a way less dangerous than the one they used. The traditional method was to fish near the shore in shallow water in which crocodile swarmed. To avoid accidents, two men stood on the right and left at a short distance from the fishermen, well hidden behind rocks or vegetation, and made a sound like 'im-im-im' which attracted crocodiles from far across the lake. Soon, their periscopic noses appeared from all directions moving towards the callers, without apparently becoming aware of the fishermen who were placed between these decoys.

31

12.   Marakwet woman dressed similarly to Suk

I found this way of attracting crocodile most intriguing, and tried to 'im' as they did, but not a single crocodile responded to my efforts till I observed that the Njemps callers blocked their noses with two fingers to achieve a nasal sound. Copying them, I at once attracted more crocodile than I cared for. I do not know why crocodile respond to the sound 'im'; they themselves make no sounds, except

KADAPAN LOKODO
MUTUTI
KADAM

KOMANJO LEKENG
MARTI. BARINGO
NJEMPS

JOY

13. Njemps warriors

for a belching noise when calling their young, yet presumably the vibration of the 'imming' carries a message to them under water.

Meanwhile the first of the Africans summoned for Gatti's visit had arrived. They were Njemps warriors (13), who approached from a distance in great leaps and then crouched behind their oval shields, pointing their spears; as they came nearer, they increased their short runs and howled threatening war cries. Their faces were hardly visible under their head-dresses made from the mane of a lion and which reminded me of busbies and were tied under the chin (14) (pl. II, p. 34). When the warriors reached us, some collapsed and fell to the ground unconscious, their limbs jerking, while others stood trembling as if ready to drop at any moment. Their frenzy was so great that it took them a long time to recover.

I have never known what to think about such frenzies. Some seemed genuine, some looked contrived, or was it only a matter of degree? The Masai are well known for throwing fits, and the Njemps are an offshoot of this highly strung people. I found it difficult, however, to reconcile such hysteria with the more phlegmatic Bantu. I remember an occasion when we were camping on the Tana

BATAN LAMBARAN
MIBURI BARINGO
NJEMPS

14. Njemps warrior

River. We had been invited by our cook to see a dance given by his people, who belonged to the MALAKOTI tribe which is of Bantu stock. When we arrived in his village after dark, everybody was already in a festive mood. Bedecked in their best ornaments, the people sang to the beating of drums while the bright moonlight glistened on the river and on palm leaves. Everybody was enjoying the party, except our cook, who seemed not popular with the girls and however hard he tried to attract their attention, was always ignored. This obviously hurt his self-respect and, since we were there as witnesses, his pride too. In despair he worked himself into such a state that he threw fit after fit, rolling unconscious on the ground with only the whites of his eyeballs showing and foam bubbling from his mouth. His friends poured water over him, but he recovered only for short spells. I suggested that we should leave while he was in one of his fits. But as soon as we rose, he jumped to his feet, looking normal, stood at attention, and asked, 'What would you like for your dinner—pancakes or banana fritters?'

Now at Lake Baringo, more and more Africans and their families arrived, glittering spears and metal arm-coils reflected the sunlight, and the excited chatter of hundreds of people drowned all conversation in our party. I thought that we looked pretty drab surrounded by these Suk and Njemps who wore leopard or monkey fur capes over their athletic bodies, crowned their heads with ostrich plumes, and carried glittering spears. Their women were equally colorful, decked in their ornaments of beads and metal.

The District Commissioner told the people of my wish to paint a few of them, and after many hours of arguing we selected some splendid models.

While this went on, the Africans made the best of the occasion; small groups of dancers formed and competed with each other to the rhythmic chanting of the onlookers. I watched the Njemps with fascination: they jumped straight up in the air, their legs rigid, and when the soles of their feet again touched the ground they instantly propelled themselves up again. It was an astonishing sight, and it made me wonder whether such hard landings must not affect their heads. The singing and dancing went on late into the night and, judging by what we could see in the flickering light of campfires, everybody had a good time.

Next morning I started painting a Njemps youth about twelve years old who, with another youngster, had joined the party only after dawn (pl. VII, p. 55). We called them Tim and Tot.

They wore a black dyed hide, knotted over one shoulder, which fell loosely to the ground and was held in position around the waist by a string of cowrie shells. The hide, I was told, had to be the property of a woman. Their faces were blackened with ash, which showed up the bright plumage of the sunbirds which dangled from a string around their heads. Two ostrich feathers were fastened behind their ears, the ends meeting at the backs of their heads. A chain of crudely shaped iron rings hung from their shoulders and each boy carried a small bow and arrow, the points covered with balls of dried resin.

I learned that these youngsters had recently been circumcised and that it was customary for them to walk about for a month in this circumcision dress. During this period they lived isolated in the bush. With their blunted arrows they shot the little sunbirds whose bodies they hung around their heads. For fun they also shot at small girls who, if hit, had to present them with an iron link from their ankle ornaments. This trophy was then added to the chain on the boy's shoulder.

Although Tim and Tot were undergoing their seclusion period, they seemed neither shy nor reluctant to be painted. Later when I tried to persuade less willing people to pose in their circumcision dress, their pictures became of great value to me.

I stayed on by the lake after the District Commissioner's party returned to Kabarnet and was provided with an Askari, a tribal policeman, to act as interpreter and to see that all went well. The local people were greatly intrigued by my work and crowded round me as I painted. A few were rather suspicious and even frightened when I started to paint their portraits; they had never sat for so many hours, at such close range, in front of a European woman, let alone one who was staring at them intensely. Having myself several times sat for a portrait, I knew what a strain sitting is. Here there was the added difficulty that I could not talk to my models to keep their minds and expressions alive. Only a few of them spoke Swahili (the *lingua franca* of East Africa). My knowledge of it was rather scanty, so even when they did I could only go on for so long asking questions concerning the number of wives, children or livestock they had. At first it was a great strain to concentrate on painting while at the same time stimulating my sitter so that he would not look rigid or bored, or fall asleep. But in time I learned to put them at ease by admiring their ornaments, making·them laugh, or offering them tobacco or sweets, and, of course, they all knew that a baksheesh was waiting for them, the amount of which I had previously fixed with the District Commissioner, when I had finished my painting.

I soon realized that my being a woman was a great advantage, for I doubt whether any African woman would have posed for a man.

Usually I painted from eight in the morning to five in the afternoon with an hour's break for lunch. It took me from ten to fifteen hours to complete a life-size portrait if there were not too many detailed ornaments. These I often had to finish after the sitter had left, adding the correct color to the endless strings of beads I had previously outlined.

I found water-color the best medium when I was travelling, as it dries quickly and I could wash off the fine mica or dust which the wind frequently blew across the paintings. My studio was usually under a tree or in a shady place. These technical problems were of less importance, of course, than establishing contact

38

JOY

MTOME LOSENG
GALEOSO IRIZE
TURKANA

LOSURU TYOCHO
SABA
TURKANA

15. Kamasya girl at Kabarnet in circumcision dress of bamboo sections

with the models. Here in Baringo the people were so friendly that it was easy to get on with them. I never felt nervous while camping amongst them and my only moments of anxiety were during the night, when the hippos in the lake came ashore and I heard their deep vibrating booms uncomfortably close to my tent.

41

iv   Turkana elder

The neighbouring Kamasya, or Tuken, are of Nandi stock and they have in common many ornaments and customs. They live on the Kerio side of the Kamasya escarpment which is so steep in parts that by 1937 it was one of the worst eroded areas in Kenya. They were the people I intended to paint next, and while in their territory I often wondered how they managed to grow any crops on their steep hills.

One day I met a girl wearing a large 'apron' of over-lapping bamboo sections. She was evidently going through her seclusion after clitoridectomy and it was very difficult to persuade her to sit for me (15). By now I was not satisfied with only painting girls in the costume they wore after clitoridectomy – I wanted to know more about these intiation rites and began making inquiries, but the people here were very evasive in their answers.

From Kabarnet I went on to Kapsabet, the Administrative Center for the Nandi.

The Nandi and the Masai belong to the most important Nilo-Hamitic group in Kenya, and from their stock many sub groups have splintered off. Although both Nandi and Masai are cattle owning people and have many common customs, they differ in many ways. To the Nandi group belong the Kamasya, Elgeyo, Kony, SABEI, KIPSIKIS, the Suk and Marakwet, all of whom live in Kenya; and the TATOG or BARABAIG who live in Tanganyika. Considerable literature on the Nandi exists, of which the works of Hollis, Hobley, and Huntingford are the most important. Aftcr rcading these books, I became increasingly interested in the initiation rites. Unfortunately, on this occasion I could not paint them as the ritual cycle was not on. I now realized that initiation was one of the most important events in the life of those Africans who practiced it, and I was convinced that one could better understand many of their customs if one knew something of these rites.

The short time I had spent painting portraits of Africans had already made me aware of the importance of studying tribal life and of comparing and recording in paintings traditional ornaments and customs before they vanished. Although I had lately been in districts where the people were least affected by foreign influence, it was clear that even in these parts it would not be long before the spears and ocher-plaited hair would disappear and bicycles and sewing machines be brought in.

I had so far painted individual Africans purely because of their merit as subjects for portraits, but now I began to think how much more interesting it would be to paint a systematic record of *all* the peoples of Kenya, which would portray their occupations, rites and traditional clothing before they adopted Western ways of life.

No amount of money would induce the people to let a stranger witness their intimate rites of which circumcision was the most secret. Only by convincing the most progressive of the chiefs and elders of the importance of preserving a record of Kenyan traditional culture for future generations could one perhaps hope to

42

16. Nandi warrior

win the co-operation of the people. To do this, I should need not only help from the government, but also funds. At the moment I had no such assistance, so I carried on as before, painting elders, warriors (16), dancers, girls, and married women (17) (pl. VIII, p. 56).

While I was at Kapsabet, a new memorial hall was being built in honor of the Nandi who had been killed while distinguishing themselves in the Burma Campaign of World War II. When the District Commissioner asked me if I would paint a life size oil portrait of a Nandi in Burma kit, I hesitated for I had only twice before used oil and then for small heads. Eventually I suggested that he would be under

17. Nandi married woman

no obligation to accept the painting if it turned out to be a failure, but that if he wanted it, I should be paid fifteen pounds.

I felt very nervous about my first 'commission', particularly as I had no idea how to compose such a large picture, besides which I needed to place the model's wide-

44

brimmed hat, his rifle and a lot of medal ribbons in their correct position. Luckily for me, the occupant of the other room of the guest-house, a government official, returned from safari just as I was trying to place the rifle at the right angle. As an ex-Army officer, he was able to come to my rescue and ensure that my model's appearance was correct. When he heard what I was doing, he asked to see my pictures. He was interested because he was the Commissioner of Social Welfare, and therefore closely associated with the Ministry for African Affairs. After seeing my paintings, he offered to show some of my work to the Governor and to try to interest the members of the Legislative Council in the possibility of commissioning me to paint a record of the most important tribes of Kenya. I agreed enthusiastically.

When I had completed the picture for the memorial hall, and seen it hung there, I made arrangements to visit Turkana, which is by far the largest district of the Northern Frontier Province, covering some thirty thousand square miles. Although I knew the eastern part quite well from previous safaris with George to Lake Rudolf, I had never been in the western area, which borders on Uganda, the Sudan and Ethiopia. The Turkana have been little influenced by the Europeans for this was a closed district and visitors needed special permits. Luckily the Provincial Commissioner knew me and gave me an entry permit, though it was against current regulations for a woman to go there on her own. He also arranged for me to travel to Lodwar—headquarters of Turkana—under the escort of a District Officer who was at the time in Kitale, which is not far from Kapsabet.

To reach the District Officer's lorry at the hotel at Kitale, I had to work my way through a crowd gathered around it admiring the spectacularly dressed Turkana tribal policemen who were adjusting the loads. These Askaris, well accustomed to arousing public attention, pretended to be unaware of the sensation they were causing. Like most Turkana, they were of slender build, about six feet tall, their muscular bodies covered only by a tightly fitting short blue loincloth, edged with a bright red band. A red 'T.P.' stitched on the front of the cloth and the traditional chignon, adorned with ostrich feathers, completed their uniform. Totally aloof, the Askaris went on with the loading of the truck.

Soon after we had started our two hundred mile journey, we left the forested hills of the Suk and descended two escarpments where the hot air hit us like a furnace. We continued across sandy plains with rocky outcrops, merged together by a haze of red dust which was now and then whipped by sudden gusts into dust-devils, that whirled like giant columns across the country until they dissolved. Thorny candelabra *euphorbia* and spiky *sansevieria* blades made up the meager vegetation which became more desolate as we drove further north. To save the tires from the heat, we only camped for a short time during the night, pushing on

45

18.   A group of Turkana at Lodwar

over ground which was covered with lava boulders until we reached Lodwar; the
fort which housed the Administrative H.Q., stood on a small hill and was surrounded by stone walls. Because of the heat the buildings had neither doors nor
windows. Tribal policemen patrolled continually along the top of its walls. A few
African shops made of mud and corrugated-iron clustered around the fort; these,
together with three flat-roofed houses for the Europeans and a dispensary, made
up the whole of Lodwar. I was offered a mud rondavel painted chrome green, with
pigment found locally, which gave a cooling effect.

Close to the *boma*[2] ran the River Turkwel, a seasonal tributary of Lake Rudolf,
which is forty miles distant. At this time of year it was reduced to a few stagnant
pools fouled by animals, and the water supply for Lodwar was pumped through
pipelines from bore-holes in the river. These also fed a swimming pool which was
the social center for the few Europeans and a great luxury in a place where the
rainfall is only seven inches a year.

The District Commissioner arranged for some elders to appear in their ornaments so that I could choose my models (18). This group of tall Turkana was

46

impressive; most were adorned only with head-dresses of ostrich plumes and ivory plugs under their lower lips; a few also wore leopard capes. The dignified bearing of these men impressed me very much, as did their capacity to do with few possessions: a two legged wooden head-rest, a spear and a wrist-knife were all they needed to carry for comfort and security in a country which is one of the hardest that men live in. Little has changed in the lives of the Turkana since they migrated some hundred and fifty years ago from the Jie country west of Lodwar in Eastern Uganda. Following the rains, they drive their camels, cattle, sheep, goats, and donkeys across the sandy plains, grazing them on the meager vegetation and them-selves living on berries, meat, milk and blood. Blood is obtained by bleeding the animals from the jugular vein or, in the case of sheep and goats, from under the eye, using a special arrow. To provide for the dry season, Turkana make powdered milk by letting vast quantities of liquid milk dry on skins. They are the only people I know of who eat crocodile and lion; we had often watched our Turkana Game Scouts eating these animals.

The Turkana can supplement their diet with fish. With wicker traps or nets they catch in the shallows the delicious Giant Tilapia Nilotica and Nile perch, both survivors of a period some fifteen thousand years ago when Lake Rudolf was con-nected with the Nile. One day we took a cooling dip in the lake, as usual keeping a sharp lookout for crocodiles, while watching the local Africans spearing fish, a skill in which they are experts.

In spite of, or perhaps because of, this difficult life, the Turkana are a most robust and virile people. They make by far the best game trackers, as they are not only exceptionally fearless, but also seem to possess a special knowledge of wild animals. They are Nilo-Hamites, but do not circumcise and are apt to look with contempt on those who do.

While selecting my models, I wondered why some of them used only brown hen ostrich feathers for their head-dresses while others used only black cock plumes. I learned that these men belonged to an age-set system whose members have to help each other in any way they can. The color of the ostrich head-dresses changes with each generation and if the father belonged to the black feathered group (19), called the Stones (*imurut*, plur. *ngimur*), the son automatically belongs to the brown feathered group, called the Leopards (*erisite*, plur. *ngerisai*) (pl. III, p. 39). The Stones are regarded as senior to the Leopards. Illegitimate sons belong to the same group as their fathers.

One morning a man arrived wearing superb ornaments; he had walked eighty miles and crossed three flooded rivers. I was struck by his serene expression and painted him, making him pose in profile to give the fullest view of his ornaments (pl. VI, p. 50). For some time he sat in silence; then suddenly he turned his head and looked me straight in the eyes and said in Swahili, 'You Europeans are very clever; you can make motor-cars, wirelesses and airplanes. But the most important thing you cannot make—"the heart".' Then he turned his head again and continued posing. I was rather taken aback by this challenge and in my limited Swahili tried to explain that indeed Europeans are unable to make what only God and Nature can create—but his remark stirred me deeply and I wondered what made him say it.

In the company of primitive people, I often feel very small; character, wisdom and kindness are not the prerogative of any race and certainly the closer a man lives to nature, the more he can absorb of its greatness. I have often experienced the impact of the 'heart' of the African people and felt their sympathy in return.

The Turkana women are attractive so long as they are young. Unlike the other Nilo-Hamites, who have delicate features, theirs are strong and heavy but express great vitality. They shave their hair at the sides and twist the top into little strands which hang like tassels from the crown down the neck. Their ears are perforated all along the edge; married women (pl. V, p. 49) put iron rings or oval-shaped plates through the lobe, but girls wear only rings. Shoulders, neck and breast are covered with coils of discs smaller than a sixpence which are chipped from ostrich eggs. It is interesting that discs of this kind are also found in prehistoric graves. It takes great skill to shape them identically, and I would not like to guess how many ostrich eggs are used to make one necklace. Once George found a clutch of twenty-two ostrich eggs close to some Turkana huts. Fearing for their fate, he marked O.H.M.S. on each with indelible pencil, and as he had expected, he found their fragments a few days later in the huts.

All married women wear a narrow hide apron richly decorated with beads; it joins a slit hide skirt at the back. The skirt is held in position by a belt of metal beads; they also ornament the skirt in such quantities that I wonder how these women can walk without injuring their legs. Each bead is cut by craftsmen into many facets. Today aluminium from melted cooking pots is used instead of the traditional soft local stone. The girls wear two V-shaped aprons made of skins: a small one in front and a larger one at the back, both elaborately decorated with cowrie shells and held together with a broad cowrie belt.

Cowrie shells are used all over East Africa as a sexual emblem representing the vagina. In all birth, circumcision and marriage rites these shells are used, and no matter how far people live from the sea, every effort is made to obtain cowries. I also found them used in Central and West Africa which explains the flourishing trade in these shells, though they are no longer used as currency.

There are two forms of marriage for Turkana women. They may become legal wives, having been bought with a brideprice of livestock, in which case they have authority and security and the first-born son is heir; or they may be concubines, who may be better loved but who enjoy no rights except the protection of the

v Turkana married woman

AKITALA LOWUI
NAWOYAPUA
ABERO
TURKANA

EBEY KORE
MAKE-ENGET. KERIO.
TURKANA

19. Turkana member
of Stone group

family to which, however, they owe no obligation and which they can leave at any time they choose. The children of concubines belong to the father; they are never of equal status with those born of legal wives.

Once I watched a Turkana sitting in front of his hut which was a flimsy construction of sticks covered with bits of hide and grass and just big enough to give

VI Turkana with chignon

shelter to two or three people. He was concentrating on throwing his self-made hide sandals into the air and eagerly studying the form in which they fell. From observing this he expected to learn whether his child, who was seriously ill, would recover. This is a typical Turkana custom and no major decision is made without such divination. The people believe in one supreme God *(Akuj)* who is benevolent. Diviners of varying degrees, skilled in casting sandals, and medicine men endeavor to interpret his will. But any Turkana may consult his own sandals without having recourse to an intermediary between himself and *Akuj*.

I well remember a case in which the sandals ended a year-long pursuit of poachers. It had been common knowledge all over the Northern Frontier District that many poachers belonged to a gang under the leadership of the great Atukan, an old Turkana. He and his followers had cost the Government hundreds of pounds; for years they had hunted elephant for ivory, giraffe for leather and rhino for horns to sell to Indian traders. (Rhino horns are wrongly believed to contain an aphrodisiac substance.) This gang of poachers was very bold and known to have rolled boulders downhill to kill anyone who tried to catch them. They operated mainly in the area around the southern end of Lake Rudolf.

One day we were camping in the South Horr Valley, which leads up to the lake and is flanked on both sides by steep mountain ranges. The Game Scouts were out searching for Atukan, who was supposed to be camping on top of the hills. Suddenly two scouts appeared with Atukan naked between them; he grinned sheepishly and seemed quite content to be captured. Apparently he had made no struggle when the scouts arrested him in his hide-out; in fact he had behaved as if he had been waiting for them. When George asked him about his strange behavior, he said that he had that morning consulted his sandals about the outcome of George's search, of which he had been warned by his informers. The oracle had told him that he was going to be caught, so he made no effort to escape and simply waited for the scouts to appear.

I was impressed by his story, which showed that belief in a preordained fate can make a man give up his freedom and normal reactions. To find out more, I asked Atukan to consult his sandals about my father's present doings in Europe. After long hesitation he announced that my father was well and sending me a lot of money. Since my father had been dead for many years, it made me realize the power of faith, and how it can be turned into good or evil, depending on the person's philosophy or character.

After I had spent some time at Lodwar, a Police Officer came from Lokitaung, some hundred and thirty miles to the north, and it was suggested that when he went back I should go with him to paint the MERILE people of that area. I had heard much of the Merile who live on the Sudanese side of the frontier and were a constant source of trouble to the Administration because of their raids.

52

The daughter of the Merile Chief, Tapo

IROJA TAPO
LOCHORANITAK
MERRILLI

53

We set off and bumped along a road which soon became a mere track, winding its way across lava, sand, and grit. The country looked like a lunar landscape.

At Lokitaung, very close to the frontier, were the headquarters of the Turkana Police. The whitewashed Police buildings stood out in contrast to their barren lava surroundings. There was also a natural swimming pool hidden among the rocks close to the mud walled guest-house where I stayed. This was a great delight, because if Lodwar had been hot, Lokitaung was still hotter; it stood in a sheltered valley and lacked any breeze.

Lokitaung is close to the Ilemi triangle, adjacent to the Turkana district, and is a buffer area between Kenya and the Sudan. It was administered by the British, although the country belongs to the Sudanese.

One day we drove into the Ilemi triangle to visit the fort Kamathia. While climbing up a mountain pass, we saw a deposit of petrified trees, broken into clean-cut blocks of three to six feet in diameter, which lay like matches fallen from a box on both sides of the pass. What faulting must have taken place to throw up such gigantic trees, giving evidence of an extinct flora.

On our return we stopped near Lokitaung at a gorge where I was shown more petrified tree trunks embedded in the cliffs, although they were of a smaller size than the ones we had seen on the pass, they were proofs of a time when this now desolate country had been forested.

Trouble along the border often arose because of trespassing around the water-holes in the area; fights were followed by raids and these sometimes ended in murder. The Merile are truculent instigators of such fights and may kill the donkey of a passing Turkana out of pure mischief. The Turkana then retaliate and kill livestock belonging to the Merile. It is after such incidents, when blood is up on both sides, that murder is liable to take place.

Tapo, the Paramount Chief of the Merile, had several times been held as a hostage until such quarrels had been appeased. Indeed, during my visit he was again a 'guest' in Lokitaung. Naturally I was eager to paint him, and he agreed not only to sit for his portrait, but also persuaded his somewhat antagonistic son (pl. IX, p. 61) and daughter (20) to pose for me. The Merile wear their chignons at an upright angle different from the hanging bun of the Turkana and the horizontal style of the Suk.

Lokitaung appealed to me greatly and I liked the local Turkana very much. One day they held a party and when we followed the sounds of their singing we found them doing a fascinating dance. A line of men moved in single file and imitated the undulating movements of the giraffe by stretching their arms and swaying slowly forward. Another group represented elephants and simulated the movements of their trunks with probing gestures of their arms; others imitated baboons, tottering about, mocking each other, and clowning, to the delight of the

54

LASAROTE LESAVOI
BARINGO
NJEMPS

CHAPKWE KIBIRIR
KAPSABET
NANDI

audience. The onlookers, in leopard capes and ostrich plume head-dresses, squatted around the dancers, singing and laughing and encouraging them to do their best.

I painted several warriors carrying the typical Turkana shield, so narrow that I could not understand how it could give protection to such big people. They also wore a circular wrist-knife; when not in use, its razor-sharp blade was encased in a leather sheath. Besides this legal weapon, they used to wear the now forbidden finger-knife, a deadly hook usually concealed inside the palm of the hand.

A drawback to Lokitaung was the number of snakes. Of course they, like any other creature, needed to drink, and as water was only available near the swimming pool and in the houses, cobra became part of my daily life. I always made a very careful approach to the room my canvas bath was in, and I often found a cobra coiled close to it. There were also a number of small, grey Sudan sand vipers, about a foot long (echis crainatus—carpet viper—saw scaled viper) which like other vipers, cause fatal hemorrhage by their bite. They are nocturnal, and almost impossible to detect on the lava, so we had to take great care when walking after dark.

After leaving Lokitaung, I returned for a short time to Lodwar, but became very ill there with water-poisoning. The temperature was over a hundred degrees in the shade, and I had a fever of a hundred and four and agonizing pains in my stomach.

This happened at Christmas time when a crowd of several hundred Turkana arrived and gathered around the fort to celebrate the season; for several days and nights their singing and merry-making never ceased and sleep became impossible. The little kitchen boy and the cook I had engaged locally joined the crowd, and when they occasionally turned up, they were so drunk that they only added to my troubles. Their behavior contradicted the general belief that the Turkana never drink, furthermore they certainly are fond of very strong tobacco.

I was spending a miserable Christmas when I received a letter from the Commissioner of Social Welfare in which he told me that the Government was prepared to commission me to paint a record of the twenty-two most important tribes of Kenya. One hundred and thirty-two portraits were to be done in the next twelve to eighteen months, for which a thousand pounds had been authorized as my fee. Would I come as soon as possible to sign the contract? With this prospect before me I made a most determined effort to recover by sheer will power, and was soon on my way to Nairobi.

VIII Nandi married woman

CHAPTER 3

THE BANTU ROUND MOUNT KENYA

Before committing myself, I went to Isiolo to discuss the offer with George. It would of course cut a big slice out of our private life, but he fully realized the importance and urgency of making such a record, and wholeheartedly agreed that I should accept the commission. So I collected my camp kit, took one of our boys, Daniel, to look after me, and also Pippin, my Cairn terrier. Pippin had been my intimate companion for the last eight years and had shared everything with me. Together we went to Nairobi where, on 28 January 1949, I signed a contract with the Government.

It was pointed out that no anthropological knowledge was expected of me, but I was asked to make notes on tribal life and record vernacular names of ornaments; the Government reserved the right to reject any paintings which were not up to standard, either technically or anthropologically. I would be paid a fee for each picture and the cost of my petrol. The models would be paid by me at rates which the local District Commissioner would decide. Finally a circular letter was written to the administrative officers of the five Provinces of Kenya asking for their co-operation in getting the type of models required for this record.

Before starting on my new adventure I had to buy myself a car in which I could travel with my equipment. I decided on a Morris Commercial one and a half ton truck which I had converted into a wired box body, large enough to put a camp bed inside in emergencies. I engaged an African driver to help me in case of mechanical trouble.

It was decided that I should start by painting the AKAMBA around Machakos. The Akamba are a large group of Bantu with two administrative headquarters, one at Kitui and one at Machakos, the latter only forty-two miles distant from Nairobi. It is the oldest *boma* in Kenya and, being so close to the capital and therefore longest under European influence, its inhabitants are very progressive and have given up most of their traditional customs. This was precisely the reason why this group had been listed as one of the more important for me to paint, as now was perhaps the last moment in which to find genuine ornaments for a pictorial record which would supplement the book about these people by Gerhard Lindblom, the Swedish anthropologist.

58

The morning after my arrival at Machakos, a lorry-load of women dressed in gaudy clothes drew up. These had been summoned as possible models but they were bedecked with cheap and modern trinkets bought in the African shops; none of them were any use for my purpose. So, after paying for their transport, I sent them back and searched for better models. One girl looked promising, but after sitting for an hour she bolted, for she found posing for me tiresome compared to being photographed, something to which the people of Machakos were well used.

Next I persuaded an old woman to sit for me, though her face and her ornaments were very commonplace; I painted her in the hope of making a friend and of using her influence to get more interesting sitters.

I also painted an old blacksmith; his profession is one for which the Akamba are famous. In general I found it easier to establish contact with older people who as a rule had good manners, which many of the young generation lacked. But I needed to paint young people as well and therefore tried my luck with a warrior. Unfortunately he dressed up specially for the occasion and when he arrived his ornaments looked so unconvincing that I painted him only because there was no alternative. The same happened with a young girl whose outfit was chosen on the basis of the brighter the better, and who had the brazen look of an experienced harlot.

I struggled on at Machakos for a fortnight but was very disappointed with the results of my work and when I returned to Nairobi and handed over my first 'official' collection of portraits I was not surprised that all were rejected. Although this was not an encouraging beginning, I was rather glad that pictures of people wearing spurious costumes should be refused, and I looked forward to going later to Kitui which is more remote from Nairobi than Machakos, and where the people still lived close to their tradition.

For the time being it was arranged for me to visit the KIKUYU at Fort Hall. They, like the Akamba, were administered from several centers. I knew it would again be difficult, if not impossible, to find models wearing traditional ornaments for these people are amongst the most advanced in Kenya. Fort Hall is one of the oldest *bomas* in the country, and is situated in the center of the Kikuyu district.

I stayed with the District Commissioner and his family who did their best to find suitable models but day after day went by and no one worth painting turned up. Finally an old man who often posed for tourist photographers near the Nairobi hotels volunteered to sit for me, but instead of appearing with his hair plaited and colored with ocher in the traditional fashion, he wore a fiber wig dyed red and a lot of meaningless ornaments.

Then, an ex-chief came in the dress worn to recruit labor, but he also did not look authentic, for his ornaments were overdone.

Fortunately there is an extensive literature recording the tribal customs of the Kikuyu. I found many interesting photographs in a book published by the Consolata Mission, one of the first to settle in Kenya. Most of these pictures showed an African, almost naked, with spear, shield and plaited hair, standing next to a converted house-boy, dressed in the long garment known as *kanzu* with a fez on his head and holding a teapot invitingly towards the camera: the *Bad* and the *Good* placed next to each other in striking contrast.

Of course I was only interested in the bad boy, as he wore all the ornaments I needed for my record—but where could I find him? It was obvious that I was wasting everybody's time here just as much as if I were looking for a medieval knight around Piccadilly Circus.

Finally the District Commissioner had an inspiration. If anybody could help it was Chief Njiri. He was a man of the old stamp and enjoyed great prestige and influence among his people. All depended, of course, on his approval of my work.

The Chief lived high in the Aberdare foothills on the edge of the bamboo forest. After the D.C. had sent word of my visit, I drove up into the hills, along thickly forested ridges with heather and everlastings growing by the side of the rivulets which crossed our way. Finally I reached more open slopes, and on one of these was Njiri's homestead (21). It looked more like a village, with its many huts and granaries perched on tall poles to be above reach of predators.

The Chief came to welcome me. He wore an ocher-dyed hide cap of the traditional type and was wrapped in a blanket to ward off the evening chill. I felt at once attracted by his face with its countless wrinkles and humorous eyes. He greeted me in Swahili with outstretched hands.

Then he took me to a little wooden hut in which he invited me to stay. I had intended to camp in my tent, but I could not hurt my host's feelings and therefore agreed to sleep in his guest-house of which he was evidently very proud.

While my truck was being unloaded, I tried to explain the purpose of my visit; it was cold and I wondered what I could offer this nice old man? It was too late for tea, nor was there a fire ready for boiling water. Then I remembered that I had some gin. Although I knew I would not be popular with the D.C. for offering spirits to any African, what else could I do? We could not just stand there and talk and freeze. When Njiri had taken his first sip, he drained the glass with one long gulp and, sighing approvingly, said, 'That beer is good; what do you call it? Please can I have some more?' Feeling a bit worried, I told him that this beer was very potent, but he seemed well used to intoxicants and, as I soon found out, could take large quantities of his potent home-made beer without ever losing his dignity.

I do not know if it was thanks to the gin or whether my wish to paint his people appealed to him but Njiri and I were soon good friends. He knew of odd bits of

IX The son of the Merile chief, Tapo

AKIENEM TAPO
LOPEHMGUAT
MEKKILLI

MUNYI SYUMA
KATHARINGU
EMBU

21. Kikuyu chief Njiri's homestead

traditional ornaments belonging to various people and collected all he could find. To give an encouraging example, he agreed to be my first model. Although he was a bad sitter and never kept still, never have I enjoyed painting anyone so much. I painted him in his official regalia as Chief, wearing his hide cap and a blue monkey fur coat onto which his M.B.E. and other medals were pinned. In one hand he held his staff of chieftainship, in the other, a bottle of his home-made beer which was always refilled. Of course, I omitted this in the painting.

While posing, Njiri held court to crowds of petitioners squatting around. As I listened to arguments, which were sometimes heated, I was fascinated to observe how he managed to disarm disgruntled petitioners with his wit, using jokes like darts. He always tried to settle a case with humor, but when he met stubbornness, he changed his tactics and, with thundering authority, mercilessly made mince-meat of the man and turned him into a laughing-stock so that he lost his case.

Njiri did not speak English, not because of lack of loyalty towards the Administration but because it was against his principles and his pride to express himself in any language other than his own; he used Swahili when he had to only as a compromise. He also refused to wear European clothes or copy the Western way of living, but being tolerant, he had no objection to his children having a different outlook; several had adopted Christianity, spoke fluent English and had accepted jobs demanding adaptation to foreign habits.

Njiri ruled his district to perfection. Though many people feared him, he was generally very popular and everybody respected him. He was not a hereditary chief, and had started his career when he was employed on the construction of the Kenya-Uganda railway. Though he was a youngster at the time, he showed great ability in handling laborers who had been recruited from all over East Africa and who were often truculent. His gift for leadership was recognized and on his return he was elected by his people as Chief. His generosity was as large as his heart. In his prime he managed a family of fifty wives, but now he was getting old and told me, with a twinkle in his eyes, that he could only cope with the thirty who all lived

63

x   Ndio six months before circumcision

22. The favourite wife
of the Kikuyu
chief, Njiri

happily together in his *boma*. When I inquired how many children he had, I realized from his evasive answer that I had made a *faux pas*, for it is against African custom to tell strangers the number of one's children. But I soon learned that every mountain-ridge I could see around belonged to, or was shared out among, his children, all farming close together in their hamlets.

23. Kikuyu bride

After his portrait was completed, I painted his favorite wife, a dignified woman with perfect manners (22). Even with Njiri's help it was extremely difficult to persuade young people to sit for me, for they had no interest in their history, and many were ashamed of it. Only after great trouble did we finally get a girl to pose as a bride (23); we checked the authenticity of her ornaments against photographs in the Consolata Mission book.

65

DULI WA KERAGANNA
KERETI
KIKUYU

24. Kikuyu warrior

I also used this book to help me when painting a witch doctor, warriors, elders, and dancers. Although I was fortunate in getting enough genuine ornaments for twelve paintings, I had to resign myself to having mostly older people posing for them. The warrior I painted had an ostrich pompon attached to his spear indicating that his intentions were peaceful. The design on his shield was his family's emblem painted in ocher, charcoal, and white ash; his leggings were of Colobus fur (24).

66

25. Kikuyu circumciser

One afternoon I had a visit from a woman missionary from one of the many missions which tried to convert the Kikuyu. She had spent most of her life among the people here and I hoped to learn from her experiences. But she was upset when she realized that I wanted to paint the traditional costumes of the Kikuyu, for she was devoting all her time to replacing them with European clothing and teaching the Kikuyu our way of life. When I asked her what she knew about clitoridectomy, she left me hurriedly without answering (25).

I wondered how anyone could hope to improve the life of these people while determined to ignore their roots. When I asked Njiri what he thought about the missions, his comment was that he would rather see them concentrating on agricultural, educational, and medical improvements than interfering with the religious beliefs of his people.

The country here was beautiful, and on my evening walks with Pippin I collected white and yellow helichrysum amongst the bracken and tree ferns and watched elephants breaking through the bamboo.

My next destination was Embu, the administrative headquarters of the EMBU and MBERE people. Coming from the south-east, they were the first of several groups, settled around the base of Mount Kenya, all of Bantu stock.

Here the altitude was only about four thousand feet, and Pippin, who had not been well lately, started heavy nosebleeding. I took him to the vet at Nyeri some forty miles away, but he could not diagnose the trouble and could only advise me to keep him quiet. Poor Pippin, he looked so ill and tried so hard to pull through.

The driver added to my troubles, for he turned out to be a drunkard and I had to dismiss him. After some difficulty I replaced him by a local man, but when a few days later he almost drove the car over an escarpment, I decided to carry on without a driver.

I started by painting two NDIO circumcision candidates; this tribe is akin to the Kikuyu. The first picture showed a youth in a costume which is worn six months prior to initiation, and which indicates to the boy's parents that he wants to be circumcised (pl. X, p. 62). The second model was dressed in the ceremonial attire worn two days before the operation. During this time he had to throw his staff into a tree *(mugomo)* and it had to be caught by a young married woman. This custom implied that he was going to be circumcised (pl. XI, p. 71).

Here at Embu I had no literature by which to check the authenticity of the costumes, and I had to rely on what the people told me. I interrogated the elderly who still knew the tribal significance of the ornaments; if they contradicted each other, I did not paint the person even if the appearance was picturesque. This was the only way of keeping my collection as authentic as possible and it became my routine practice.

Among the Embu I painted a young man who posed as a trumpeter for the important *kibata* dance, a ceremony held when the elders meet to settle judicial cases. After him two warriors arrived, carrying shields made of buffalo hide, showing very large markings so that they could be easily recognized by fellow-clansmen (26). Another model was a witch doctor; his profession was indicated by a white line along his nose and temples (28). Except for him and the two youths in

26. Embu warrior

circumcision costume, who were actually undergoing the rites, all the other men who posed for me wore traditional ornaments which had been collected from various owners.

The women were more conservative and did not have to be dressed up in borrowed ornaments. I noticed many cicatrizations on their stomachs and faces.

69

27. Embu woman circumciser

Here for the first time I painted a woman circumciser (27), whose paraphernalia was heavily decorated with cowrie shells.

Next on my list was Chief Muruatetu, who was also Vice President of the Embu Local Native Council, and had held this position since 1924. As he lived some distance away I camped near his home. He was a fat, thick-set man and obviously fond of food. Although he liked to laugh and chuckled readily, we never got beyond conventional conversation. I painted two portraits of Muruatetu, one to be presented to the Governor of Gambia who had been Chief Native Commissioner in Kenya, and knew the Chief well. Both pictures showed him in his monkey coat and ostrich feathered head-dress.

One afternoon I heard the noise of a large crowd and learned that the Chief's niece was going to be circumcised. I asked if I could see the operation, and with Muruatetu's consent, his wife took me to the scene.

70

xi Ndio two days before circumcision

NGAIRE MITHAMO
KANOGU
EMBU

MUTHORO KIBURI
INJERU, KARUNDINI
THARAKA

JOY

28. Embu witch doctor

It was a cold, rainy afternoon and I was shivering in my raincoat. When we arrived, a dance was in progress attended only by women, although there were also a few young 'warriors' watching at a distance. Many of the women carried green branches, waving them as they rushed back and forth towards the center of the crowd. I was not able to see what was going on there. After a great deal of noise and dancing I was told that the operation was about to start. From as near as I could get among the whirl of shouting women I saw a girl of about twelve

73

years old, standing naked, rigid with fear and cold in the drizzling rain. She was as frightened as a child of twelve could be but tried desperately to keep her composure: her mouth was firmly compressed. An elderly woman circumciser pressed a bunch of leaves between the girl's clasped hands and helped her into a sitting position with her legs wide apart while two assistants seized her by the arms and legs and held her tightly. By now the girl seemed in extreme tension and completely stiff. She kept her eyes wide open and stared to the side, trying to hide her feelings. This, I was told, was the test of her courage and the slightest flicker in her eyes betraying fear would reduce her chances of a good marriage. The circumciser washed her hands in filthy greenish water which certainly did not improve their cleanliness; then she took a handful of dry chicken droppings and rubbed it over the sexual organs of the girl to render the skin less slippery. Out of a banana leaf she unwrapped a spatula with white markings and with a few deft cuts removed part of the clitoris. There appeared to be no bleeding during the operation. When later I tried the sharpness of this spatula on my arm, I found the blade so blunt that it left hardly a mark on my skin.

I was deeply impressed by the girl's behavior during the whole ordeal; she controlled her reactions to pain and fright with such determination that not the slightest change in her expression conveyed what she must be going through. As soon as the operation was completed, she was dragged away by the assistant circumcisers and made to jump three times in order to make sure that there was no bleeding; it is the custom to pay a fee of honey for a bloodless operation and a goat in case of bleeding.

While all this went on I noticed that a group of old women were bending down round the circumciser and examining the severed clitoris which was lying on the ground. One of them picked it up and, wrapping it in leaves, placed it between the first and the second toe of another woman who was led off into the bush where she kicked it away.

During all this time the noise of shouting, dancing and singing was deafening and many women threw their branches at the girl while the young 'warriors' danced in a rather obscene manner around a stick about four feet long with a wooden disc of four to six inches in diameter at the top.

The last I saw of the girl she was sitting utterly exhausted on the ground, surrounded by the yelling crowd of women. Their dance continued for at least another two hours, until darkness fell.

When I asked Muruatetu how he reconciled the clitoridectomy of his niece with his position as Chief and the critical attitude of the Mission and Administration to this custom, he only shrugged his shoulders and assured me that no girl would find a husband unless she had been initiated and that only then would her bride-price be paid.

74

29. Mbere drummers

The next people I visited were the Mbere who live in the plains below Embu, which border immediately on the thickly forested slopes of Mount Kenya. The change of climate there is as abrupt as that of the vegetation. Leaving the cool shade of tall trees and dense undergrowth, one enters the grilling heat of sandy plains with gigantic baobabs towering over thorny scrub. I drove in the company of the D.C. and his party who had summoned a large crowd for a dance during which I was to choose my models; and splendid dancers they certainly were. As far as we could see in the dust they churned up, the place was filled with people decorated with feathers and beads, and covered with grease so that their skin glistened beautifully. The men used very large drums, and I was fascinated to see them jump and dance while holding the drums between their legs (29). Although the people looked impressive (30), most of their ornaments were modern and even

75

30.   Mbere dancers

the drums were copied from the neighboring Akamba tribe and had replaced the old-type tambourines.

I was puzzled by the expression of the girls whose eyelids were swollen and inflamed; instead of looking straight at you they blinked. I was told that this was the result of plucking the eye-lashes in order to develop a 'modest look'.

Here too it was only among the older, more conservative women that I could find traditional clothing; my first model was a mother whose shaven head and ear ornaments indicated that her child was undergoing circumcision. This was also shown by metal decorations at the edge of her skirt, which otherwise would be made of beads.

The girls wore traditional short hide skirts fitting tightly to their bodies (31, 32); these would only be split open after marriage, by the husband.

I noticed that some of the warriors carried their elaborate ostrich plume head-dresses at a horizontal angle (33), while others wore them upright, and learned

31.   Mbere dancers: note the traditional short hide skirt of the women

that the former indicated a peaceful approach while the latter was a sign of war.

I camped at the District Commissioner's rest-house which was built of wooden poles whose interstices were stuffed with grass. These walls were alive with insects, and I often picked off ticks; their bites gave me a reaction like a chill. But as the rest-house was cooler than my tent would have been, I remained there while I painted the Mbere.

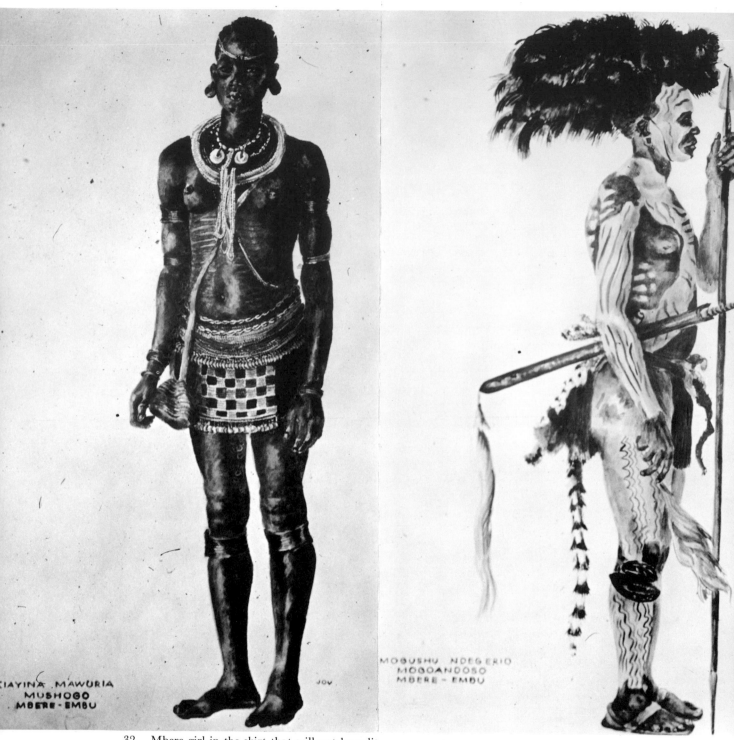

32. Mbere girl in the skirt that will not be split until marriage

33. Mbere warrior

They were a cheerful lot, and I would have enjoyed my stay with them if poor Pippin had not become desperately ill. I was so worried about him that I sent a runner to George who happened to be in the neighborhood dealing with game offences. Soon after he arrived Pippin died. To help me over my distress, George gave me a baby serval cat which his scouts had found abandoned in the bush. It was the most charming little creature, and though it could not replace Pippin, it won my heart at once. I called it Shockerly.

As soon as I had completed my record of the Mbere I drove higher up the mountain slopes to paint the CHUKA. Although I did not feel well, I managed to pitch camp and greet the many hundreds of people who had been sent to meet me. Several came from great distances and were naturally keen to return home as soon as possible. After selecting suitable models, I arranged for one to come every second day, after which I sent the people home. I only hoped they would be punctual as I had had enough experience to know how one sitter arriving late upset my schedule, obliging me to paint by lamplight so as to be able to catch up. While talking to the people I suddenly felt very ill and took my temperature; it was a hundred and three degrees. I wondered if I was going to have an attack of malaria. Luckily George visited me next day and, after making the necessary arrangements with the Chief to postpone my painting, he took me to a doctor at Meru and, on his advice, on to Isiolo, to get fit again.

CHAPTER 4

WITH GEORGE ON A RECCE THROUGH THE SAMBURU, TURKANA AND SUK COUNTRY

George had been asked to reconnoiter a route which would provide enough water to repatriate, on foot, several thousand Turkana with their livestock who, during the War, had moved illegally into other parts of the Northern Frontier Province, where they interfered with the grazing rights of the local tribes. I was naturally keen to join George on this safari which would take him into areas where few Europeans had ever been. I hoped that in these remote places would be tribesmen whom otherwise I would have no chance of painting for my record.

It was to be a foot safari with donkeys to carry the loads; fortunately our leading donkey-herd, Ngobus, who was a former member of Atukan's gang, had just recovered from a witchcraft-spell that almost had killed him. He was a robust Turkana with a strongly developed Casanovan temperament. This had got him into trouble with a rival who had engaged a witch doctor to cast a spell on him intended to make him die within a fixed period. For many days he lay unconscious, kept alive by his mother who poured milk into his mouth. After great trouble and partly thanks to George's interventions, another witch doctor had been persuaded to counteract the spell; whereupon Ngobus recovered. He was a firm believer in witchcraft and on several occasions had given George a charm, imploring him to carry it as a protection when he was going away to deal with dangerous animals.

The combination of superior physical abilities and psychological weakness shown by Ngobus and other Africans often perplexes me. Any one of our Game Scouts can walk for a whole day in the hottest weather without a drink; detect vultures high up in the sky which we can hardly see with field-glasses; carry on a lively conversation over a long distance when we can hear only a faint sound and they often walked barefoot into inch-long thorns without showing any sign of pain. (I well remember the guide who went with me up Mount Kilimanjaro walking barefoot over sharp, ice-covered lava near the summit, at an altitude of 20,000 feet. When I offered him my spare boots, he flung them promptly across his shoulder to save them for showing off to his village.)

Wounds caused by predators, unless immediately treated with sulphanilamide, are fatal to Europeans within forty-eight hours because of the blood poisoning caused by the decayed meat adhering to the animal's claws from its last kill. But on several occasions, we treated Africans mauled by lions or crocodiles many days earlier; the wounds were rotten with gangrene, and yet they had not succumbed to blood poisoning.

It is very curious that in spite of these enviable physical qualities, many Africans lack resistance to psychic suggestion, and easily succumb to witchcraft. Only recently we had lost one of George's best Game Scouts as a result of a spell. He was an intelligent, middle-aged Akamba who had previously served for many years with the Kenya Police. His wife had run away with a lover who, wishing to get rid of her husband, had arranged for a spell to be cast on the poor scout; he was to die within a certain time limit. We visited him and found him in a state of advanced emaciation. We tried our best to talk him out of his conviction that he must die, and we took him to the hospital where the doctor assured him that there was nothing physical the matter with him. Nevertheless, he died on the day forecast by the spellbinder.

Here I would like to stress that the term 'witch doctor' is often misused in connection with evil witchcraft. The profession of witch doctor is a benevolent one, like that of the medicine man. The person who is hired for a shady purpose is the sorcerer who always works in the dark and conceals his activities.

When Ngobus and I were well again and all was ready for the safari, we set off together with Shockerly, the serval cat, in the company of a young District Officer. The trip was expected to last six weeks. Our route took us along the base of the General Mathews Range, one of the loveliest parts of the Northern Frontier Province, but, since it is off the beaten track, it is hardly ever visited; indeed, when George joined the Game Department in 1936 he was the second European to explore these attractive mountains.

The range is sparsely populated by the DOROBO, a primitive hunting group who, like the equally primitive SANYE at the Coast, are the aborigines of Kenya; they subsist on the results of hunting, and on wild honey and berries.

When George first visited the General Mathews Range, each family owned one mountain and guarded its domain jealously. Any person wishing to pay a call on a neighbor carried a bundle of specially marked sticks; by placing these 'visiting cards' along his track he showed that his visit was a friendly one. Whereas, if the owner of the area found strange footmarks without any sticks, he knew that the trespasser was an enemy who must be hunted and killed.

George had seen many of these visiting cards; he had also had reason to know how severely honey thieves were punished, no doubt because honey provides these primitive people with their only form of sugar and is therefore greatly prized. It is collected from beehives made of hollowed tree trunk sections hung on trees. Once the bees have settled in the hives and produced their honey, the natives smoke them out.

One day George found an old man hiding near his camp; he was on the verge of starvation. Both his hands had been mutilated and reduced to crippled fists, so he depended on what food he could get without using his fingers. He told George that as a youngster he had been caught stealing honey. To punish him and prevent further thieving, the tendons of his fingers had been severed and his fists tied together until they grew into useless lumps. Since then he had lived the cruel existence of a crippled outcast.

Soon after our marriage, George had taken me on a four week foot safari through the General Mathews Range. We often found hot ashes and fresh antelope bones in caves or under overhanging rocks, obviously left in a hurry by the Dorobo who had vanished into the bush on hearing our footsteps. Most of the huts we saw were flimsy, impoverished shelters made of a few branches tied together to serve as a temporary home until the people moved on.

After passing the range we went through country inhabited by the SAMBURU. This tribe is one of the Masai group and consequently they have common customs. They are a very graceful people and the women especially often have remarkable charm. The country around was hilly, very eroded and broken up. Here and there we noticed *manyata*s and *enkangs*³ perched like dark rings on the hillsides. At sunset it was a lovely sight to see the herds of livestock, streaming like white rivulets across the sun-baked red soil, as they returned from every direction to the *manyata*s.

One afternoon while George was busy in the camp, the young District Officer and I went to visit a *manyata*. There were no men present but plenty of women. Full of curiosity they came out of their huts and we soon found ourselves surrounded by attractive chattering girls, their brass-coiled bracelets and stiff bead collars adding vivid touches of color to the scene. They seemed to find the good-looking District Officer attractive, for they formed a giggling circle around him and sang a song which caused them great amusement. When we insisted on having it translated by the Samburu Game Scout who had come with us, he was extremely embarrassed, but finally told us that these naughty women were hinting that such a handsome father would be sure to produce nice babies.

I bought a few ornaments and, while I searched for the money, asked a youngster who was standing next to me to hold them. He refused to help, and I was told that if he had it would have brought him bad luck as he was not yet circumcised and was not supposed to touch any woman's ornaments before his initiation.

82

We camped near a spring, which bubbled from beneath a deposit of limestone; it was the main water supply for this arid area. The many animal footprints around it gave us a good idea of those who would be sharing the spring with us. Unfortunately I could not watch the nocturnal visitors, as again I suddenly ran a high temperature and felt very ill. It seemed odd that I should have a fresh attack of malaria when I had hardly recovered from the last one. Luckily by next morning I was fit enough to ride all day on the mule.

We passed through Baragoi, a small shopping center at the entrance of the South Horr Valley around which lately many Turkana had settled illegally. The local population had found temporary jobs building a Catholic Mission. Up to now the missions had kept out of the Northern Frontier Province with the one exception at Marsabit, where the Church Missionary Society had tried, with little success, to convert the Borana.

As I watched the Samburu with their ocher-plaited hair and their spears, and the Turkana tribesmen, walking about aloof, proud and independent as this vast, hard country had made them, I wondered whether this new attempt to turn them into Christians would be more successful than the previous one.

Leaving Baragoi, we continued through an almost waterless and unexplored area. We met very few tribesmen, but found many petrified tree stumps of about one foot in diameter with clearly marked year-rings. To get any water for the donkeys, we had to dig deep holes in the dry riverbeds and spend hours bucketing it to the surface. Unless there were exceptional rains, it seemed out of the question to make three thousand Turkana and some thirty thousand livestock trek through this lava desert.

Our route took us across the Suguta Valley, which is part of the dried-up lake bed of what was once a vast sheet of water connecting Lake Rudolf with the Nile. Flanked along its sides by steep lava escarpments, no breeze comes in, and dehydrating heat hit us as soon as we entered the ten miles wide valley. All that remains today of this once vast lake is a narrow trickle called Suguta River, which winds its way through the silted-up bed, passing by steamjets and one formidable geyser. This region is not only one of the hottest, but also one of the most volcanically active parts of Kenya. We had often experienced tremors when camping at the southern end of Lake Rudolf which is only some thirty miles away though separated by a twenty mile wide barrier, pushed up by a volcanic eruption. On a previous safari we had crossed this barrier and found it a truly forbidding place; the earth's crust consisted of fairly recent lava flows, pierced in places by steamjets, or cracked by deep craters. The last eruption took place in 1888, but fine cinder and sulphur fumes proved that the volcanic action was even now far from dormant. On this safari I had searched for signs of previous life in the Suguta Valley, but had not found any traces which suggested that living creatures had once dwelt here. This surprised me as, on the other side of the barrier along the shores of Lake Rudolf, we had found many fossilized fishbones, as well as fragments of pottery embedded in the lava tuff. Two sites of rock-engravings, which we discovered at the south end of Lake Rudolf, were most interesting. One was near the Surima waterhole, here we saw pictures of Oryx, buffalo, flamingo and various small gazelle; the most startling was one of a herd of giraffe led by a man. All these rock-engravings were in an exposed position, high up on the walls of a gorge. In order to make tracings on cellophane, I had to balance on a ledge only a few inches wide, forty feet above the bottom of the gorge. As this was full of large rocks, I supposed that they must have broken off since the engravings were made, at which time the ground level must have been much higher.

The second site was some twelve miles from Teleki's volcano on an overhanging basalt cliff. These engravings showed more developed varieties of technique, and a greater range of animals as well. Here we found mammoth, rhino, giraffe and several types of long-horned antelope *(see page* 88*)*.

These engravings are the only ones so far discovered in Kenya, and have been identified, in Cambridge, as closely related to engravings found in the Sahara, British Somaliland, and Ethiopia. When on a trip to Europe we visited several of the Spanish caves, famous for their rock-engraving, we saw a mammoth identical with the one we had found in Kenya.

Now we camped at the Suguta River. The heat was almost unbearable so we enjoyed a bathe in its shallow water. Next day, to make the best of the cool hours, we started before dawn to climb the escarpment on the far side. I was riding ahead when I suddenly lost my balance and George was only just in time to prevent me from falling off the mule. I then discovered that I had a temperature of a hundred and four degrees so we had to pitch camp on the spot, though there was no shade or privacy. I was very sick and felt near dying so, amidst the braying donkeys and the dust they churned up, George wrapped wet sheets around me to bring the temperature down.

This was the third time that I had had a sudden violent attack during which I had been almost delirious but which had lasted for only one day. I realized that these attacks could not be due to malaria and when I checked the dates in my diary, I found that they had occurred at intervals of twelve days; I hoped this might give a doctor some indication of the nature of the illness.

Next morning I was as fit as ever, so we continued on our safari. As we scouted across lava escarpments the going became extremely rough; often we had to unload

34. East Suk girl

the donkeys as they could not pass through narrow rock-passages without breaking their load of wooden boxes, or we had to lead them step by step along precipitous ledges.

Soon after we entered southern Turkana I was lucky enough to find several models who belonged to sections different to the ones I had met in the North. Here the women wore their hair in another style and seemed to be rather lighter in color. They were greatly intrigued by my serval cat whom I usually kept in my lap while painting. Up to now he had stood the safari very well, travelling during the hot hours in a shady box loaded on a mule which trotted close to mine. At other times he sat on my shoulder or in my lap. During the day he was usually half asleep, but before sundown he woke and then made up for his previous laziness, and at night I had to keep him shut up or he might have got into trouble with prowling predators. By now Shockerly had become the pet of us all and he proved invaluable as entertainment for my models, by preventing them from falling asleep. But I had to keep a sharp eye on him, as they often hinted in no uncertain way what nice ornaments his spotted pelt would make.

Later we passed through country inhabited by the East Suk (34). They were administered from Kabarnet which is at the far end of the Suguta Valley. I had painted some of these people when I camped on Lake Baringo.

Since this was not the period of circumcision, I could not paint the candidates, but was told that their clothing during their two to five months seclusion was similar to that of the neighboring Njemps.

Our route took us close to Seker, the sacred mountain of the Suk, 'the navel of the Suk', as they call it. On our way, we passed many large stone cairns, most of which marked graves. But I knew that not all Suk were buried; after death many were just left out for the hyenas. The bodies of those who are buried are laid so that their stomachs are tilted towards Seker.

The Suk believe in a God called the sky *(terorut)* and his son called the rain *(ilat)*. They also revere snakes and if a snake enters a hut, it may not be killed but must be given milk.

Although the country here resembles that of the Turkana and food is scarce, only the very poor eat fish and on no account will any Suk eat a beast of prey.

I painted a few men (35); one posed for me lying on the ground, with his head on his neck-rest so as to save his chignon from getting damaged. He carried a shield identical to the Turkana type and also wore a magnificent leopard-skin cape for the occasion (36).

A Suk may have as many wives as he can afford and the number of children we met everywhere proved that they prospered.

86

35. East Suk man

36. East Suk with neck rest

From here we went on through very broken and uninhabited country until we reached the Lorogi Plateau, where the Samburu live.

On the last day of this safari I went in the afternoon for a stroll with Lambradan. He was a Samburu and one of George's oldest and most loyal Game Scouts, who had shared many critical moments with us in our encounters with dangerous animals. By African standards he was a wealthy man who owned several wives and lots of livestock, all living close to where we now were. He had no need to work for money, but preferred the life of a Game Scout to staying at home.

He was an old friend of mine and I liked his company better than that of any of the other scouts. When the sun began to set, we sat on a rock and I watched its last rays lighting up the country until all the color drained away, everything became dim; the twitter of birds gradually faded and all grew still. Talking to Lambradan, I remarked on the low wages paid by the Game Department and asked him why he did not choose to take a job with either the Police, the Veterinary Department, or National Parks, which offer their employees much better terms. He replied simply that he liked helping George. I probed further and asked what he would do if one day George should have an accident or get killed, as was not impossible since he so often risked his life with dangerous animals. Lambradan looked up at me not only with surprise, but with anger as he replied: 'How could the *bwana* (master) do anything without *Mungu* (God) helping him and protecting him? Is not all we do controlled by God?' I accepted the rebuke and remembered another occasion when the pagan Lambradan had also put me in the wrong. I had asked him to help me carry a giant lobelia from the higher moorlands of Mount Kenya to my camp, which was pitched at a lower altitude and where I

87

wanted to paint it. It was a cumbersome plant to carry, some eight feet high and very poisonous and when we reached camp, our eyelids and lips were swollen from the fumes it had exuded. To show my gratitude for his help I offered him a shilling. Lambradan looked at the coin and at me with a puzzled expression, then he returned it with great dignity, saying, 'Would you not also help me if I needed help. Why should I take money from you?'

As we were already overdue in Isiolo, I could not paint the Samburu now, but decided that I would return later for a longer stay to make a proper record of this attractive people.

During all these weeks I had carefully watched out for every twelfth day when I expected my fever to break out and we always tried to find a shady camping site for the attack which returned with unfailing regularity. As soon as we had completed our safari I went to see a doctor at Nairobi who diagnosed this illness as relapsing fever, a tick-borne disease, which I had probably caught from the 'chilly tick-bites' at the Mbere camp. I was cured with injections of arsenic and recovered very soon.

While I was staying at Nairobi for the treatment, George wrote to tell me the upsetting news that Shockerly had died. He had found him one morning with a broken spine from which he could never recover. To put an end to his misery, George gave him the *coup de grâce*. I found it very hard to be once more without a pet, especially as my next location promised to be a lonely one.

CHAPTER 5

THE MERU PEOPLE

One of the tribes I had been asked to paint was the THARAKA (37). They live in the remote, hot plains below Meru. They are a very interesting Bantu group, with unique ornaments and customs, that differ from any of the neighboring Bantu. With the exception of an article by A. M. Champion[4] little is known about these people. I reached their territory, taking the road through Meru, on the slopes of Mount Kenya, from where they are administered.

After driving across hilly, rocky country, I finally pitched my camp at the foot of a large mountain close to the District Commissioner's rest-house, from which I had a superb view over the plains below. The Chief and many people came to welcome me. I was struck by their long extremities and knock-knees, which were especially noticeable in the women. First I painted the Chief's wife, who by the brass coils around her legs proved that she had borne him children. Like all the married women, she wore a triangular apron richly embroidered with cowries, the number of these shells being indicative of her husband's wealth (38).

The Tharaka are polygamous. The brideprice is carefully calculated and staggered: for the first wife it amounts to sixty goats, each worth fourteen shillings, or five head of cattle, valued at a hundred shillings each. For the second wife thirty goats or three head of cattle are given. The brideprice is not purchase money for a wife, but is a guarantee of the stability of the marriage and compensation to the wife's group for the loss of her services. When a man has chosen the girl he wants to marry—she is expected to be a virgin—he arranges for his father to call on the father of the girl. It is the custom for the girl to refuse four times; when she finally accepts the offer, the two fathers start discussing the brideprice. The full amount, however, is only paid if the girl is provided by her father with a proper dress for ceremonial occasions. When all is settled, the bridegroom calls on the girl and her parents. After this, both parents exchange visits for three months or longer, then the brideprice is paid. Finally the marriage is celebrated by a feast given at the husband's home. Should the first wife have only daughters, the eldest son of the next wife will become heir.

My next model was a circumciser who was said to be eighty-five years old; he had started his career fifty years ago under District Commissioner Horne, one of

37. Tharaka girls

the first administrators of this area. I was told that, when Horne shot off a revolver in 1908, the Tharaka had never seen one before and they called it maize, as it burst out like a maize cob. It puzzled me that the old man carried a spear with his very elaborate paraphernalia, but I was told that the way to call on his services for the initiation of a warrior was to send a person who would plant a spear in front of him. His ornaments and white paint are intended to impress the uncircumcised youth and to stress the importance of the circumcision rites.

The old man showed the usual white markings as a badge of his profession, but also wore a sheathed finger-knife, allegedly to wipe off sweat. He worked with a group of young warriors, all wearing special clothes and rattling boards to intimidate the candidates. I was impressed by the artistic taste displayed in their choice of ornaments which blended in perfect color harmony (39).

A rather amusing sitter was a witch doctor with a large collection of tortoise shells, monkey claws, snails, pebbles, and other objects (pl. XII, p. 72). He explained that he carried his medicines, which had been previously boiled, in a

90

38.   Tharaka married woman

calabash. To administer them a portion was put into a hollowed antelope horn which was of ritual significance. Then he poured water over it and made the patient drink the mixture from the horn. Afterwards he dipped a tiny bow into the medicine and touched the body of the patient all over with it to drive out the evil spirit. When he was asked to cicatrize, he would pour the medicine over lucky beans previously placed on a tortoise shell; with a minute axe dipped into this liquid he would then make small incisions which resulted in raised scars. To make all his medicines more effective, he inserted a monkey's paw into a small snail shell and, waving both three times above the medicines, asserted that this would increase their potency. Elaborate paintings, white and red blotches, all over his own body enhanced his prestige with his patients.

Though I tried, as I thought with considerable cunning, to find out what ingredients he used for his medicines, he was evasive in his answers and did not disclose his secrets. But since the Tharaka are famed for their witchcraft, I was glad to have the co-operation of this cheerful man as far as it went.

While I was painting the Tharaka, I became aware of the importance of including the neighboring tribes, although they were not on my list. All those tribes administered from Meru are grouped as Meru, although this general term comprises the Chuka, Tharaka, MUTHAMBI, IGEMBE, IMENTI, IGOSHI, MWIMBI, and TIGANIA; all are Bantu, except the Tigania who are Nilo-Hamites and an offshoot of the Masai from the time when they roamed around this part of Kenya.

The earliest of these people to arrive were the Chuka, who may have come here from the Coast about A.D. 1300. Their exodus was provoked by an invasion from Somalia, which drove the people living round Shungwaya, north of Malindi, away (they had originally come from the Teita Hills). Some of them then fled further south to the Coast and today these are the NYIKA tribes; some settled along the Tana River and are today known as the POKOMO, while the rest crossed the Northern Frontier District and became part of the Meru group. Their migration route left its mark on them, since they still have certain words and rituals in common with the people inhabiting the Northern Frontier Province.

I heard that a Meru chief had recently tried to interest his people in their history; together with the Church Missionary Society mission he had arranged for the performance of a Christmas play, which described the history of their migrations. The rehearsals at first went well. Then suddenly they came to a stop. Apparently the Africans got worried that if the fact that they had immigrated to this well-watered, fertile country became known in high quarters, they might be repatriated to Shungwaya which, by comparison, is a barren, semi-desert country. Finally the play had to be dropped.

My Government contract limited the number of my paintings for each tribe to six, although it was left to the discretion of the D.C. and myself to alter this number by agreement. I was not strictly bound to a date-line, so long as I worked within the limit of the money which had been allocated. If I decided to paint more pictures than money had been allowed for, I did this at my own risk; I felt justified in doing so in this instance, for these Africans were likely soon to abandon their traditional way of life, and it seemed a pity not to record all that still remained of it while I was in this area.

After finishing with the Tharaka, I went to Meru and discussed my problems with the D.C. He very kindly offered to help and we arranged that I should go to Maua, some forty miles away, high up in the Jombeni Hills, to paint the Igembe. In Maua there was not only a Police post and a Methodist mission, but also a new Welfare hall near which I pitched my camp. It is a most attractive place situated at an altitude of about seven thousand feet at the end of the fifty mile long volcanic Jombeni Range. With an average rainfall of a hundred and twenty inches a year,

92

KANYARU   KIAMBATI
RONDONI,   KIOGOJI
IGEMBE

M. KUABI M. IKWINGA
NTURA,   URINGU
    TIGANIA

JOY

39. Circumcised Tharaka youth dressed to intimidate a younger boy undergoing circumcision

it is one of the most fertile parts of Kenya. The few houses of this small station
nestled among hills and extinct craters, all densely forested; there were patches
of phoenix palms and, as one went higher, of bamboo. From the hills one has a
view over the vast plains and mountains of the Northern Frontier Province bordering on the Jombeni. The climate is brisk, and owing to the heavy mist I was often
chilly until midday, when it usually cleared up.

95

40. A Njuri elder of the Tigania tribe

Among the Africans who daily crowded round the Welfare hall I noticed some men wearing sheepskin coronets, their eyes and foreheads painted with white and yellow markings of an unusual design (40). I was told that these were *Njuri* elders (41), and that all the tribes round Meru had a well organized age-set system from which the High Council of Government for clan and tribal affairs is recruited.

41. A Njuri elder of the Igembe tribe

This Council, known as *Njuri Nchkeke*, is extremely powerful and functions as the liaison between Government, the local Native Council, and the Meru people and exercises control over land, forest, water, and native customs. Its members are chosen from the wiser, richer, and more influential members of the *kiama*, which is the usual council of elders.

97

I noticed that the younger *Njuris* had paint only around their eyes, a sign that they had only recently been initiated as *Njuris*. During this period the older *Njuris* added markings to those on their foreheads, which proclaimed: 'The *Njuri* is having children.'

After I had painted three of these men, I found it difficult to get more models, and was told by the rather sophisticated African clerk of the Welfare center that the population here was too advanced to practice traditional customs. The nearby mission had also influenced the people. I was delighted when a sorcerer arrived who had been summoned by the Chief to sit for me (42). I was told that his ornaments were foreign and belonged to the Pokomo and DURUMA people; this was interesting as it proved a link between the Meru, Pokomo, and Nyika group, to which the Duruma belong, before they all split up in the fourteenth century.

One morning I went to the market, hoping to find models. Luck was with me; I saw two youngsters who attracted my attention not only by their peculiar clothing, but also by their singing. Apparently they were in a stage, several weeks prior to their circumcision, when they wander around the villages in imitation warrior clothing, made of material such as grass stalks, cock feathers and bamboo strings, thus announcing their impending initiation. In response the women present the candidates with small gifts and food (pl. XIII, p. 93).

I painted these young men and with my fees added considerably to their gifts. Unfortunately I could not find a girl during her initiation period and had to paint one especially dressed up as she would be during her seclusion. I was told that after clitoridectomy she would be kept for six months in a special hut under the care of a 'mother' whose duty it is to make her as fat as possible. During seclusion the girl wears no ornaments and allows her hair to grow so long that it may cover the eyes. She has few visitors and it is made very difficult for her future husband to see her; she marries almost immediately afterwards. Coming out of seclusion, she is shaved by the tutor, encouraged to widen her ear-lobes, puts on strings of beads, and on special occasions may wear a white painted stripe.

After I had completed this picture, a woman posed for me in a dress worn for circumcision dances. Among other ornaments she carried a colorful painted wooden shield of minute size, which on these occasions she would beat with a sword.

Altogether I painted twelve people in various costumes, but most of them had to be specially dressed up for me.

Amongst the Igembe, no young woman was allowed to expose her breasts, only older ones did so.

I called frequently at the mission to add to my knowledge of the local people and was told by the doctor that he found it difficult to get the women to enter the mission hospital; only the wives of government employees came to the maternity

42. Igembe sorcerer

ward, obviously wishing to please the authorities. Soon I could add my own observations.

While I was painting a witch doctor, the clerk of the Welfare center strolled by. As he saw the old man spreading out his monkey fur, cowries, bells and bird-skulls, and explaining their powers, the clerk assured me that no one any long paid attention to all the rubbish, and that everyone went to the mission doctor to get aspirin.

However, I knew that there existed a sacred lake near the summit of the Jombeni Hills which was frequently visited by witch doctors in order to recover their powers. Several District Commissioners had tried with the help of a guide to locate this place, but had never succeeded in finding it.

My curiosity was aroused and I tried my best during the three weeks I camped in Maua to get a guide to lead me to the lake. Although several men promised to come, each at the last moment was detained by some urgent job. This strengthened my determination and, knowing that one of George's Game Scouts belonged to the Igembe, I asked him to bring him when next he came for a weekend. I hoped that thanks to his influence we might get a guide to show us the sacred lake. Isiolo was not far away and the Jombeni Hills were within George's control. My plan was successful and soon after George arrived with the Scout we were all climbing the steep foothills which lead to the summit. The higher we went, the more impenetrable the forest became, and when we reached the bamboo belt, we had often to crawl on our hands and knees along narrow tunnels, while buffalo crashed through the woods, far too close for my liking. Though we had rifles, it was frightening to be so close to these animals and I could imagine how the witch doctors, who are usually older men and have nothing but their witchcraft for protection, must have felt as they approached the lake.

Later it began to drizzle and the dripping bamboo soaked us to the skin. We were by then at an altitude of about eight thousand feet and it was bitterly cold. As we had walked since dawn, everybody was tired. But when the guide suggested that we should turn back as it would soon be dark, I insisted on carrying on. Determined not to be defeated, I told the guide that, if he did not find the lake today, I would stay overnight and continue the search tomorrow; he, of course, would have to remain with me and there would be no reward if he failed to find the place.

I do not know which of these alternatives impressed him more, but within a few minutes we reached the spot. We must have circled around it for hours, and it was plain that the guide had intended to mislead us. Although there was no lake, it was strategically a well-chosen spot for ritual ceremonies, for it was easy to protect against unwanted visitors. At the far end of a semicircular, sheltered gorge a small spring dripped and formed a little pool out of which the water trickled

43. Tigania warriors with shields

over two rocky ledges and ran into the forest. Near the pool were a few chicken bones, no doubt remains of sacrificed animals, as well as several small bundles of sticks, each marked with different cuttings at their ends. As we were frozen, I told the men to light a fire with the sticks and make tea. My suggestion horrified them; they explained that the sticks belonged to various witch doctors and that a curse would fall on them if they burned them. Since they felt like this, there was nothing to do but to return home as cold as we were.

The following morning a noticeably hushed atmosphere greeted us. Even the sophisticated clerk was subdued and came to tell me that George and I would die within the next six months, as we were the first Europeans to see the sacred lake and by doing so had broken its spell. However loyally the clerk wanted to be 'progressive', he reverted instinctively to his old beliefs when the tribal spirits were threatened.

I was sorry to have unknowingly transgressed the local spirit's law, but it made me aware of the powerful hold which superstition has over these people.

From Maua I went to paint the Tigania, who are the neighbors of the Igembe. I had sent word of my coming and on my arrival found a large crowd waiting (43),

101

44. Tigania warrior

dressed up in anything they could find. It took a lot of sifting, in which the Chief helped, before I could select fourteen people worth painting. The Tigania still use some of the Masai insignia such as shields, ostrich feathered head-dresses and women's ornaments (44, 45), and the grass skirts they wear on ritual occasions

45. Tigania warrior

46. Tigania war leader

show Coast influence. But they have also developed customs of their own. I was enthralled by the attire of a warrior, who was acknowledged as the bravest man of the clan and in time of war would be chosen to lead his people (46). The apron covering his back, lavishly decorated with cowries, was the equivalent of a regiment's colors, and should on no account fall into the hands of the enemy. A quiver

TWAMIKWA RECHE
URINGU NKOMO
TIGANIA

47. Tigania hunter lighting a fire

holding ostrich feathers was attached to it, and both were blessed before the battle
by the medicine man to protect the wearer and make him lead his men to victory.
The mere sight of this apron and quiver was believed to throw the enemy into
confusion. But since he wore it on his back, perhaps its main purpose was to
encourage his men to follow him (pl. XIV, p. 94).

Another interesting man was a hunter in a hula-hula grass skirt, with a bamboo rattle for scaring birds hanging from his shoulder. He belonged to a guild of hunters, as despised as it was feared. Their curse was believed to be so powerful that many wealthy and respected men preferred to join this guild rather than risk trouble from their curse.

I painted two pictures of this hunter, one showing him shooting with bow and arrow, the other lighting a fire (47). His method was the ancient one used before matches were introduced. Twirling a stick in the notch of a piece of dry wood, he finally generated a spark which, falling on tinder, was blown into a flame. I tried to copy this method but found it beyond my skill to make a spark.

Of the many missions around the Meru district, I found the Church Missionary Society the most helpful. One missionary in particular was interested in my work and asked me whether I had a picture of a girl wearing a *gitaita*. He explained that this was a fringe of tiny metal chains worn across the eyes immediately after clitoridectomy. This made me very keen to find such a girl. For many days my inquiries drew a blank until finally in a remote valley I heard that high up in the forest such a girl was living in seclusion. The following weekend George came to visit me to demonstrate his newly bought Land Rover. It was the first to be used in the Northern Frontier Province and he wanted to show me what this fabulous car could do. Of course I suggested driving into the forest to find the girl.

We bumped across forbidding country for as far as even a Land Rover could go and then continued on foot, accompanied by the local headman. He guided us to a tiny hut which seemed deserted, for nobody answered our calls. While we were waiting for someone to turn up, the headman told us that here in Tigania a girl lives in seclusion for two years with an older woman who instructs her in her future duties and all that married life will entail. During this period the girl has to behave in a helpless manner, is only allowed to speak in a whisper, and has to keep her eyes downcast under a fringe of metal chains; she is made as fat as possible and, when she leaves the hut, has to be led by her 'mother's' hand and walk extremely slowly.

All this seemed to me to indicate a symbol of rebirth, the fringe across the eyes intimating that she has not yet learned to see, the whisper that she does not know how to speak, nor can she walk alone. During these two years she sometimes occupies herself by looking after a small child or making string-bags or ornamenting calabashes.

If her bridegroom wants to visit her during her seclusion, he has to bring costly presents, not only to her but also to her family; in consequence he cannot afford to see her often. At the end of the period he marries her within a week.

48. Tigania girl in seclusion, back view   49. Tigania girl in seclusion, front view

After a while the old woman in charge of the girl appeared, but was so alarmed at seeing us that she ran to the village to get the girl's parents. When they had arrived, the headman explained the purpose of our visit, dissipated their worries and persuaded them to let me have a close look at the girl.

I hardly could believe what I now saw. When I entered the tiny hut I almost banged into a partition facing the entrance. After my eyes had become accustomed to the darkness inside, I realized that this was one of the walls of the girl's sleeping room which was only just large enough for her to crouch in. On one side of the cubicle, between it and the outer wall of the round hut, was a small storage place for her belongings. The inside walls of the hut were plastered with mud on which representations of ornaments such as a man's armlet made of buffalo horn or a design of women's skirt-embroideries were painted.

Most intriguing were little mud receptacles, plastered like swallows' nests on the wall and painted white. Each contained three different seeds, probably charms. I was told that these were taken away by the bridegroom when he finally came to get the girl. From the roof hung pieces of wood which, when burnt and allowed to smoulder, gave off a pleasant scent.

The girl herself was very plump and covered in a long, charcoal-blackened skin, decorated with cowries and blue seeds. Her head was shaven except for the top where the hair was shaped into a crown. From the back of her neck across her skull and hair ran a broad white mark painted with a strong-smelling substance, which was also painted on her nose (48, 49). Her 'mother' showed a similar line across

107

her shaven head. In the girl's hand I noticed a piece of string with many knots and was told these had to be unravelled by her bridegroom or his supporters before the marriage could be consummated.

I was fascinated by the girl who stood silent, like a statue, staring at the ground. Of course I wanted to paint her, but as it was not possible for me to do it here, I tried, with the help of the headman, to get her family to agree to letting her come to my camp. After a long consultation, helped by considerable baksheesh, it was decided that all of them, including her bridegroom, would accompany her to my camp and remain with her until I had painted her.

The next problem was how to bring the girl to the car which was too far away for us to carry her there. When I looked at the soles of her feet, which were as soft as those of a newly born baby, I realized that she had not walked for some time, and it seemed to me that, considering the pace at which she would now be able to walk, she would never be able to reach the car that day.

The headman came to my rescue and suggested that George and I should walk ahead and he would see that the girl followed. So we went along and, after a while, I looked back to see what was happening to the little procession. To my surprise I saw that they were coming along splendidly, the girl walking vigorously in the middle of the group. But when we finally got her into the car and started driving, she was sick and we all were glad when at last we reached my camp. We installed the party in as much seclusion as possible and arranged that nobody except her own people could see her during the time she stayed with me. I also saw to it that she and her family got all the special food they required.

After Tigania I visited the Imenti (50) (pl. XV, p. 111), the people who live very close to the Administration Headquarters at Meru. It was all the more surprising that in spite of their daily contact with numerous Europeans, many of the Africans were completely untouched by their influence.

Barely a mile away from all the hustle of traffic, offices, and schools, I found a girl sitting in front of her hut, obviously undergoing her seclusion period. In contrast to her counterpart in Tigania, who had looked as if she had been dipped in black paint, this one looked as if she had been dipped in ocher. Not only her eyes but her whole face was covered by a fringe of seeds which merged together with her ocher-colored braided hair hanging all over her head (51). She was as fat as the Tigania girl, even more loaded with seeds and cowries, and wore a belt of a bamboo pattern identical with the bird rattle of the Tigania hunter; under her hide clothes she was painted with the same striations, resembling a jacket, as he was. Though her hut was close to a village and right in the open so that everybody could see her, she behaved as helplessly as the girl in Tigania.

108

50. Imenti
circumciser

51.   Imenti girl in seclusion during circumcision rites

xv   Imenti circumciser

M. RINGERA   KUNGANIA
MAGUNDU,   NTAKIRA
IMENTI

LUKHOLO SHIRISIA
HAMUKUYA, MIRONJE
ISUKHA

JOY

52. Imenti boys
before circumcision

I had no difficulty in getting her to my camp to paint her, but of course I
respected her state and kept her as isolated from onlookers as I could.

The circumcision candidates (52) also observed customs similar to their counter-
parts among the Igembe and Tigania, except that they wore grass skirts and their
chests were painted white. One showed a small decoration on his temple which
was caused by staining the skin with the juice of a cashew nut. Since this tree grows

113

only on the Coast, the custom, as well as the grass skirts, may have been a survival from the time when the Meru lived there.

The country all around Meru is very fertile and though it is thickly populated one hardly sees the huts among the dense patches of bananas, maize, beans, coffee and indeed any crop which can be grown aided by heavy rainfalls in that rich volcanic soil.

Meru itself is a very attractive district, situated on the slopes of Mount Kenya with its beautiful forest in which one often sees Colobus monkeys, buffaloes, elephants, and antelopes of various kinds. The *boma* is at the lower end of the forest and from there one overlooks the undulating plains leading up to the many volcanic hills of the forested Jombeni Range which borders on the semi-desert of the Northern Frontier Province.

On one of my afternoon walks, which I took regularly to relax from the day's painting session, I came across a large pottery. This was run by women; though they used no wheel but moulded each pot by hand, these were beautifully shaped and often very large. Having done some ceramic work myself, a long time ago, I could appreciate the quality of the pottery and the proof it gave of the skill of its makers.

Honey hunting was another favorite occupation here, and I painted one man with the rope he used to climb trees, a skin drum to collect the honey, a bundle of green sticks to smoke the bees out of the hive, and an axe for bush clearing.

One day, after having completed the picture of an elder wearing a large head-dress of ostrich plumes, a monkey coat and a spear, I took a stroll. Walking up a lonely valley I must have come close to his home, for suddenly he appeared on the top of a hill, still dressed in the clothes in which he had posed for me. As soon as he spotted me, he came tearing down the slope, shouting and waving his spear excitedly. For a time I thought he was doing this for fun, but when he came closer I realized that he was out to charge and I had to run as fast as I could to escape his spear. Yelling and waving it threateningly, he followed me; luckily he aroused the attention of some Africans who came to my rescue. Only after considerable trouble could they bring the 'old warrior' under control and take him to the Chief. I did my best to secure his release when the Chief wanted to tie him to a tree to sober him up. The only explanation that I could think of to explain the strange antics of this elder, who had behaved with very good manners throughout the day, was that wearing traditional ornaments must have gone to his head and that, perhaps stimulated by a little home-made beer to celebrate the occasion, his mind had switched back to the time when he was still fighting tribal wars.

Among the neighboring Mwimbi I painted a woman wearing an ocher-dyed thick hide roll around her neck which indicated that she could no longer bear children.

114

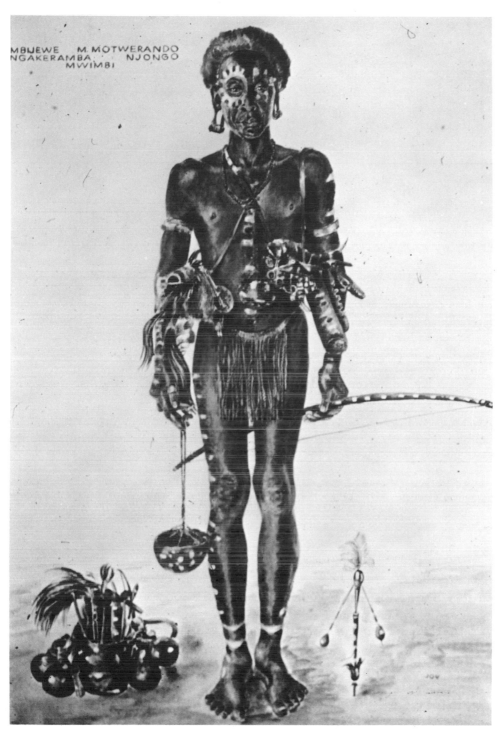

53. Mwimbi sorcerer

115

54. Mwimbi girl weaving basket while walking

I also painted a sorcerer (53) who among his bulky outfit had a small instrument which, he believed, represented his heart. It was made of two tiny *dikdik* horns, balanced one on top of the other and kept steady by two grass stalks with little resin lumps at their ends. These grass stalks were fastened to the tops of the horns, pointing to the sides. The whole structure was extremely delicate and was used as an infallible test to prove the reliability of a man. Though it moved at the slightest breeze, if this 'lie detector' showed the faintest movement while a 'client' spoke, he was dismissed as a liar. The sorcerer never dealt with any person without first consulting it. I was relieved to learn that this test was only used in connection with witchcraft and never when medical help was needed.

116

55. Very old Muthambi witch doctor

Basket weaving is done by girls and married women, mainly while they are walking around (54).

Moving south along the base of Mount Kenya, I visited the Igoshi and Muthambi, two small groups whose customs are similar to those of the other Meru people, though they use fewer ornaments originating from the Coast. I passed several missions on my way, and it was probably owing to their influence that I found it

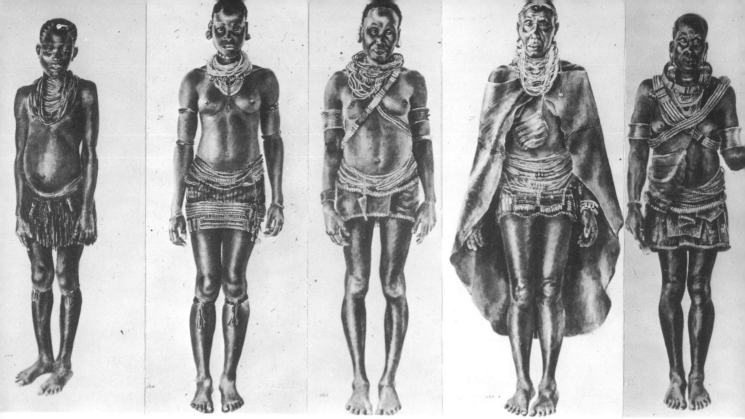

56. Chuka girl before initiation   57. Chuka girl after clitoridectomy   58. Chuka young mother

59. Chuka woman past child-bearing age   60. Chuka woman circumciser

difficult to get sitters and had, for my purpose, to paint models dressed up in traditional clothing for the occasion.

I was fortunate in finding a very old witch doctor to pose for me (55), and a Muthambi girl, indicating the transition period between initiation and marriage by a white and red ring painted round her eyes.

Last on my list were the Chuka and with them I completed my portraits of the Meru group. My first visit had ended abruptly because of my illness; now the Chief welcomed me back and proved of great help. I painted a sequence of a woman's life, beginning with a small girl before initiation (56). When a girl wants to be initiated, she calls on her relations for ten days, and receives small presents from them. These visits are called kuratia. On the eleventh day she visits the young warriors in their house (gari) whom she also informs of her intention. These warriors take her to a special ground (itiri) and a big dance (ntayu) is held for her which lasts until the early morning. After the girl returns home, she washes and until three in the afternoon prepares herself for her initiation, by which time women of all ages arrive, dancing and singing the song of Njei. No man is permitted to be present, but men can look on from a distance. At 6 p.m. the operation is performed, during which no man is allowed near. Afterwards the girl is taken to a

118

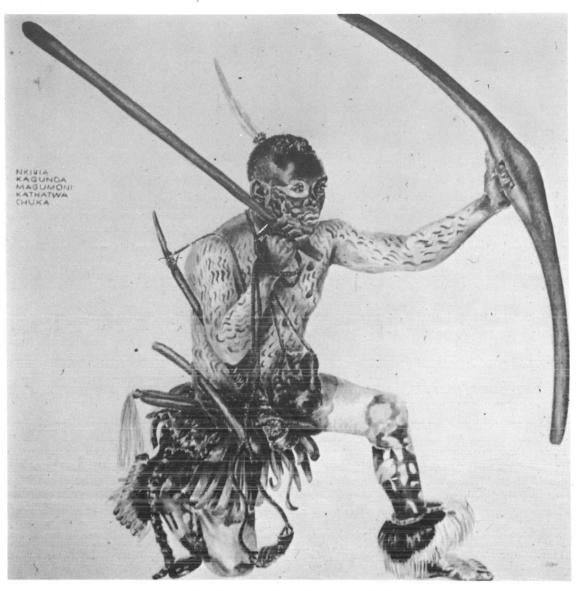

NKIRIA
KAGUNDA
MAGUMONI
KATHATWA
CHUKA

61.   Chuka warrior with parrying shield

special hut *(gichiere)* where she remains for three to six months. During this period she helps to cultivate a small compound nearby, but if she wants to go further off, she has to cover herself from head to foot with a large bag. So she lives until she marries.

I painted a girl before and after the operation (57), then a young woman whose children had not been initiated (58), and elderly woman past bearing children (59), and finally a woman circumciser (60). All these phases were symbolized by their ornaments.

119

About the boys' circumcision rites I learned that they were performed in the old days between the ages of eighteen and twenty, but are now done between twelve and fourteen. A short time prior to the initiation each youth can carry a gourd, bow and arrow, but only one or two are allowed to blow a special hide-covered horn *(choro)* which is always kept inside a hut. Should any other boy wish to blow it, he has first to bring a chicken as a gift, otherwise he will be punished.

The day before circumcision the candidate dresses in special clothes and calls in the morning on the elders. Without saying a word, he jumps three times in front of them. In response the elders shout, whereupon the boy runs home. Now the elders are supposed to blow a bugle to inform the neighbors of the forthcoming initiation, but they rarely do so, waiting for the boy's father to present them with a goat and apologize in case his son should have offended them. When they see the goat, the elders blow the bugle without fail, assure the father that they have heard his son, and return with him to his hut. The boy is then taken to a special ground *(itiri)* where he will be circumcised next morning. In the meantime a big dance is held which lasts from 4 p.m. until next morning. Then the operation is performed. When all is over, the elders take the youth to a banana plot where he remains until 6 p.m.; only then can he go to a special temporary hut where he sleeps and is looked after, until he recovers, by a boy appointed to do so.

Among the warriors I painted one using a wooden parrying shield of a very narrow, bow-like shape. This, together with a long wooden club, is as deadly as the stone-sling which this warrior also carried (61). Among all the tribes and customs I recorded, this was the only time that I came across these weapons.

The Chuka claim to be brothers of the Tharaka, both having the same father. Both lived originally in Chuka country, from which the Tharaka later moved into their present location. Some evidence of contact may be found in the fact that the same kind of long, wooden rattles are used by young men of both tribes when they go to a dance (62).

By now the rainy season had started and it interfered a great deal with my painting. As I had completed my record of the Meru people, George and I decided to go to the Congo until the weather here improved. On our way through Nairobi I showed my latest paintings to the Government officials, who seemed pleased with them and agreed that I should go on painting whatever interesting models I might think worth recording, even if I should exceed the number stated in my contract. Of course I understood that I should do this at my own risk.

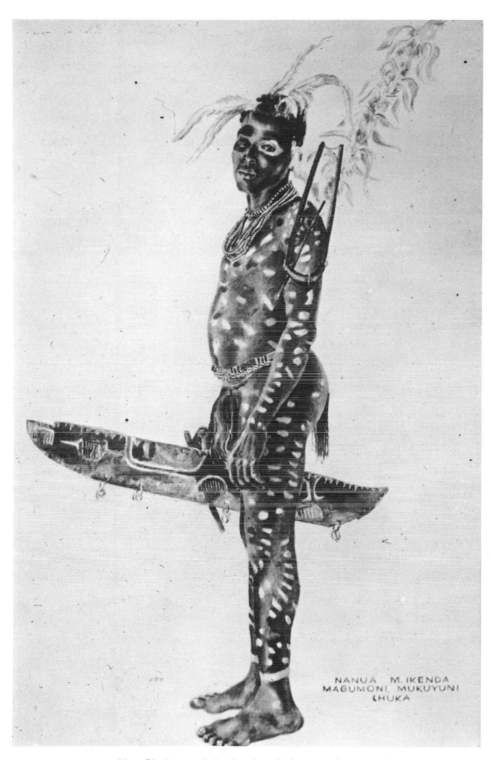

62.   Chuka youth in dancing clothes carrying a rattle

121

CHAPTER 6

AMONG THE LUHYA

On our return from the Congo I was asked to continue my record with the KAVI-RONDO LUHYA, a large Bantu group comprising the KITOSH (BUKUSU), TATSONI, KABARASI, KAKELELWA*, TSOTSO*, ISUKHA*, and IDAKHO* (collectively KAKUMEGA), TIRIKI*, MARAGOLI*, HANGA, MARAMA, KISA*, NYALA, XAIYO, MARACHI, SAMIA*, NYOLE, who came from Uganda.

On my way I had to pass close to the MASAI DOROBO who were also on the list to be painted and had been selected from amongst the twelve Dorobo groups who live in Kenya because they had more distinct characteristics than the rest.

Little seems known about the origin of all Dorobo, and theories vary; some say that they inhabited Kenya before the present tribes invaded it and later mixed with the neighboring tribes. All Dorobo speak dialects of Nandi no matter where they live. Any people claiming to be Dorobo who do not speak Nandi are not Dorobo.

All Dorobo used to live in the forest, where they feel safer than in open country and exist on hunting for which they use bows, poisoned arrows and traps. Sometimes they also grow tiny patches of crops to supplement their food; they are great lovers of honey, which provides them with their only form of sugar.

The Masai Dorobo here had their home high up in the Mau forest above Njoro, and I camped there. They had many ornaments in common with the Masai and Nandi on the other side of the Mau escarpment, but having adjusted their weapons to forest life, they had neither spear nor shield, only a long knife in a leather sheath, or a wooden club for their protection. They also lacked any sort of head-dress and wore their hair in little plaits or ocher-greased pigtails.

A youngster, whom I painted in his circumcision stage (63) wore two hawk feathers instead of the two ostrich feathers which are the typical Nilo-Hamitic emblems of this state; obviously there were no ostriches at this altitude. The boy was painted white all over; he wore black-dyed hides like the Masai and wandered

*I painted the tribes whose names are marked with an asterisk.

122

63 Dorobo youth in circumcision dress

64. Dorobo married woman immediately after
giving birth

through the forest during the seclusion months in the company of one or two other candidates, shooting little birds with resin-blunted arrows.

The girls remained, during their seclusion period, inside a special hut and showed their state by parallel striations painted in white across their foreheads, temples and cheeks. The same design, but with only one line, was painted on married women for one day after they had borne a child (64). Both these markings differed from the ones the Masai used in the same circumstances.

I visited the little homestead of the nearest Dorobo family, who lived in flimsy grass huts in a forest glade. There were many children about, and I was interested to find out if they played games, to teach each other hunting, similar to those we

123

had watched among the Pygmy children playing in the Ituri Forest of the Congo. There they trained themselves to hit a fast moving target with their tiny arrows by standing in a circle around a youngster, who whirled a small fruit on a string past them, and we were amazed how often the children succeed in hitting the target. Here I found nothing of the sort, nor did I see any net-hunting as the Pygmies practice it. They use a kind of long tennis net stretched from tree to tree over a considerable distance and hanging close to the ground. Beside it the hunters are placed at short intervals and go for the game which is driven into the nets with loud shouting by the women. As this method involves a great crowd and a lot of noise, it is understandable that it is not used by the Dorobo, who, since the introduction of the Game Laws, have always to hunt illegally.

I noticed that the women here had far greater authority than is usual among Africans, probably owing to the fact that there are fewer women than men among the Dorobo. As they are consequently held in high esteem, I was worried when I noticed that my boy developed a distinct liking for one of the girls. Daniel was a Bantu from Meru, who had been in our service for many years and was acting as a 'man of all works' for me since I started on my painting commission. He had been educated at a mission, was married, had several children, and by, African standards, was well off, owning a big holding and livestock, which his family managed while he was away. Lately he had been absent for several nights and, though I tried my best to control him, he continued to sneak off after dark. I had by now spent four weeks at this lovely forest camp, and in spite of Daniel's misbehavior, had almost made friends with these shy Dorobo. When the day came to move on, I was touched when they presented me with some of their delicious wild honey as a farewell gift.

Now I drove on over the highlands, crossing the equator at an altitude of about nine thousand feet, and passing through beautiful, partly forested, country. Finally I descended a steep escarpment with a drop of some six thousand feet to Kisumu on Lake Victoria. Here were the headquarters of the Nyanza Province and the change of climate from the chilly forest to the humid heat around the lake was very noticeable.

I called on the Provincial Commissioner, who had already organized my stay in his area, and arranged to have my first camp established at Vihiga not far from Kisumu. There I would be close to several tribes, would be looked after by an African District Officer, and also be near to a big girls' school.

To reach Vihiga I drove up an escarpment from where I had a wonderful view over Lake Victoria, which is almost like a sea. I well remember the reply of a patriotic Swiss to whom I mentioned that this lake was six times larger than Switzerland; his answer was: 'not if you iron Switzerland out'.

I pitched my camp within a few hundred yards of the house of the D.O. of whom I had already heard, since he was one of the first Africans to join the Administration. We decided that I should first paint the Maragoli. I had to wait a long time before finding any suitable models, so I tried to make the best use of this time by calling at two local missions; at the first I drew blank stares when I asked for photographs or notes on traditional customs. One elderly missionary, who had been here for forty years, even denied having any knowledge of circumcision, which I knew to be practiced by most of the Luhya men, though not by women. The other mission was more helpful; I was shown early photographs which gave me an idea how people dressed in the past.

While we were discussing this, we heard the wailing of women; although the person whom they mourned for had been buried with Christian rites, the traditional wailing continued and was still going on when I called again the next day.

I also often called at a girls' school—the first one of its kind in Kenya—where some thirty carefully selected African girls were educated for three years. Not only did they learn to become good housewives and look after their future children properly, but were also taught to stimulate, by their example, the women of their villages to improve their way of living. By talking to the girls and their schoolmistress, I learned a lot about the problems confronting women of the old and present days.

On my walks I saw many deposits of neat little baskets which were made for transporting quail (65); these birds are caught in season by the thousand, partly for eating by the local Africans, partly for sale all over Kenya; they also provided a good income for the huntsmen. The people here are great experts in wickerwork and use baskets of all sorts for various purposes.

Most of the round huts had a stick projecting from the top of their thatched roof, which was there to keep the evil spirits away; when it hailed, a special slippery grass was tied around to direct the hail.

The Maragoli are fond of beer which they make by fermenting millet or sorghum. If a man wants to visit a friend in the hope of being invited to a beer party, he first spits reverently in all directions, then takes his youngest child to show him the way he should go. If it chooses to step to the left, he takes this to be a good omen and follows that direction. But if no beer is offered him on his way, he will turn back and rely on the next child to give him a better start. Spitting is of great importance, and the elders do it each morning when God is asked to bless the new day.

The Maragoli believe in one God, *Nyasaye*, who is helped by several spirits. To these, offerings are made in a special shrine which has at its center a five-foot pole, surrounded by eight large round stones. Once a year, preferably in August around

65. Maragoli quail baskets

harvest time, the elders mix millet and water and spit this mixture onto the heads and feet of the women and children assembled under the eaves of this shrine, to prevent the evil spirits from harming them. Then a white or black fowl is killed and the blood, dribbling from its beak, is also smeared onto their heads and feet as well as on the eight stones. Afterwards the chicken's beak is cut off and a hole is pierced into it by which it is hung around the neck of the youngest child. The rest of the fowl is then roasted until it is almost black and the flesh, mixed with millet, cooked to a thick paste which is placed on the eight stones. What remains is eaten by the children and men. Similar rites are performed in cases of illness to appease the angry spirits responsible for them.

126

66. Maragoli potter

On special occasions the elders congregate at a sacred tree called *murembe*, walk around it three times, then kneel on one knee and pray for help. This they do as a rule on Mondays or Tuesdays.

In the old days a sheep was sacrificed before a raid, and a witch doctor was asked which way to go. He may well have had his secret sources of information but he performed the necessary rites and the raid was usually successful. When the

67. Maragoli warrior

men returned with their loot, they had to spend the night outside their huts close to their poisoned arrows and spears which they were not permitted to take inside. Next morning these were hung in a safe place on the wall outside and remained there.

No man should marry before he was circumcised and had proved himself in raids or war. In case of war, a horn was blown at dawn as a signal for the start. If this horn was heard again in the evening, the people knew there had been a disaster and that many had been killed.

128

68. Maragoli
circumciser

A widow is given her late husband's spear and shield; she carries them during his funeral, and hands them afterwards to his eldest brother. The Maragoli bury their old men lying on the right side and the young ones on the left.

The wives do all the planting of the crops and start at dawn; they watch the shadow of the sun, and when it is at its shortest they go home and give the children porridge. Men eat only fat at midday, it is stored in a bullock horn. Their main meal, which they eat close to their cattle, is taken in the evening.

I learned that while in the old days the men always covered themselves with a skin hung from their shoulders, the women used to wear nothing but a tiny fiber fringe for modesty in front and one at the back. They were experts in making pottery and I watched them doing it (66), but although they used a framework of sticks as moulds for the clay, their pots were less shapely than the ones I had seen made by the Meru women who used no support.

By now the D.O. had produced a few models, among whom was a witch doctor. He looked a bit of a fake but made up for it by telling me the story of a monster which rises from Lake Victoria and disappears into the sky. I suppose he meant the thin curtain of rain one could often see hanging over the lake which, whipped by a storm into fine whirls, could easily give rise to such a legend.

I found painting my next model, a musician, more enjoyable. He had an instrument like a lute, but it had its seven strings stretched across a frame. Next came a warrior with an elaborate head-dress made of wickerwork and a shield of buffalo hide which, as I was told, would be painted if it belonged to a young man (67). A circumciser posing for me (68) told me that the Maragoli, Tiriki, Kakelelwa, Isukha, Idakho, Nyala, and Kitosh tribes only circumcise the men.

Close to the Maragoli live the Tiriki who, being neighbors and related to the Nilo-Hamitic Nandi, have adopted some of their ornaments. I painted a youth in seclusion costume who was almost invisible under a fiber hood which had only eye-holes (69). The circumcision cycle is repeated every four or five years, the candidates' age varying between twenty-five and thirty years. After the operation all live together in a special hut for six months during which period they are not allowed to be seen by women of childbearing age. They are fed by the men of the previous circumcision cycle, who instruct them in their future duties as warriors and useful members of the community. After two months the candidates are permitted to leave the hut, under the cover of a hood and under the protection of two guardians, one walking ahead and one in the rear, to keep intruders off the path; if these are not Tiriki, they are often beaten. The candidates are allowed to attend dances, but may speak only to each other on such occasions. The hoods are made by their tutors and are handed over to the group of the next circumcision cycle to be worn by the new candidates until fresh ones are provided, which again will be handed on.

I painted a circumciser who wore a head covering of cowrie shells and a ram's horn as his emblem (70). His fly-switch was a cow's tail and his coat was made of cowhide. He told me that he seldom gets a fee except from men who marry before

130

69. Tiriki youth in seclusion during circumcision

131

being circumcised; in such cases he receives a bull. If he operates on a cripple, he may also get a heifer or a bull.

Should a candidate father an illegitimate child before he is twenty-five, the baby will be cared for by the grandmother of the girl, who is married off to an older man but can never rank as first wife.

All tribes in this area are polygamous, and each man may marry as many wives as he can afford to keep. When twins are born a special emblem is placed on the front door and anybody entering the hut has to give a present of grain or a piece of iron to the babies. In the past the mother was kept in seclusion for two weeks, after which she was allowed to leave the hut but had to kneel down and drink with the cattle out of a trough. A ram was killed on this occasion. Afterwards she was not permitted to visit another village where cattle were kept; she was never again allowed to go near cattle, and therefore she usually remained confined within her village until she died.

One day, while I was painting, my vision suddenly became blurred by a dark red circle in one eye which followed in whatever direction I looked. It was painless, but a great nuisance. As it did not clear up, I drove next day to see a doctor at Kisumu who gave me a penicillin injection. But the red patch got worse, so, when I heard that there was an eye specialist at Eldoret who had recently retired there from the Sudan, I drove the one hundred and six miles to consult him. He diagnosed it as a hemorrhage in the retina; a septic focus somewhere in my body had affected this weak spot, no doubt overstrained by prolonged concentration and painting under difficult conditions. He did a thorough X-ray test but could not find the focus of infection so he advised me to stop painting and continue with the penicillin injections.

Before leaving Eldoret for home, I stopped at a garage to get a minor repair job done on my car. A terrific storm was building up in the direction in which I had to go, and I did not feel too happy at the prospect of driving through it in the dark with my poor vision. While waiting for the car, I met Princess Sapieha, whom I knew slightly through our mutual interest in botany. She told me that she was now helping on a farm while the owners were on holiday and, hearing of my eye trouble, invited me to spend the night there so that I could avoid the storm. I accepted eagerly.

Next morning I found her clearing a patch for planting vegetables. She used a rake with great skill and smoothed the soil until it looked like velvet. When I tried to help her I made a frightful mess. She watched me smiling and said, 'It took me many years to learn from my old gardener how to use a rake; like using a paint brush, it is an art—if you do it properly.' I admired the Princess for the way in which she had adapted herself to a new life—so very different from her old one in pre-war Poland.

132

70. Tiriki circumciser

One day when I called at the girls' school at Vihiga, I noticed a great hush over the place. I was told that the day before the girls had been asked to clean their lockers and they had refused, considering it too low a task and, when reprimanded, had run away. Of course this was only an excuse to cover a deeper motive. They had heard rumors that none of them would find a husband as the young men were suspicious of girls with too much education and doubted their ability to bear children, and this was why they bolted. There may have been some truth in their fears, for it is a recognized fact that many of the qualified African midwives remain unmarried.

The hemorrhage in my eye dissolved after five penicillin injections. As soon as I

133

71. Kisa warrior   72. Kisa warrior

could paint again, I continued with the Kisa, a group living near Vihiga. Here it is the custom for the men to pull out four of the lower incisors and many tribes, including those of Nandi stock, extract the two lower middle incisors. The common explanation for this custom is that, in case of tetanus, the victim can be kept alive by being fed through the gap. The Kisa do not circumcise.

I painted a few warriors (71) carrying enormous shields of wildebeest hide which could conceal more than one man (72). These were embossed in individual patterns, for which unripe banana skins were used to soften the hides.

134

73. Tsotso blacksmiths

Then I moved some thirty miles to paint the Tsotso, Kakelelwa, Idakho, and
Isukha peoples around Kakumega. Thirty years ago Kakumega was the center of
a gold rush but, although a few mines are still worked in the district, it is now
reduced to a small township and a *boma*, which is one of the largest in Kenya. I
was asked to pitch my camp a few miles away in a lane of houses in ruins, remains
of the gold rush period. Some of these had their water supply still intact, and that
was the reason why this area was chosen for my camping site. Kakumega is
notorious for its snakes and I imagined ruins would be ideal lodgings for them,
so I picked a place where only a fireplace remained of former luxuries. As a further
precaution we cut all the bush round about, but had to kill the first cobra even
before my tent was up. Next morning I heard the twittering of birds flying agitated-
ly round a branch of a tree above my tent. When I looked closely, I saw a mamba
blending to perfection into the green foliage; the birds were mocking it. We killed
it with a shotgun I borrowed from the D.O.

I started by painting the Tsotso and got a blacksmith and his assistant to pose
for me (73). Although the blacksmith provides the people with their most essential

implements, such as spears, knives, axes and, among agricultural tribes, hoes and cowbells, the profession is usually despised among Africans. In the old days they collected iron ore from dry riverbeds, nowadays they use scrap metal, but their methods of melting it remain primitive.

The assistant worked two bellows made from a hollowed, forked log. The straight end was inserted into a crudely made funnel of baked clay and pointed at the embers. The forked ends were covered with goatskins tied in the center to a long stick by which they were worked to keep the embers aflame. The blacksmith squatted, reheating the iron and beating it into shape with a crude, hand-made hammer.

Some years ago on Mount Kulal near Lake Rudolf, we surprised a Samburu blacksmith and his wife who was acting as his assistant. We had heard the faint sound of hammering and, following it, found the pair working in an underground hollow covered with branches, which concealed the forge. The woman was working bellows very like those of the Tsotso, except that she had no sticks, but squeezed the wind into the bellows by working the skins with her hands. This pair supplied most of the Samburu district with spears. They kept their workshop hidden on the remote mountain as the Government had imposed a temporary ban on spear-making in this district because a European had recently been speared.

The Tsotso are one of the few tribes among the Luhya group who do not practice circumcision. Here I came face to face with a woman witch doctor; although I knew they also practiced among the Meru group, I had never before seen one. She was timid and, I think, rather frightened that I might give her away to the District Commissioner.

Then I painted a man representing a herald announcing war or death by blowing a bugle which was higher than he was tall (74). It was a combination of several gourds stuck together and when blown resounded with a vibrating boom.

When I asked about funeral rites, I was informed that the Tsotso are buried lying on their left side; the right ear is blocked with a pebble to prevent earth falling in.

The Kakelelwa were next on my list. I painted a young woman who showed that she was only recently married by wearing wooden ear-plugs and a string of metal rings with bells attached to indicate that she had not yet borne a child (75). By the type of her bracelet one knew that she was the daughter of a wealthy man. She also wore a cowrie-ornamented leather strap across her shoulder to ward off evil spirits.

The Kakelelwa are of Nilotic origin, but they have intermarried with the Bantu and have adopted their customs and language to such an extent that they now appear more like Bantu than Nilotics.

136

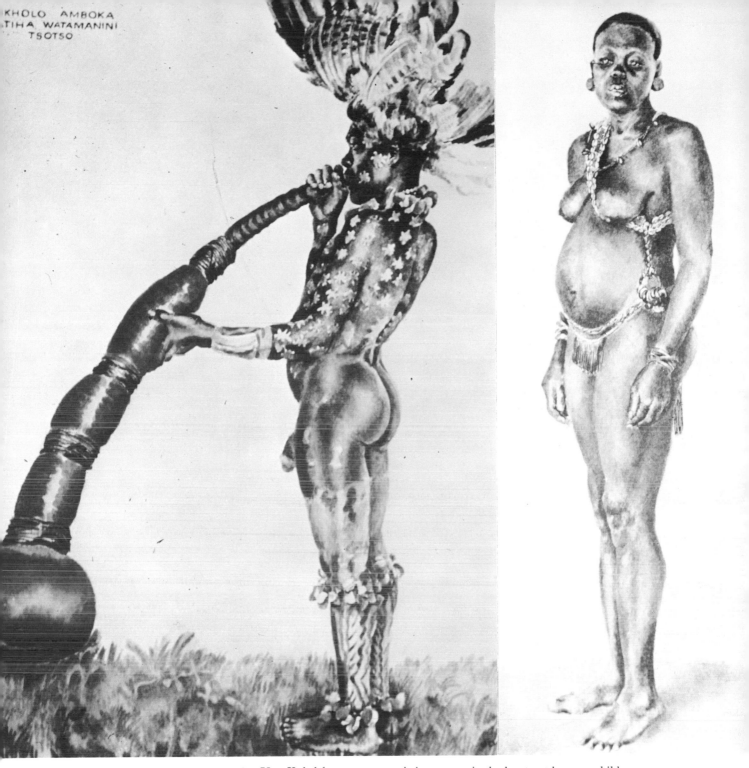

74. Tsotso herald blowing his bugle   75. Kakelelwa young married woman who had not yet borne a child

The two main groups at Kakumega are the Idakho and Isukha (76). They, like the rest of the people between Kisumu and here, are very progressive and almost every model I painted in that area had been especially dressed up in traditional costumes. Yet I knew that circumcision and other rites were still practiced and that even the

137

76.   Isukha musician

local Chief's son had recently been initiated, although his father wore European clothes and drove his own car. This Isukha Chief was most helpful in producing models to illustrate a sequence of all circumcision stages among the Isukha (77a–f), which were similar to those of the Idakho.

The first stage showed a boy between twelve and fifteen years old, holding a small tree *(lusui)* with roots above his head, supposed to give him strength during the operation. The roots in particular were of ritual significance. He was protected against evil by his 'godfather' blowing millet mixed with water over his chest. The operation was performed by a circumciser and his assistant, both painted all over with red and white dots; they also beat a drum to intimidate the boy, who, should he show fear, must pay a goat.

The next stage showed a candidate after the operation wearing a skirt made of branches of *cassia didymobotrya*, held in position by a ritual belt of black, white and red dyed fiber. To prevent the wound from becoming septic, a fiber ring was wrapped around the penis until it was healed. The youth also carried, hanging from his belt, a small roll of leaves containing medicine in case he had to doctor his wound. All this was burnt after seclusion.

For three months a group of thirty to forty candidates lived together in a hut (77) during which time no old man was allowed to see them. The hut had only one door for entrance and exit. After one month the boys could leave the hut, but had to hide themselves under a grass hood held together with vertical fiber bands which must be of the same colors as their belts. These hoods were made by men who belonged to the previous circumcision cycle and looked after the group.

Food, consisting of grain and water, was supplied by a specially chosen girl (77e) who regarded it as a great honor to be selected for this task. During this period she wore a grass skirt and a belt similar to those of the candidates, and in addition the fiber of a special tree around her neck, arms and legs. Nobody was permitted to talk to the girl during the three months, after which she received a small present from the young men.

When the seclusion period comes to an end, the candidates go secretly to a river where they wash thoroughly, as if to free themselves symbolically of their boyhood. Then they wrap around their loins a banana leaf, which has previously been softened over smoke by the elders. During the few hours these are worn, nobody is permitted to see the candidates. Finally all go to the elders who present the leader of the group with a spear and shield and declare that they are now all adult men. The rest of the group has later on to buy their spears with a goat.

If a man marries prior to circumcision he has to pay a goat for the operation, as this is regarded as a disgrace.

Kakumega has a plentiful rainfall and I certainly got my share of it. Daily cloudbursts swamped my camp, and everything got damp. Painting became very

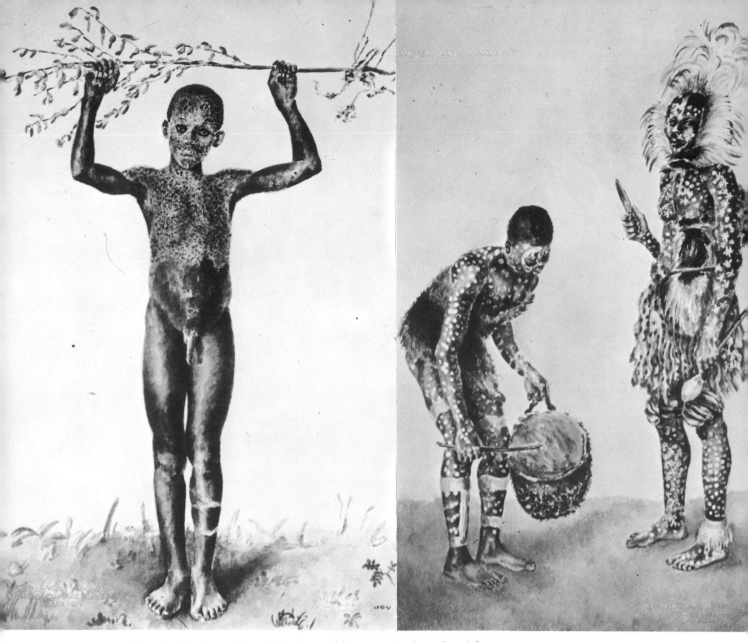

77a.   Isukha boys during their circumcision stages (a, b, c, d and f)

tiresome so I felt excited when one day the Chief brought a woman rainmaker along (pl. XVI, p. 112). He told me that she attracted the element by going to a sacred place where she waved her ritual staff with its thicker end up. In addition she boiled medicine in four large, special pots to which she added the ash of burnt thatching-grass. If the brew boiled over, then rain would come—but if there was no spilling, there would be no rain. Should the rainmaker be annoyed by people and want to stop rain, she would dip her staff with its thin end into the pot and then turn this end up to the sky. As long as the staff was kept in this position, there would be no rain. When people wanted to appease an angry rainmaker and get rain, they usually brought presents until she was conciliated and turned the staff around—which apparently produced the desired result.

140

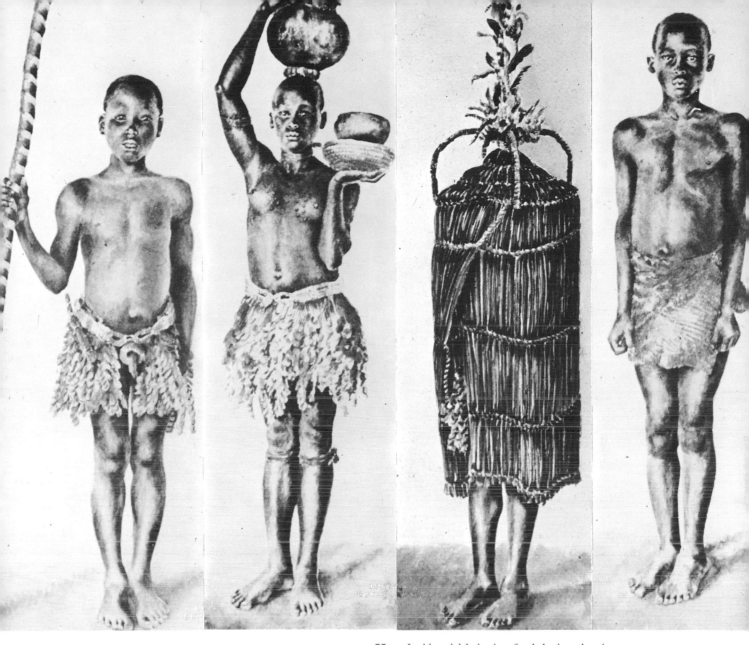

77e. Isukha girl bringing food during the rites

I was more interested in how she could stop the rain, and I was told that she would then move her stick up again, repeating simultaneously, 'I don't want rain, I don't want rain,' until it stopped.

Unfortunately I could not test her powers as on the day I painted her it did not rain, and I did not want her to ask for rain.

The rainmaker's profession is hereditary and this woman had come from quite a distance to sit for me. She wore many charms and had an eagle's claw on her monkey-fur head-dress; owing to the number of her ornaments I could not complete her portrait in one day and asked her to spend the night in camp. But she was in a hurry to get home and insisted on returning. When the Chief intervened, she got angry and threatened to make so much rain during the night that I would

141

78. Isukha sorcerer and witch doctor   79. Isukha potter

drown. This threat seemed quite likely to come true, as black clouds were closing in from all sides. However, I told her that as I could swim I would risk her flood, and at last she agreed to stay. It was bad luck for her that during the night there was not a single drop of rain. When next morning I teased her she had her answer ready and told me, in the most convincing manner, that she had taken pity on me, a woman alone, and had therefore controlled the rain so that I should be safe.

Next I painted a queer old witch doctor who used pebbles for divination (78). If, for instance, he were asked to find a man who had poisoned someone, he would throw his pebbles, naming each after a person who he suspected might be the culprit. The pebble which most frequently rolled close to him gave him the clue to the murderer's identity.

Although witch doctors and sorcerers co-operate, they are seldom seen together (78). There are also female sorcerers who work in competition with men; both sexes acquire their profession by heredity.

Another inherited skill is the making of pottery which among the Isukha is practiced by men (79). They own the clay site and work all year around. They believe that the quality of their pots depends on the white markings with which they paint themselves–if they did not do this their pots would break.

The Isukha and Idakho excel in enormous, gaily painted shields; some made of wickerwork are used for training, large ones of wildebeest hide for dancing, and smaller but much heavier ones of buffalo hide for fighting. They also make huge

142

head-dresses of unbelievable variety, mostly on basket bases into which feathers of all kinds are stuck. These have the advantage of being light, although they look ponderous enough to impress anybody (pl. XVII, p. 145) (pl. XVIII, p. 146).

The tent which I used as a studio was designed to make allowances for such high head-dresses, and in addition I could open all four sides to get the best light. But during the rainy weather the sky, even between the frequent cloudbursts, was always overcast and the light correspondingly bad, so I spent most of my time either adjusting the tentsides or closing them to avoid being drenched.

These conditions must have affected my health, as I had another hemorrhage in the same eye, this one more serious. Since my oculist had recently moved to Nairobi, I stored my camp kit with the D.C. and left to go there. I underwent three weeks' treatment with penicillin and had many X-ray examinations. But the hemorrhage persisted stubbornly so, as I could not paint, I went to Isiolo to join George until the eye improved. This was disappointing, but I had the satisfaction of hearing that the Government were so pleased with my pictures that they had bought the lot.

One day while I had been recording the vernacular names of tribal customs I had been struck by the similarity between the title *Umwami* which the Luhya use for their chiefs and war leaders, and that with which the WATUSSI in Ruanda Urundi address their king: *Mwami* Charles Nutara Rudahigwa. Might this suggest that both races had met on their migration when, some thousand years ago, the Luhya moved from Lake Chad via Uganda to their present country?

CHAPTER 7

THE MUKOGODO AND RENDILE

After a few days I set off with George on a trip to the Mukogodo Range, where he had to deal with poachers. We camped in a glade in the cedar forest at an altitude of 7,000 feet; there the climate was brisk.

One morning, while we were having our breakfast, a local African arrived clutching a tiny animal in his fist, of which only the head and hindlegs were visible. We identified it as a female hyrax, only a few days old. The hyrax are known for their soft fur, and trade in their pelts has almost exterminated these animals in South Africa. To provide pelts for making one coat alone, up to a hundred and twenty hyrax must lose their lives. Although in Kenya they are protected and classed as royal game, they are often killed illegally. This man had caught the baby hyrax in the hope of selling it.

George threatened to put him into jail should he ever do such a thing again, but this would not help the little orphan, so I adopted it. First we thought it was a tree hyrax, of which there were plenty about; their nocturnal, piercing screams had often prevented us from sleeping. Unless one has watched them at it, it is difficult to associate these loud shrieks with such small creatures. But our little orphan was far too young to utter such a scream and – as I wanted to be polite to her – I thought of her rather as a singer than a shrieker and named her after the Italian prima-donna Adelina Patti.

I carried Patti on my shoulder by day, and during the night she curled round my neck like a little muff. Only later did we realize that she was a rock hyrax, which do not scream like their arboreal cousins, and are not nocturnal. But as the name Patti suited her, we stuck to it even though she hardly ever uttered a sound. Readers of *Born Free* will remember that Patti helped to bring up Elsa.

The Dorobo of the Mukogodo Range are notorious poachers, since Game Laws have been enforced and they are all hunting tribes[5]. They are administered by a District Officer at Doldol. In addition to bows and poisoned arrows, they use poisoned drop-spear-traps, and poisoned harpoons. The poison is made from a small evergreen tree called *acocanthera schimperi*, which grows locally and in other parts of Kenya, at an altitude of 5,000 to 7,000 feet; the twigs and leaves are boiled until

144

ANDALA MWAVALI
MAKHOKHO, BUSHUMULI
IDAKHO

JOY

AMBALUIA KHASIMWA
HILALA, MIRONJE
ISUKHA

JOY

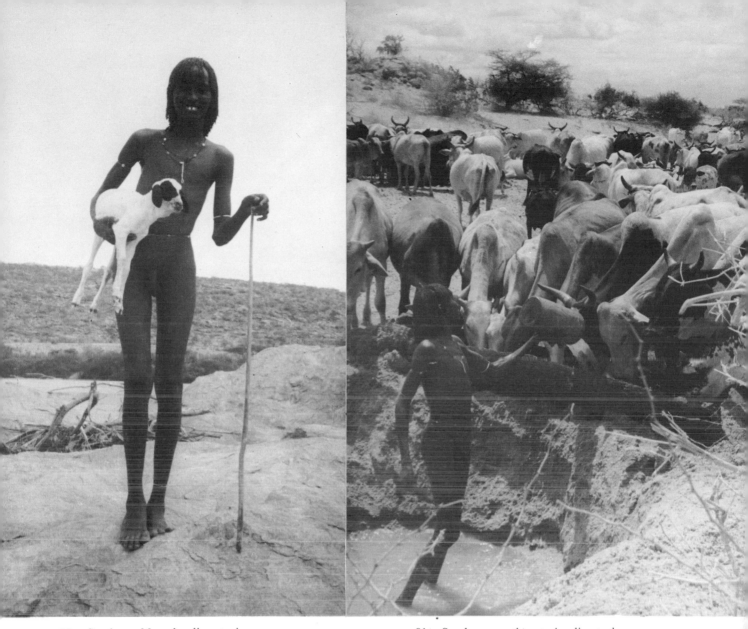

80. Samburu *Moran* herding stock   81. Samburu youth watering livestock

there remains only a pitch like residue which is smeared onto the weapons. As the use of this poison is strictly forbidden by law, the hunters hide it in the mountain caves in which they sleep. All trophies such as rhino horns and leopard skins are also stored in these caves until the owners find an opportunity of selling them, illegally, to Somali traders.

Another safari took us to the Rendile country near Laisamis, about a hundred miles north of Isiolo. To reach it we had to cross wide plains sparsely covered with thorn bush until we reached the Kaisut Desert. On the way, we met several Samburu tribesmen with large herds of livestock (80, 81), also on their way to Laisamis which borders on their district.

147

XVIII Isukha warrior

82. Recently married Rendile woman who has not yet borne a child

Laisamis is important in this desert country because of the springs that bubble up from a deposit of limestone. Close to them are a few mud huts where Somali traders sell sugar, salt, beads, unbleached cotton, and other essentials. Here we met up with the Rendile who follow the rains with their stock across their vast country stretching from Lake Rudolf to Marsabit and as far south as Laisamis. They are Hamites, a very handsome people with natural grace and proud and free as only desert nomads can be (82). For the short time a family remain in one

83.   Married Rendile woman after bearing her first son   84.   The same woman

place, they make a strong thorn enclosure within which they keep the livestock during the night, doubly protected by the huts put up around. These they always carry dismantled on their camels in the form of poles, hides, and grass matting; they can be erected as quickly as they can be pulled down. When the family is on the move, they lead the camels in single file, linked together head to tail, their wooden bells responding to each step with a muffled sound.

On previous safaris we had often been woken up by their fascinating noise and watched a string of camels silhouetted against the morning sky; with the wooden poles protruding from the loads, they are aptly called ships of the desert.

The Rendile are Mohammedan. They are the only tribe in East Africa whose women wear a most becoming coxcomb. As soon as the first wife has borne the heir, she moulds her hair with fat and ocher into a large cockscomb, which is sometimes perforated, sometimes solid, and runs from the forehead to the neck, where it ends in a little stump (83, 84). This the woman keeps in perfect condition until

149

85.   Rendile camels with water containers

her son is circumcised or her husband dies, when she removes it.

While we were camping close to the springs, we had ample opportunity to watch the watering of livestock which needed much organizing because of the many hundreds of animals and people involved (85). The Rendile make their water buckets from giraffe hide and are also experts at plaiting fiber vessels to hold milk and water. As they live chiefly on camel milk, blood, and occasionally meat, there are always plenty of these containers loaded on the camels. If in the dry season the water level at the springs is too low, the men bucket it from a great depth to the surface where they pour it into hollowed palm logs which they use as troughs. During an exceptional drought we once counted ten men standing on a tree ladder above each other, singing a monotonous chant, as they rhythmically bucketed the precious liquid up to ground level. Usually a watering place is very noisy with people chattering and laughing and animals bleating.

Strolling among the crowd one morning, I noticed, carved in the limestone, a double line of eleven holes parallel to each other. A little farther was another set of holes and farther on still more. I recognized these as used for the ancient game of *bao,* played all over Africa in the old days and still popular among primitive people. It is a gambling game played between two opponents and needs quick

150

86. Rendile playing the ancient game of *bao*

thinking. Indeed it is by no means a game for primitive minds, and many Europeans who have tried to play it have failed. Pebbles are thrown in turn into the holes and one has to count several moves ahead to add up the right number for the final throw and outwit one's adversary (86).

Here at Laisamis there must have been quite a club of *bao* players since they found it worth their while to carve the holes into the limestone instead of carrying along the wooden blocks which usually serve as a gaming board.

At the moment there were many Rendile round Laisamis including an important Chief. Taking advantage of his presence, I asked him what his people's circumcision customs were. This was a shot in the dark, as I knew very little about Rendile customs. When he replied that the new cycle was starting next day not far from here and that some twenty men were going to be initiated, I could hardly believe my good luck. Almost nothing is known about Rendile ritual, as it is always performed in remote areas and at irregular intervals. Perhaps the impending ceremonies explained the gathering of so many tribesmen at Laisamis.

From the Chief I learned that in the old days the age for circumcision was between twenty and twenty-five years, after which the initiated men immediately became warriors and had to take on the responsibilities of mature men. Now, as

151

87.   Rendile circumcision scene

tribal warfare is forbidden, the operation is done between the ages of fifteen and twenty. Each candidate presents the circumciser with a goat.

When I asked if I could paint one of the candidates, the Chief was evasive, but after I assured him that other peoples had co-operated and showed him photographs, he agreed to give us a guide to the place of initiation, but he advised us to camp at some distance from it and to be discreet. We drove nine miles across country and camped two miles from the spot where the circumcision rite was going to be performed before dawn next day. When we carefully approached the place next morning, we saw through our field glasses the men who had been operated on squatting in a semicircle with their bows and arrows (87), and the circumciser going from one to the other, inspecting their wounds and spitting on them; he gave each man his blessing. He also talked for some time to all of them, as though giving them a lecture. Of course we concealed ourselves and none of the men knew of our presence; I was able to photograph this scene with my powerful telescopic lens.

Then the candidates dispersed (88) and spent the day in the shade of a bush to recover from the operation. Towards sunset they returned, walking and singing in small groups.

Through the mediation of the Chief, I was able to paint one of the candidates. He wore a black dyed hide, fastened on the right shoulder and falling loosely to

152

88.   Rendile circumcision candidates withdrawing after initiation

his feet, only partly covering his body which was smeared all over with charcoal. Attached to his shoulder knot was a bunch of dried grass, an offering to the divinity, and a protection against the evil eye as well. This is worn only on the day after the operation. He also wore two ostrich feathers stuck behind his ears and tied together at their ends (89). Later, during his two months' seclusion, he would shoot sunbirds with blunted arrows and tie these round his neck. I was surprised that these Hamitic people practiced circumcision rites similar to those of most Nilo-Hamites. Although the Rendile have lately intermarried with the Nilo-Hamitic Samburu, they speak a language almost identical with that of the Hamitic Somali.

But I was even more startled to find a similarity between the Rendile and the Bantu Igembe. Among the latter I had painted a father whose child was undergoing circumcision, during which period he had to wear a sheepskin coronet, have a mark in white paint across his skull, and carry a stick.

Here the Rendile fathers help their sons for two days after circumcision with food and advice and, during these days, wear a black goatskin coronet (90), paint a white mark across their skull, and carry two sticks; in addition they have two skin straps round their loins and tie a lionskin strap below each knee. Did the Igembe on their migration from the Coast through the Northern Frontier Province meet the Rendile and adopt their custom, or was it the other way round? I was delighted to be able to add these Rendile circumcision paintings to my collection.

153

89.   Rendile boy after circumcision

As soon as we returned from this safari, I went to Nairobi to see the dentist as I had been suffering from toothache. He extracted a tooth with a root so badly infected that he reckoned it must have taken a year for the abscess to develop.

154

90.   Rendile father of boy in circumcision holding one of his two sticks

Here, then, was the cause of my eye troubles, which the X-rays had not traced
and which penicillin had not cured. Now, with the 'septic focus' removed, my eye
cleared up and after two months I was able to continue with my record.

CHAPTER 8

THE LUO

I went to the Government Office at Nairobi and received instructions that I should now paint the Luo, the only Nilotic people in Kenya who came from the west some three hundred and fifty years ago, round, or perhaps across, Lake Victoria. After pushing the local Bantu further inland, they occupied most of the southern lake shore. A large proportion of the people remained on the White Nile. Though originally pastoral, they soon took to agriculture and also became expert fishermen.

I set off with Patti and Daniel and drove to Nyahera and pitched my camp close to the lake. I was welcomed by the Chief and a few elders who began by assuring me how lucky they regarded themselves at having their history painted free of charge. They promised their help and certainly kept me busy.

The Luo, when dressed in their traditional ornaments, deserve their reputation of being the most picturesque people in Kenya (pl. XX, p. 164). My first model confirmed this; he was so loaded with feathers, hippo teeth, Colobus furs, and other ornaments that I wondered how he could walk (91).

My next sitter, a very old man, was introduced as the son of the great hero Okore Oganda, who had died some twenty years before the first European arrived here. His life has become a legend, and many heroic fights are attributed to him. At the age of eight, while he was still herding cattle, there were already signs and portents of his future leadership. When he was eighteen, he often successfully fought single-handed against ten men, and by twenty-one his reputation as a hero was established. He then adopted the name *Chieng*, meaning sun, while one of his assistants got the nickname *Otiende Luoch*, meaning mist. Between the sun and the mist the enemy was thrown into confusion, and the battle was won. All the followers of Okore were known as 'fighting he-goats' and became a terror to their enemies. Finally, on his return from a victorious fight with the Tiriki, Okore was ambushed from a tree by a treacherous Tiriki who killed him with a poisoned arrow.

And now his only son was here in front of me (92), in the kind of attire that he would wear at a funeral. I was struck by the resemblance between his ornaments and the basic design of the royal insignia of a Pharaoh, only that these were made of local material (fig. 1). The regal wig of a Pharaoh was replaced by a broad,

156

91. Luo elder in dancing dress

beautifully carved ivory frame, and the regal beard had become a solid ivory tusk. Instead of the golden chains of the Egyptian kings, he wore strings of python vertebrae, but the brass ear-rings were almost identical with Egyptian designs (fig. 2) and so were the bluish-green beads.

Next I painted a married woman also wearing funeral attire; her head-dress made me think of that of Queen Nefertiti, with the difference that hers was made of beads.

If the ornaments of these two models recalled emblems of one of the most highly developed cultures, my next model did just the opposite. He was a witch doctor

157

92. The son of the great hero Okore Oganda in funeral head-dress which bears a strong resemblance to that of the pharoah

whom I met close to my camp (93). His face was almost invisible under a wooden head-dress which he could use alternatively as a drum or a stool. To this were attached seven antelope horns, and more of them dangled from his face and neck; altogether I counted seventeen. The rest of his body was covered by so many charms that I lost count. He was on his way home and in a hurry, but in the best

158

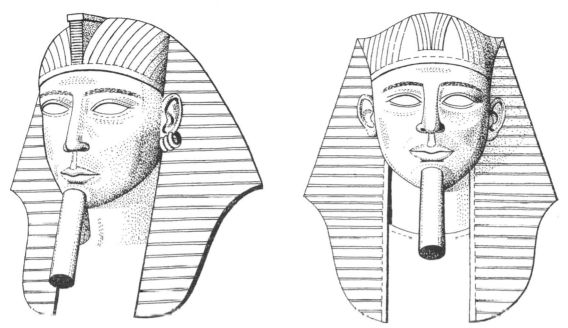

Fig. 1 and 2.   The Royal insignia of a pharoah

of moods, having just earned 250 shillings' worth of cattle for a successful cure. I asked him to sit for me, and when the next day he did so, he showed great interest in Patti, who watched him from a safe spot between the middle pole and the outer fly of the tent. He told me happily that he was the best-known witch doctor in the area, earning between 200 and 300 shillings' worth of cattle for every successful treatment. When I inquired about the secret of his witchcraft I was told he owed it to his diet which consisted of cats, dogs, leopards, hyenas, lizards, geckos, chameleons, tortoises, snakes, crocodiles, and other delicacies. As he recorded this menu, I could not help feeling very worried about Patti.

When I expressed my disbelief in the source of his powers, he invited me to watch him having dinner. So we went together to his hut, which was not far away, and there he produced a large pot from which he took a dried, blackened snake which he broke and pounded to the last bone. Then he ate it—obviously enjoying his meal—until no morsel was left. Watching him I had to control myself so as not to be sick; but he looked quite content and only complained that he was forced to prepare his food himself as his wife refused to do it. What astounded me was not only his belief in his diet, but the fact that his hut was almost door to door with the home of an African clerk who, dressed in European clothes, spoke perfect English and worked in an office at Kisumu not more than six miles away.

The Luo huts are round and much bigger and better built than the ones of the neighboring Luhya. Some are partly painted and partly ornamented with a pattern incised into the wall before the mud has hardened.

93. Luo witch doctor whose head-dress can also be used as a stool or drum

94. Old Luo woman smoking a long clay pipe

It was interesting that the Luo, like the Maragoli, also believe in a lake monster, but here it is a giant serpent. If it rises from the lake with its head in the water and tail in the sky, it is taken as an omen that great sickness will befall the people. In order to prevent it from appearing, the Luo stick a pole of some fifteen feet every few miles along the water's edge, and on to these they tie a special rattling grass. This they sprinkle with the blood of sacrificed sheep or goats, the meat of which is later eaten on the spot. This custom is usually practiced in November when one can see the poles along the shore.

In the old days the Luo women (94) were as scantily dressed as their sisters in Luhya country, but had more ornaments and sometimes wore a rich bead-embroidered skin apron tied to one shoulder. All are very fond of smoking long pipes and it is an amusing sight to watch an old crone filling the bowl of her clay pipe, which is set at the end of a thin reed some three feet long.

After three weeks at Nyahera, I moved nearer to the Uganda border in Central Nyanza, and camped at Rata. Here the people had rather different ornaments

95. Luo head-dress of white painted
impala horn

and my models surpassed in picturesqueness those I had recently painted. Gigantic basket-hats, hardly visible under ostrich plumes; hippo and wild pig teeth of all sizes, which must have been uncomfortably heavy; antelope horns (95), ivory ornaments, cowries, palm-seed rattles, seashells, metal beads, python vertebrae, bells, and decorative animal skins produced a variety of designs and I was fascinated by

96. Luo man in funeral dress   97. Luo going to a dance

the artistic sense with which the Luo instinctively chose the right color combinations or texture of materials for their costumes (96, 97).

A woman witch doctor was particularly impressive (98). Though with all her ornaments, charms, and white-painted body she looked rather alarming, she was utterly feminine and appealing. She was highly regarded in her profession but she did not let this interfere with her very normal family life (pl. XXI, p. 169).

While camping at Rata, I received an invitation from the Provincial Commissioner to join the annual Luo regatta held at Homa Bay, which this year would

162

XIX   Rendile woman

KURE KOROKOLE
LEGATSHO, LAISAMIS
RENDILLE

JOY

OMBOGO OKO
APWONJA SINYOLO
LUO

98. Luo woman witch doctor

coincide with a farewell party in honor of his retirement. I had heard a great deal about these famous regattas and accepted with joy. So I drove via Kisumu, where I was joined by a D.O., and from there we continued over an escarpment to Kisii and farther across hilly country until we descended again in the late afternoon to the lake at Homa Bay.

The sun was setting and tinted the country with a warm glow; the shore was rather broken and the view across the lake most attractive with the hills from the opposite side of the Kavirondo Gulf outlined against the deep red sky.

We found a large crowd busy preparing for the next day's event; it was a bright scene, the bay crowded with boats gaily painted in decorative designs, some with exquisitely carved prows, to which colorful Africans were giving the last touches. Although these boats were long enough to hold a crew of twelve or more, they had not a single nail in their construction, the planks being held together with wooden pegs.

Among the many guests, I recognized several old friends and we celebrated with a grand party in the evening.

xx   Luo warrior

99. Luo boat racing

Next morning everybody assembled on the Provincial Commissioner's launch, from which we watched the races (99). It was magnificent to see the ornamental boats shoot past, the muscles of the crew bulging under their glistening skin, each team working frantically to the rhythmic shouts of onlookers. When finally the victorious crew won the race, by a few inches only, there was such a din and excitement, such dancing and clapping, that it took some time before order was sufficiently restored to award the prizes. Then everybody relaxed and among speeches, drinks, reunions of friends and celebrations, the day passed most pleasantly—in short, it was one of the grand occasions where everything went splendidly, only it lasted for much too short a time.

The Luo certainly excelled in boat racing and soon I had proof of their fishing skill too (100). I had moved from Rata to South Nyanza and had camped close to the shore at Doho Kosele from where I watched the men fishing in the shallows, standing on rafts and poling themselves with long sticks through the reeds in order to investigate the grass traps they had previously set up. If these were not wriggling with fish the men used the harpoons, which they always carried on the raft, to fill their baskets. I painted such a scene since it was typical of the Luo fishing methods.

166

100. Luo fishing

Like their Nilotic brothers further north along the Nile, the Luo rest by standing on one leg and pressing the foot of the other leg against the inside of the knee. One can see the men standing in this position for hours while herding stock or relaxing.

Here I came for the first time across masks. There are very few recorded in Kenya and these were found among the KURYA or BATENDE, a small group of whom live in Kenya along Lake Victoria, while the majority have settled across the Tanganyika border. So it was surprising to see, in Luo country, a man walking into my camp wearing a mask which was part of a funeral costume (pl. XXII, p. 170). It was made of hide with cow's teeth stuck into what were supposed to be lips; he wore the typical Luo crown, a small pointed skin cap, decorated with cowries, which is commonly used by elders. To complete this costume, it was here surmounted with two cow horns.

In South Nyanza I ran into difficulties with some missionaries. They not only worked the population up against me, but even threatened to expel anybody from the Church who posed for me. Pressing their point that it was a sin to wear as few clothes as was customary with the Luo in the old days, they now objected to the women showing even a bare neck. Finally the Provincial Commissioner had to intervene on my behalf and we reached a compromise: I agreed to put up a large

101. Luo elder in dancing dress

102. Luo warrior with impala horn head-
dress

circular grass screen and to paint within it, so that nobody could take offence
when my models wore their traditional costumes which had been their usual dress
only one generation ago.

I made many friends among the Luo (101, 102, 103, 107) and I remember a call
I made unexpectedly on one of my afternoon walks at the home of a man I had
recently painted. He gave me an overwhelming welcome, pressing on me all he

168

XXI Luo woman witch doctor

NYAUNDI OMULU
NGULU, KAKELO
LUO

OCHARA MBOI
KACHIEN KADITONG
LUO

103. Luo prophet

could think of that might be of use to me: eggs, oranges, milk, and even a chicken; only with great difficulty could I stop him from also sending along a sheep.

Several of my Luo models were so interested in my work that they offered their livestock in return for a painting and years later I received a letter from a Chief, asking if he could buy his portrait or any of the thirty-two pictures I had painted of his people.

XXII Luo wearing mask for funeral

CHAPTER 9

THE SAMIA, KISII, KURYA, SUBA AND KIPSIKIS

I went on to the Samia, who live on either side of the Kenya-Uganda border and are noted for their skill in working iron. Although they belong to the Luhya group, they are supposed to be of Nilotic stock. They inhabit the country round Port Victoria, which was originally intended to be the terminus for the Kenya-Uganda railway; but when the cost of draining the local swamps, to provide solid ground for the railroad, became prohibitive, Kisumu was chosen instead. The country round Port Victoria is beautiful parkland, but the many swamps make it into a veritable paradise for the tsetse flies which carry sleeping sickness to human beings. Recently it became possible to eradicate the fly, but at the time of my stay there, the country was still very thinly populated.

I called at the local mission, an austere building perched on a hill overlooking the lake. The three Fathers who ran it were friendly but of no help and after my initial call we saw no more of each other. They were the only Europeans I met during my stay of over a month among the Samia.

I found it difficult to get models though the Chief did everything to help. But I was lucky to discover another mask which was also made of skin. The eyes, nose and chin were formed by lucky beans stuck on with honey which afterwards was hardened. By the same means a few rodent's teeth were secured to indicate the mouth. Although this mask was meant to be worn at a dance (104), it looked rather gruesome with a large bird skull attached to its top and a wild pig's lower jaw dangling underneath round the man's neck. Another interesting model was a warrior carrying an enormous wooden shield, painted with unusual designs (105). It was not only of a rare shape, but also painted in a pattern more common to the west of Kenya, as was also obviously the case with the wooden shield of a woman witch doctor (106).

In the end I was able to paint ten people, all wearing costumes that, even if influenced by the Luo, were unusual (109, 110).

104. Samia man with funeral dance-mask (above left)   105. Samia warrior with unusual shield (above right)

106. Samia woman witch doctor (below left)   107. Luo in dancing dress (below right)

108. Samia warrior (left)   109. Kisii bridegroom (above)

From here I moved to paint the Kisii. I camped some distance from the little township, on a hill overlooking lovely country. The climate, at an altitude of 6,000 feet, was very pleasant after the humid heat by Lake Victoria, and rich vegetation covered the hills as far as I could see. The Africans made good use of the soil's fertility and patches of crops could be seen all around.

The Kisii, one of the GUZII group of Bantu, came from the south; they differ in many ways from the Luhya, not only in their ornaments but also in their customs and type of language. As in most fertile areas that can easily be reached, there were also several missions here of which the Catholic ones seemed the most popular.

I soon made friends with the Chief who spoke English and wore European clothes. From him I learned that the Kisii practiced—and continue to do so—a sort of test marriage as do the Keyo, but with the difference that here, once a girl and a young man wanted to marry and had got the approval of their parents, the bride was 'kidnapped' by the two best friends of the bridegroom (108) and the pair lived for ten days together, prior to the wedding. If, after this time, the couple

174

110. A rich old
Samia woman

approved of each other, the wedding was performed. The ceremony was simple
enough: the bridegroom, elaborately dressed for the occasion, held a basket with
both hands while the elders interrogated him as to the honesty of his intention.
Simultaneously the girl was asked similar questions by her parents. If both replied
satisfactorily, the bride rushed to her future husband, took the basket, and left the
scene hurriedly, thus ending the wedding rite.

Should the pair, after their ten day experience of living together, decide against the marriage, the girl would return to her parents without a stigma and wait for another proposal. This custom prevented divorce later on which would involve complicated compensation for the brideprice. When I asked what would happen if the girl got pregnant, or what would be the fate of an unattractive girl, I was assured that in either case she would be married to an old or otherwise undesirable man and get a lower brideprice, but that under no circumstances would she remain single.

This applied also to widows, who, after one year's mourning, could look for another husband. As soon as a widow had chosen a man, she brought him a plate with food and presented it in silence. If he accepted her gift and ate, she knew that he was willing to marry her and would visit her the following night.

This system seemed to work well in a community with far more women than men, and prevented the existence of destitute spinsters or widows. With the arrival of the missions, a great change took place. Although the Kisii were very willing to adopt Christianity, they soon found out that it interfered with their code of morals and with their economy. Christianity demanded monogamy. What then were they to do with all the surplus women? The only profession open to these unfortunate creatures, who were not trained for earning a living, was prostitution. Another drawback to monogamy was the fact that a single wife could not bear as many children as several wives; and quite apart from sentiment, children represented labor and wealth for the family. Also, one wife could not work the fields single-handed. In short, monogamy created so many difficulties that the elders approached the missions for advice on how to combine Christianity with their social needs. They were told that God would look after them and that education would do the rest.

What, in fact, happens is that if a mission-educated girl intends to marry a mission-educated boy, ten days prior to the Christian wedding she asks to leave the mission, giving as an excuse that her mother has suddenly become ill. If the missionary, knowing what is going on during those days, pretends to ignore the fact, he creates an atmosphere of hypocrisy among his pupils which is not in accordance with Christian teaching. Statistics which reveal an increase in prostitution appear to indicate that education has not yet solved this problem. On the whole, the Kisii regard the mission rather sceptically, and would prefer them to confine their work to improving their standard of living.

The witch doctors (111) here used the same device as the Meru people for lie detectors: two *dikdik* horns balanced by two sticks whose movements indicate whether a man is honest or not for if they move he is dismissed as a liar.

Another interesting sitter was a woman who had lost three children (112). In despair she consulted a witch doctor and on her advice a bull was sacrificed,

111. Kisii witch doctor

the skin of which was used to line a ring which the woman now carried hanging from her waist as a charm to prevent the loss of more children. She also wore a leather roll round her right ankle, a sign that her husband was alive.

I went on to paint a musician (113), with an instrument commonly used by many tribes, and a warrior holding a shield made of buffalo hide embossed with markings of the clan (pl. XXIII, p. 179). The warthog teeth signify that he has killed a man.

177

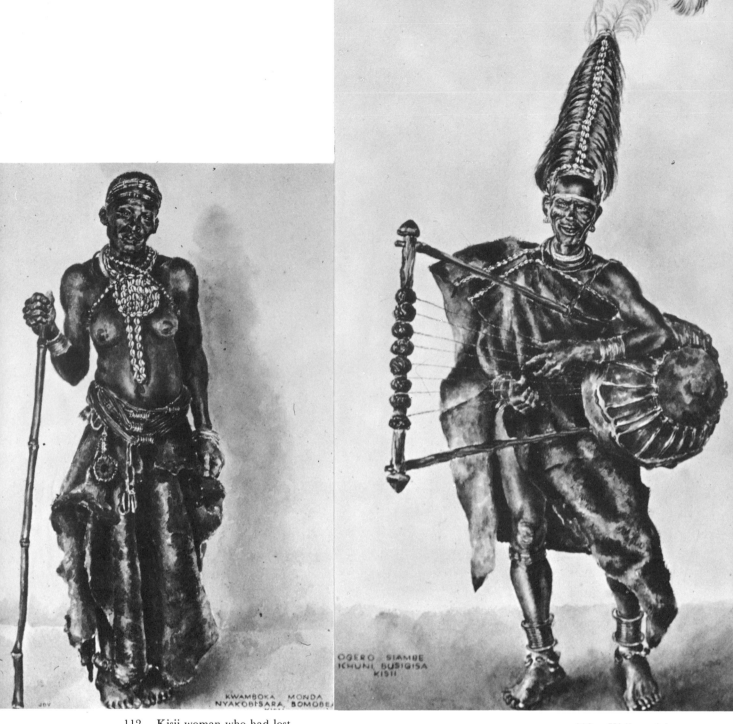

112. Kisii woman who had lost
three children

113.   Kisii musician

While painting one day I heard wailing and soon saw a procession approaching; they were mourning the death of a woman. Close behind the people followed a small herd of cattle, decorated with flowers and branches for this occasion.

In response to my questions about funeral customs, I was told that before Christianity was introduced it had been the duty of the father or husband to carry a

178

XXIII   Kisii warrior; the warthog teeth indicate he has killed a man

MOGERA OKINYI
NYONSIA BOMOBEA
KISII

MWITA KICHAINE
MASABA, BUGIBETI
KURIA

114. Kurya dance

relative who had died away from his home back to it so that the body could be buried near the hut.

The Kisii initiate both sexes, but as the cycle was not on during my stay, I could not paint the costumes.

I had better luck with the Kurya or Batende whom I visited next. I drove for some fifty miles through open bush towards Lake Victoria; the country soon turned flat, and large, rocky outcrops in grotesque formations occurred frequently. Close to these clustered small villages, taking advantage of the strategic position these rocks offered. Although it was not far from Kisii, a completely different atmosphere prevailed; while around Kisii the country was densely populated, here the African huts were tucked away in the bush so that the area looked almost uninhabited. The people seemed little affected by civilization, but were certainly among the most picturesque I had come across; they are famed for their elaborate ear-ornaments and masks.

I pitched my camp at Utende, close to the Chief's home and within walking distance of the Tanganyika border, across which the main bulk of the Kurya live.

The Chief had arranged a dance to celebrate my arrival, and as the local Africans welcomed any excuse to have some fun, this seemed to make me popular from the start. Early next morning a large crowd appeared from all directions, swarming like ants towards a big rock, next to which the party was going to be held (114). The women and children looked highly polished, as their skin is well

181

115.   Kurya dance

oiled, and they were loaded with metal coils and beads from their waists upwards. They could hardly control themselves until the dance began, which was to my surprise a very organized affair–at least to begin with. With almost military precision the women and girls lined up in a circle until each was in her proper place, the women in the center and the girls on the periphery. First they jumped in slow rhythm, but gradually they worked themselves up to a frenzy faster and faster, twisting their abdomens vigorously until the greased back-aprons skipped from side to side at each jump, making a fascinating counter-movement to the jumping bodies (115). When they all were in full swing, a procession of giants appeared, walking stiffly on large wooden blocks more than a foot high, which were tied to their feet (116). These were the young men come to join in the dance. Covered with Colobus monkey capes, and heightened not only by the blocks but also by wearing tall head-dresses of ostrich plumes, they towered over the girls by several feet and slowly they encircled them. Having walked around them, they too started jumping, lifting their heavy wooden clogs with astonishing ease, and twisting their bodies at the same time until their back-aprons decorated with metal, swung in rhythm with those of the girls. Soon there was one mass of glisten-

182

116. Kurya dancer with blocks tied to his feet   117. Kurya drummer

ing, wriggling people leaping to the sound of drumming (117), oblivious of time and fatigue. How they could carry on this strenuous exercise for the whole day, and yet seem to become livelier the longer it lasted, was beyond my comprehension.

While we watched, the Chief was constantly being asked when the next dance would be held and finally he promised one for the following week. I selected many

118.　Kurya warrior with raffia palm-nut necklace

119.　Kurya musician

120.　Kurya women going to a dance near Utende (opposite)

models (118, 119, 120, 121) from the crowd, and when they arrived next morning they seemed none the worse for their party which had lasted till the early hours.

The beauty culture of the Kurya women struck me as somewhat odd: they regarded it as a great enhancement to pluck out their eyelashes and eyebrows, and thereby achieved a strangely naked look. The men competed by chipping their

121. Kurya warrior

teeth to narrow points. Both sexes had greatly elongated ear-lobes from which dangled a large variety of ornaments made of metal, wood, beads, ivory, all of outstanding size.

186

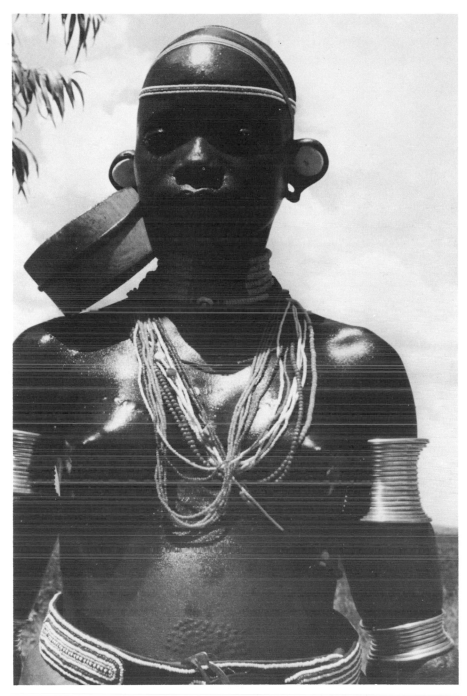

122.   Kurya girl after circumcision with wooden ear plugs

To stretch the ear-lobes to the required length, the initial hole is gradually widened by inserting wooden plugs of increasing size until they reach a diameter of four inches. This is usually regarded as sufficient for women (122); but the

123. Kurya youths with wooden blocks hanging from their ears

men are more ambitious and I painted a youth who carried a solid wooden block weighing eight pounds hanging through his ear-lobes like a roll on his neck (123). For many months he had used this block to weigh the ear-lobes down and it seemed incredible that such a thin piece of skin could be stretched to such length without tearing.

One of the witch doctors differed from other colleagues of his I had met, as he not only consulted various assortments of charms but relied mainly on a stringed instrument, pulling the eight chords in sequence and listening intently to their vibrations which seemed to answer his queries (pl. XXIV, p. 180). Among the Kurya women witch doctors (124) outnumber their male colleagues. Each sex uses different charms.

I found two impressive dancing masks (125, 126). They were made of skin and hardened honey, with which the features were moulded, and were much more skillfully executed than the two I had found among the Luo and Samia. I bought these masks for the Nairobi Coryndon Museum, but it needed a great deal of patient bargaining as the people were reluctant to part with them.

188

124. Kurya woman witch doctor

The circumcision customs varied here from those of other groups (128) in that the girls and boys wandered together through the bush while in seclusion. Both sexes wore similar, heavily fringed hide skirts, longer at the back, and painted their bodies all over with grey mud, and both carried large bows (127). The boys were not allowed to eat unless they had touched the food with a special wooden ladle which they carried round their necks. The Borana have a similar custom.

I also met a woman rainmaker (129). She carried a pot on her head which she used to 'mix' rain. Her hair was plastered with fat and ochre and partly shaven.

189

125. Kurya dance mask made of skin and honey   126. Kurya dance mask

The leather ring attached to her largest necklace signified that she had had children.

Lately I had had cause to worry about Daniel, who had taken to disappearing at nights and often also during the day. The few African shops nearby seemed to have a magnetic attraction for him, and often he returned drunk. He began to dress extravagantly and, when asked how he managed to buy so many clothes, he assured me that everything was so cheap here that he even sent dresses to his wife in Meru – which I found rather touching.

One day I missed twenty shillings; however, as I always kept the money locked in a suitcase I thought I had made a mistake in my book-keeping and blamed myself. But a few days later when I found I was short of fifty shillings, I started watching Daniel, as he was the only one who had access to my tent. One morning while going out to clean my teeth, I left the suitcase unlocked and on my return

127. Kurya circumciser   128. Kurya boy and girl in circumsicion dress

found a hundred and twenty shillings gone. When I tackled Daniel about this, he only laughed at me and asked how I could accuse him without having a witness. There was nothing left but to put an Askari on his trail.

He soon found out not only that Daniel owed the shops a lot of money for clothes but also that he treated the local Africans to free drinks in the beer bar; his paying-coupons amounted to more than three hundred shillings of which only a few were paid up.

191

129. Kurya woman
rainmaker

I had a long talk with Daniel and tried to make him see that he would get into trouble if he continued in these new habits of stealing and drinking and that, even if I dismissed him now and he found another job, these habits would wreck his life. He only grinned and again challenged me to produce evidence against him and said the coupons were faked and that the people in the shops were liars.

In the circumstances, what could I do but hand his case over to the D.O.?

As Daniel had been with us so long, I felt rather like a mother with a naughty son and on our drive to the D.O. I tried to talk some sense into him. But he con-

192

130. Suba in dancing dress

131. Suba elder on his way to a beer party

tinued to mock me and assured me that he did not mind going to jail as I could not prove anything against him. When we parted at the prison gate, it was I who had tears in my eyes, while Daniel grinned at me and wished me a cheerful good-bye.

This unfortunately was the end of his career not only with us but also with his family who refused to bail him out after he got into more trouble of the same kind in Meru. The last we heard of him was that he had disappeared.

I felt very sorry for Daniel as he was intelligent, quick minded and a good worker, and only twenty-eight years old, but he lacked will-power. Having lately met all the rich chiefs of Nyanza and seen their higher living standards—earned by hard and honest work—the sight of their wealth had gone to his head and, wanting a similar life, he took a short cut. So my four weeks' stay with the Kurya ended on a very sad note; otherwise this would have been one of my happiest times with the Africans.

Before leaving the district I painted two tribesmen of the neighboring SUBA (130). One of them was an elder dressed for a beer party (131), who kept his eyes covered under a giraffe tail attached to his head-dress. When I asked the reason, I was assured that this would prevent him from knowing how much beer he drank.

With the Suba I had completed my record of the Guzii Bantu, and now I moved on to the Kipsikis. They are Nilo-Hamites and neighbors of the Nandi, with whom they have many customs in common.

Driving up into chilly highlands, I arrived at Kaptaket where I was welcomed by a Chief who suggested that I pitch my camp close to his new Welfare hall, the social center, of which he was very proud. He had prepared a big dance, but when the crowd arrived I was disappointed to see that not a single ornament they were wearing seemed traditional and that they had just put on fancy dress to please me. The only way to get authentic types was to start with the older people and with their help to find genuine costumes.

As we were at an altitude of about seven thousand feet, they were dressed in long furs or hides impregnated with grease and ocher.

My first model here was an old man who turned out to be the only surviving male in his family; this was indicated by a blue bead bracelet on his right arm, which otherwise would have been worn on the left.

Walking through the forest one afternoon, I met an elderly woman who had a crown of cowries on her head and round her neck a thick collar of fiber strings with a few cowries attached. She was in a hurry, but stopped when I asked her why she was dressed in that fashion and replied that she wore these ornaments because at the moment one of her children was being initiated; each string on her collar represented one previously circumcised child. I counted them and they numbered sixteen, which I thought a splendid effort. She promised to sit for me next day (pl. XXV, p. 217).

While I painted her she asked leave to attend a ceremony from which she returned with a new, brownish-colored cowrie on her collar.

My next endeavor was to paint the initiates. I was lucky; not far from my camp was a hut in which a few girls were spending their seclusion, and the Chief arranged that I should see them. When I approached the place, I saw a hooded figure completely covered from head to foot rushing toward the hut and disappearing inside it. Of course I was not permitted to enter, but while waiting for the girl to re-appear, I was myself instructed by my guide in the mysteries of the initiation. It fell into seven distinct periods:

The first, *rotinyotet*, is concerned with the operation of clitoridectomy.

In the second *lapet ap eun* (washing of hands), the girl has to undergo a test – probably to prove her self-control – during which she has to carry earth simultaneously on her head, in both her hands and on her abdomen. If she drops even the tiniest particle, she is disgraced and will have difficulty in finding a husband.

Third is *tienjinet* (singing to them) during which she is taught discipline and manners by two elderly women tutors.

Fourth is *kayaet* (casting away uncleanness) which involves baptism in a river, on which occasion the girl is given a new name for her future life. During the following month she carries a small bundle of sticks in her hand which she places above the door of the hut when entering it. This is a sign that no man is allowed to come inside while she is there. Should anyone ignore this warning, he is disgraced and fined an ox.

Fifth is *yatet ap oret* (the opening of the way), the opening to womanhood.

Sixth is *tilet ap kirokwet* (cutting of the stick)[6].

Seventh is *ngetunot* (at the end of the seclusion).

An old custom, no longer practiced, was that before initiation, but after reaching puberty, the girls used to live with young warriors but had to take precautions not to get pregnant or their chances for marriage were greatly reduced.

When a girl finally emerged from the hut which she shared with several others, I saw nothing of her but her eyes staring through tiny holes in the hood (132). Later, when I painted her and we were alone, at my request she lifted the hood (this she frequently did when among her own sex); I was even able to paint her in this pose to show the beautiful bead and cowrie decorations on the hides which she wore under the hood.

The boys' initiation also had seven stages, named like those of the girls; they last up to one year.

The first stage is the operation of circumcision *(rotinyotet)*; during the second *(lapet ap eun)* they learn to fight, to herd, and to defend livestock; in the third *(tienjinet)* they are taught manners and discipline; in the fourth *(kayaet)* they are baptised in a river, where they have to swim for a short distance under water; if they lose their direction they are disgraced; if they succeed the prefix *Arap* is added to their name, meaning 'the son of'. In the fifth stage *(yatet ap oret)* they become men. In the sixth and seventh stages *(tilet ap kirokwet* and *ngetunot)* they have their heads shaved and become freed from ritual uncleanness.

During the circumcision period, they live under the guardianship of two elders in a special hut. If they walk for short distances, they too cover themselves with a

132. Kipsikis girl in seclusion dress after
circumcision

133. Kipsikis boy during circumcision

hooded mask (133). They carry a bow and a green stick, with which they beat the
ground when they want food since they are not permitted to speak during this time.

All day long while I was painting these initiation pictures, I heard the chattering
of young people from inside the Welfare hall, which was always full of youngsters
who had endless leisure on their hands. They spent their time playing cards,
pingpong, or sipping Coca-Cola; in the past they would have been training to

196

134. Kipsikis warrior going to a dance

become warriors. I could not help thinking that this leisure might now well have been used for studying or learning trades.

The conflict between the practice of initiation and other rites, and the prevailing eagerness to adopt a foreign way of life seemed to result in an unbalanced compromise. Western habits were superficially copied, while traditional customs were adhered to secretly but outwardly denied. Nobody would want to turn back the clock and revive the past, but at least one could make these youngsters conscious and proud of the great wealth and value of the tribal life out of which their present and future will grow.

I hoped so much that my pictorial record of their past would help to make Africans proud of their tradition, but judging from the reaction of the young generation to my work, they were often ashamed of it. This worried me, and my discouragement was not eased by a letter I received from the Secretariat in Nairobi, asking me to stop painting, as the fund for paying me had been exhausted. In reply I asked for an interview with the Chief Native Commissioner as I wanted to finish the record at my own risk.

While waiting for an answer, I completed the series of the Kipsikis with a warrior (134), a witch doctor, a circumciser, and other types; but when no reply came, I broke camp, announced my arrival by telegram, and drove to the Secretariat at Nairobi. Here I was told that the Chief Native Commissioner had no time to see me either now or at a future date. As I believed my offer was a reasonable one, I got angry and told his secretary that I would camp in front of the Commissioner's door until he found the time to talk to me. This had the desired effect, and I was at once admitted.

We agreed that I should wait for a few weeks before continuing with the record while the Commissioner tried to raise more funds. In the meantime I would join George on one of his safaris and paint some tribesmen in the Northern Frontier Province, at my own expense. That seemed a fair compromise and I left for Isiolo.

CHAPTER 10

SOME NORTHERN FRONTIER TRIBES: SOMALI, BORANA, GABRA, ELMOLO

While I was at Isiolo, I painted some of our Somali Game Scouts, starting with Yusuf, who belonged to the Abdwak section and had worked loyally for many years under George. While he sat facing me, he wiped his nose with a piece of silk which I recognized as a remnant of one of my dresses. As I kept the remnant-box locked up, I asked him how he had come by it. He tucked it away quickly and pretended not to know what I was talking about and when I asked him to show it to me he was unable to find it. Although it seemed silly to make a fuss about this, as I had lately suspected our house-boy of stealing, I took the opportunity of getting evidence. I did not suspect Yusuf of being a thief but wanted to know who had given him the remnant. As he continued to deny ever having seen it, I called George, who had his pockets searched and out came the piece of silk. Even then Yusuf refused to say how he got it, and when George threatened to dismiss him if he wouldn't speak up, he resigned. Whether this was due to loyalty to the thief or to stubbornness, we never knew, but he chose to leave his job and George and he loved both.

During those days Korani Elmi, an Aulyehan Somali from the Tana, passed through Isiolo, coming from Nairobi, where he had just been made an Honorary Game Warden and given a rifle by the Game Department. He was one of the few Africans on whom such a distinction had been bestowed.

Korani Elmi claimed to have shot some thirty lions with his bow and arrow; on each occasion he had put up a kill and, lying on his stomach within a few yards, had waited for the animals and killed them. As one never knows from which direction lion will approach, or retreat if alarmed, it needs outstanding courage to keep flat on the ground at such close range. He demonstrated most convincingly how he kept his bow in a horizontal position to conceal it in the grass, and won our admiration. Korani Elmi was about fifty years old; he had amber-colored eyes like a lion and was very goodlooking and dignified. He agreed to sit for me. Although he found it a great strain to remain inactive for so many hours, he endured the ordeal with great courtesy, but when it was over he told me that he would sooner ambush a pride of lions than pose for a picture.

I like Korani Elmi and the Somali in general; these Hamites are proud and independent people and, though often unpredictable and quick-tempered, are seldom petty (135). They claim to descend from Arab men and Galla women.

They are a nation of many tribes, some of whose branches invaded Kenya from the north about a hundred and fifty years ago, and have since then occupied most of the eastern section of the Northern Frontier Province, with Wajir and Garissa as centers. In both these areas there are several large dams and at Wajir and further north deep wells, cut into the limestone with such a small diameter that one is at a loss as to how they could be made. Obviously all were constructed by a race far more advanced in engineering techniques than the present inhabitants. The Somali attribute these dams and wells to the Mahadanle—a race of giants, whom they believe to have come from Persia, Egypt and Southern Arabia about two thousand years ago. A few moved on to Tanganyika where they became known as the Magadi, AMBURU and WATATIRO, while others went to Ruanda Urundi where they settled and were called the Watussi. They certainly look like descendants of a giant race and are still termed *Malalo* by the Somali. Somali elders told me that the Watussi women's dress is similar to that of Somali women; both use an eighteen foot length of material wound around their bodies. They also make *ghee* and separate milk by identical methods and every Watussi woman covers her face when seeing a Somali.

All Somali are Mohammedans and may marry up to four wives. While at the birth and death of a man meticulous ceremonies are observed, no fuss is made about women who, although they have no official status, often exert great influence over their men.

I learned that at the birth of a boy a sheep is sacrificed and the baby's head anointed with the blood; its umbilical cord is tied with the hair of a camel's tail, and the animal itself is later given to the child. For the forty days following the birth, the mother is considered to be impure and may not leave the hut, or receive her husband. The baby stays inside the hut for a full year, after which he is carried by his maternal uncle across the door; by this rite, called *kalaqad*, the taboo of the hut is broken, and the Jinn of the threshold overcome. Twins are considered lucky, but any abnormal child is immediately killed.

On our previous safari through Somali country I had often found a tall swamp grass with a strongly scented, bulbous root locally called *oboro*. No Somali, Rendile, or Borana woman would give birth without its help. As soon as labor begins she is put on a bedstead made of palm-leaf ropes, under which a basin containing smouldering *oboro* roots is placed. The smoke is supposed to relax her muscles and to have a healing effect. So that no fumes should escape, the hut is tightly shut and,

200

135. Somali man

as many women helpers are always present, the air becomes so suffocating that the mother is weakened rather than helped; as a result, hemorrhages are frequent.

Several midwives who worked in local dispensaries told me that it was impossible to improve these conditions, as Somali women will not come into hospital for their delivery, and Government regulations, for hygienic reasons, prohibit demonstrations of medical help in native huts.

However, the Somali use some remedies which are effective: I was shown an aloe which they call *shipir*, whose bitter juice is a powerful emetic. They appear

201

to treat malaria successfully by cutting a vertical line across the forehead to let the bad blood run out and afterwards dressing the wound with a mixture of the powdered bark of a tree called *tirah* (arabic *harmal*) and sheep's fat.

The Somali initiate both sexes. The boys are circumcised in groups of twenty to fifty. In the old days fifteen years was the age for initiation, but today it is performed as early as eight. To celebrate this occasion, a feast is held and then the boys are left to recover for a few days before resuming normal life.

The girls are infibulated at the age of six to eight. They are operated on individually in the family hut. Only an informal feast is given to the women who attend the operation. This is performed by excising the clitoris and then stitching the vulva together with thorns, which are removed after seven days when the wound has closed.

The Somali told me that apart from themselves, infibulation is practiced only by the DANAKIL and some of the Galla.

As soon as a girl starts her menstruation, she changes her hair style into little plaits (136), thus inviting prospective suitors. She is usually married between the ages of twelve and fifteen and even today one rarely meets a woman of twenty who is not married.

As soon as a man has chosen a girl, he has to ask his and her parents for their consent. He starts with his own father who, if he approves, talks to his wife. After this the boy's mother discusses the matter with the girl's mother. Then both fathers confer together and, when all are agreed, the elders are informed. Only after all these parleys is the consent of the girl's father officially requested and formally communicated to the suitor's father. A few days before the wedding, the bride retires into a special hut where she discards the clothes and ornaments of a maiden. The bridegroom then presents his betrothed and both mothers with coffee and butter as contributions to the wedding feast. He also holds a party for his friends. Finally the girl is again asked whether she truly agrees to the marriage. If her answer is positive, the bridegroom is led on horseback outside the village and then returns to the entrance of the marital hut; while this is taking place the bride too is led outside her hut and brought back to the marital hut. Before entering it she cleans herself and changes into new clothes. When she goes in she is first examined by the bridegroom's mother to ascertain that she is a virgin. If she is, then the couple are at last left alone. Before the marriage is consummated, the husband has to beat the bride with his horsewhip to assert his authority, after which he defibulates her. Next morning she will find a present from her husband under the pillow.

For the next seven days the wife is not allowed to leave the hut, but the husband has to show himself. Later her vulva is partially closed and only defibulated for each childbirth. All this seems a rather complicated procedure and I was relieved

202

136. Somali girl

to learn that only the first wife has to endure it and that later wives get away with fewer ceremonies. All married women cover their hair with a black cloth.

There are outcast groups among the Somali, the chief of which are the Yibir (hunters, leather-workers, and sorcerers) the Midgan (hunters and leather-workers) and the Tumel (blacksmiths). It is generally Midgan women who infibulate the Somali girls.

The Yibir live all over Somali countries, and are despised as much as they are feared. According to legend they are descendants of a Jew called Borbaer who lived forty miles west of Hargeisa and practiced magic and witchcraft. He was killed by a certain Yusuf Kaunen, but left two sons, Turyar and Yibir. When they demanded blood money for their father's death, Yusuf asked if they wanted it now or for ever. Turyar preferred his share now and got fifty camels, but Yibir insisted on having it for ever, and since then the Yibir receive a present at the birth of every boy and at

203

the wedding of every girl. If it is withheld, he curses the people and his curse is so much feared that no Somali would provoke it willingly.

When I inquired how one could tell a Yibir from other Somali, I was told that they use a dialect which no self-respecting Somali would speak, that they have certain mannerisms and do conjuring tricks. When a boy is born to them, they tie a tiny tree-root to the baby's neck, the significance of which will be recognized by another Yibir and so assure the child's identity.

In spite of all the precautions they take to ensure a happy marriage, divorce occurs quite frequently among the Somalis but no pregnant woman can divorce; nor after divorce can she remarry until three months have elapsed in order to make certain that she is not with child.

As a rule, the children of a divorced couple remain with the mother till they are four years old and then go to the father; but this custom varies considerably among different sections of the Somali.

The Somali are spotlessly clean and whenever I have been asked inside a hut, even without previous warning, I have always found that I could have eaten off the floor.

They make two types of huts; one is built of mud and wood and is intended to be more or less permanent, and the other, used by nomadic Somali, is made of fiber matting fixed over a framework of sticks, which can easily be folded up and loaded onto camels.

Once I surprised a Somali near the Ethiopian border, reading the Koran while watering his camels. The book rested on a little wooden desk which he folded up when he moved on. I thought it rather a cumbersome thing to carry around but I was told that the Koran must never be put on the ground in case it should get dirty.

Most Somali carry a little wooden head-rest attached to their wrist. This they use not only to support their head when sleeping, but to protect their long curly hair from getting full of sand when they rest in the open. These head-rests are also used by the Rendile and Borana. All are ornamented with a carved interlacing pattern. Among the Borana I found a few with carvings of snakes and scorpions as well; these designs are supposed to protect the sleeper from what they portray. (Identical head-rests have been excavated from the tombs of the Egyptian pyramids.)

While we were at Isiolo, news came of a disastrous drought in the north, estimated to have caused the death of forty-five per cent of the Somali livestock. George was asked to recover the ivory of the elephants who had died of thirst in the Lorian Swamp, and to protect weak survivors from poachers.

The Lorian is in Somali country halfway between Isiolo and Wajir and under normal conditions it is a true game paradise. On previous safaris we had

137.   Sheep grazing near a dead elephant in Lorian swamp

often watched the animals standing up to their bellies in the water. The swamp is about eight miles long and fed by the Uaso Nyiro River. Both the swamp and river had now been dry for two months. A few wells in the heart of the Lorian were the only source of water, and the entire population and livestock of several hundred square miles depended on them. Crazed by thirst, the people were on the verge of attacking each other, and it was only owing to the influence of Chief Abdi Ogli that no serious fighting had broken out.

We set off along the Wajir road toward the Lorian 150 miles east. The closer we came to it, the more people and livestock we met, dragging themselves toward the swamp. Near it the carcases of the animals (137) became so numerous that driving grew difficult, and the stench was such that we had to cover our noses. Walking apathetically between skeletons, blown-up carcases, and dying animals, people silently held out their empty water containers towards us. It was a gruesome sight and made me feel ashamed to be well. Abdi Ogli came to greet us (138) He was middle-aged; the tautness of his skin over his delicate features expressed the tragedy of his people better than words could have done.

He told us that the water level of the wells was now so low that people arriving half dead from their long waterless journeys had to wait for days to get their fill, and even when they reached the wells, elephants, frantic because their trunks were not long enough to reach the water, would chase them until they dropped their precious water containers. Not content with this, the elephants would follow the men until they shed even their wet loincloths. On three occasions there had nearly been an accident; people had remained at the bottom of the thirty foot well hoping that the elephants would go away instead of which angry animals had trampled the earth loose and nearly buried them.

205

One bull in particular made a habit of returning every night and chasing the people away until he got his water. Although Abdi Ogli sympathized with the thirsty elephants, he asked George to shoot this one.

The scene around confirmed only too sadly the Chief's story. Contrary to the usual gay atmosphere at watering places, the people stood silent and despondent in the fierce sun from which there was no shelter. In each of the thirty wells which still contained a little water, we counted at least eight men standing one above the other on tree ladders bucketing the muddy liquid into troughs for their animals.

While waiting for the evening and the arrival of the elephant, we walked along the Uaso Nyiro; here we saw horrible animal tragedies. Turning a bend we came face to face with an elephant; he was too weak to move at our approach and only lifted his trunk as if to ask for mercy. Next to him were two dead elephant cemented into the mud of the riverbed into which they had been sucked before it had hardened. Close to them was the head of a camel, the rest of its body buried under mud; to all appearances it was dead, but the Somali told us that though it had been in this defenseless position, exposed to the sun, for thirty-six days, it was still alive. George touched its head, and slowly it opened its eyes—asking for the *coup de grâce* which he delivered.

In the deep crevices which patterned the dry riverbed many animal carcases caught by the sucking mud lay embedded. Further on we found an almost dry mud pool with a wriggling mass of catfish and decaying carrion. Close to these stood two elephants knee-deep in mud next to a dead one; they were surrounded by goats and cattle staggering in search of food among rotting carcases. Nearby a few children were herding their stock. The need for water eliminated all fear, and man and beast were equally intent on assuaging their thirst. We counted twelve dead elephants.

As soon as it got dark we returned and saw the silhouette of the dangerous elephant. Moving swiftly from well to well, he nearly bumped into the angry, shouting crowd of Somali. I had never seen Africans so careless of an elephant at such close quarters; the craving for water had certainly made everyone reckless. We tried to find a position from which George could kill the bull with a shot through the brain, for we could not risk a wounded animal stampeding among the crowds. The situation was very dangerous until we got so close to the elephant that there was only a well between us. While he sniffed the air for the scent of water, I switched on the torch. Then George shot, a crash followed, and the bull fell over. When we examined the carcase to make sure the bull was dead, we found a sheep buried under it which had been too weak to move away.

With the death of the elephant the place became alive, and the excited chatter of hundreds of Somali rushing to the scene came as a relief after having seen nothing but death and decay since our arrival.

138. Somali chief
Abdi Ogli

During the following days while we were trying to help the Somali, the long overdue rains broke and one morning we woke up to hear them shouting, 'The river is coming!' Like everybody else we rushed to meet the 'head waves', but found only a thin trickle running slowly along the parched riverbed filling cracks and waterholes as it went. The banks were already crowded with herds of camels, sheep, and cattle, and their bleatings mingled with the laughter of the Somali. What the rain meant to all of these people could only be understood by someone who had witnessed the scene that had preceded it. I felt like crying for joy. Now I thought we could leave, knowing that life had again returned to these people.

Soon after we had gone, the rains broke properly and flooded the country to an unprecedented extent. Even plains which normally were desert turned into soggy morasses. The rains lasted for many weeks and brought a new disaster to the country, which was as terrible as the previous drought. Reports came in saying that Abdi Ogli and his people were isolated by a lake ten miles wide, that the bridge across the Uaso Nyiro stood solitary in the mud as the torrent had carried the approaches away, and that the river had changed its course. Lorry-convoys, sent out with food supplies, returned defeated or were marooned for weeks. Aircraft dropped food, but most of it fell into the water; then donkeys and camels were mobilized, but their loads got soaked in the rain.

George was asked to go back to Lorian to investigate the Game situation in the area, but halfway there we were held up by a lake which had flooded an area that normally consisted of sand dunes. We tried to cross it in our rubber dinghy, but could find no transport at the other side. This was the very spot where just three weeks ago we had been picking up people who had collapsed from thirst and heat. Now there was nothing we could do but wait for the waters to recede; during this time I painted some of the local people.

We were stuck in Borana country. This large Hamitic group is a branch of the Galla, and most of them live in Ethiopia; but at the turn of the last century, some hundred and thirty thousand to a hundred and fifty thousand crossed into Kenya and settled around Marsabit. Later some forty-five thousand Borana moved south, some to the Uaso Nyiro, others to the base of the Jombeni Hills; these Borana became Moslems, while those who stayed near Marsabit remained pagan. The Islamic section is less nomadic than those who stayed in the north.

George had known several of the families in this area for many years, and one of his old friends soon turned up with his children—a lot of charming little girls who were most intrigued by our dinghy. After we had taken the party for a cruise, they wanted to stay on in our camp and so I made them pose for me. While I painted one, her father carved a small camel bell for me which I still treasure (139).

All camel-owning tribes make bells varying in their shape and in the number of clappers. The Rendile carve the largest and flattest of all the bells.

139.   Borana girl with camel bell

One day we were invited to the hut of our Borana friends, and there I saw decorative hide panels of a narrow, triangular shape, richly ornamented with cowries, hanging around the walls. Our host explained that these were made for ornamental use in huts, but sometimes the women would hang one panel from their shoulder when attending a wedding or other important event.

The weather conditions were such that George had to limit his operations to the immediate vicinity and soon we had to leave for Marsabit where he was asked to deal with similar problems.

On our way we had to stop several times to dig the cars out of the mud and on one occasion were helped by Somali who happened to come our way. One of them was a friend of our Somali house-boy, Abdi, and both seemed overjoyed at meeting each other. After the initial hand-clasping was over, we heard Abdi's pal asking him how often he had been in jail. With a sideglance at us, Abdi confessed to three times. That provoked a pitying smile from his friend who boasted that he had a far better record, having been seven times the guest of the Government. Obviously he regarded jail not as a stigma, but as a proof of courage and enterprise, just the price of risking what others were afraid to do.

In Marsabit I found a pagan Borana woman willing to pose for me; she looked as if she had stepped out of the Old Testament. She wore the typical Borana necklace, a long string of aluminium beads wound tightly around her neck until it looked like a stiff collar which extended partly over her breast (140). In the old days the beads were cut from a soft stone found near Lake Rudolf, but nowadays special craftsmen melt aluminium into rectangular bars about half an inch thick, from which they cut small sections and hammer them into the required shape. I watched a jeweller at this work and was amazed to see how quickly he turned out a hundred of the many faceted beads, for which he charged two shillings.

I inquired when the circumcision cycle would start again, and was told not before 1955. Although this meant waiting for four years, I determined that I would return to paint the ceremonies connected with this unique rite.

While at Marsabit, George received a report of severe poaching at the south end of Lake Rudolf, so we set off to deal with it. Leaving the luxuriant forest of Marsabit behind, we crossed a very rough lava plain until we reached the Chalbi Desert. For the next ninety miles we saw nothing but sand and mirages which shimmered in the distance but dissolved at our approach. At the end of this dried up lake bed was North Horr, a small oasis with a Police outpost and a District Commissioner's rest-house. Further on we came to Guss, another fresh water spring, where we met with the Gabra tribesmen (141) and their camels (142). The Gabra are Somali and still speak this language, but some time ago they split off, mixed with the Borana, gave up Mohammedanism, burnt the Koran, and became pagan. The main group lives in Ethiopia, but some crossed into Kenya and now live in the

140. Borana woman

Huri Hills close to the border where they find good grazing for their camels. During the rainy period they sometimes come into the plains below and this is where we now met with a few of them. The women wore a handsome double band of white metal round their heads, which is characteristic of the Gabra (143); otherwise they share many ornaments and customs with the Borana.

141. Gabra man

As the noise and dust of the many watering animals was appalling, we moved on and went down a very rough lava escarpment until we reached the lake just opposite the Elmolo Islands. The ELMOLO rushed forward to welcome us, and since they knew us from previous visits, they brought us presents: delicious giant tilapia fish, a speciality of the lake. The generosity of these primitive people is most endearing. Little is known about the Elmolo who number only about eighty. They are supposed to be Masai who later mixed with the GELABA (a tribe living at the northern end of the hundred and eighty mile long lake) the Rendile, and the Samburu. By now their customs are such a mixture that it is difficult to sort them out. In the past they lived along the eastern shore of Lake Rudolf, but they

142. Gabra watering scene

143. Gabra woman

were driven south and almost exterminated by more virile tribesmen until they
finally sought refuge on little islands where their small community has survived.
Their diet is limited to fish, turtle, crocodile, and an occasional hippo, and they
drink only the alkaline water of the lake. Close interbreeding has caused symptons
of degeneration to develop among them, and almost everyone suffers from rickets
or scurvy, and crutches are common. The Elmolo are the poorest of the poor,
and it was embarrassing to accept the offer of everything they possessed made
with such unselfish friendliness and without expecting any return except for a little
tobacco. Knowing their passion for it, we had brought some with us, and it was
touching to see their response to our present.

213

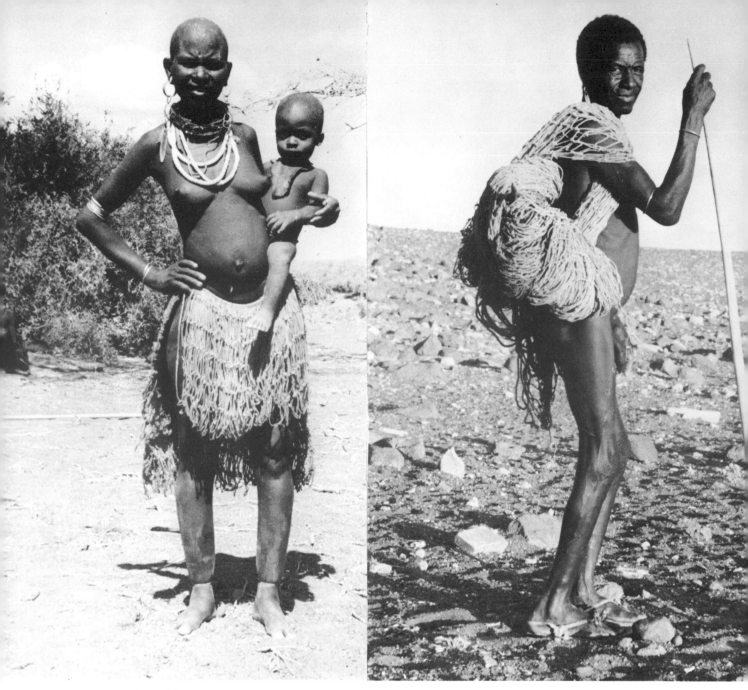

144. Elmolo woman and baby

145. Elmolo fisherman

The Elmolo live in primitive huts made of branches tied together and covered with lake-weed. A few stones secure these flimsy shelters to the ground, otherwise they would be carried away by the gales which often sweep across the lake at a speed of ninety miles an hour.

During the next few days, while George dealt with the poachers, I painted a few of our Elmolo friends, who never came near our camp without bringing a present of fish.

The women wore a short apron in front, a longer one of doum-palm fiber at the back, and a few crude ornaments made of fishbones (144). The men wore orna-

146. Elmolo on his raft

ments only. They made fishing nets of doum palm fiber (145), the only material which does not rot in the alkaline water, and used clumsy iron harpoons. On fragile rafts made of three doum-palm logs lashed together (146), they venture out on the lake spearing everything edible within reach.

Turtle shells are used as plates, and precious plates they are, as they belong to the Trionyx genus, which occur elsewhere only in the Nile and of which the British Museum could only recently obtain a perfect specimen.

Whenever George shot crocodile, which cruised in large numbers in the shallows near the shore, there was great excitement among the people, and I found it difficult to secure the skin for handbags, as the Elmolo found it just as delicious to eat as the rest of the reptile.

One day I explored a small peninsula. It was recorded as an island by Count Samuel Teleki and Ludwig von Höhnel when, in 1888, they discovered Lake Rudolf, the level of which has since fallen. At the far end is a plateau on which I saw eighteen stone cairns varying between ten and twelve feet in diameter. I was told by the Elmolo that these had been there as long as they could remember. Hoping to discover traces of earlier inhabitants, I started excavating. After removing the stones lying on the ground, I came on a layer of large boulders covering a pit filled with loose sand. In this I found a bone. Carefully brushing away the sand,

215

147.   Grave on Elmolo peninsula

I exposed a complete human skeleton (147) in a crouching position, turned to the right, with knees doubled up and hands near the face. I saw that the sand was loose only around the bones, and filled a pit just large enough to hold the skeleton. I took several photographs *in situ* and then removed the bones, wrapped them carefully in cotton wool and put them in containers.

I dug up two more graves. In one I found another skeleton, but it was in poor condition, so I could only collect the skull and the larger bones; the others fell to dust when I touched them. The third grave was the smallest and contained only bone splinters. I took all these to the Coryndon Museum at Nairobi and was told that the bones belonged to a people different from those who now live in this area.

Close to the Elmolo Islands I found fragments of pottery embedded in the lava tuff (148); I cut them out; they bore four different types of ornamentations.

The landmark of the south-east end of Lake Rudolf is the conical hill, Porr, some two miles inland. One day as we walked toward this hill we found a large deposit of oyster shells about four miles distant from the lake and some eighty feet above its present level. Some time later we were shown tracings of rock paintings found by Mr Plant at the very top of Porr: they looked like picture-writings similar to the ones we had seen in the Sahara. I wondered whether these could have been made by the same people who did the rock engravings I had previously discovered on the southern end of Lake Rudolf.

216

xxv   Kipsikis mother of girl in circumcision

JOY

148. Digging for pottery

Far too soon for my liking we had to say goodbye to the Elmolo and return to Marsabit by a different route along the lake. Driving off the track along a dry riverbed near Kagi, we came upon several large stone structures. Some were round with parallel terraces terminating in a cone. Some were rectangular, up to twenty feet in length, and had a platform and others were just stone cairns. When later, in Marsabit, we asked about these monuments, no one seemed to know of them, no doubt because they were off the beaten track. Some years later we found similar structures near Merti on the Uaso Nyiro River.

I had now been for more than five months in the Northern Frontier District; during this time I had written repeatedly to the Chief Native Commissioner about continuing my work on the tribal record.

At last I got a letter asking me to come to Nairobi and discuss the situation. There I learned that in spite of efforts to raise funds, none had been forthcoming. The Chief Native Commissioner now suggested arranging an exhibition of my paintings in order to arouse public interest in my work and hoping thus to provide money to complete it. He also advised me to see the Governor and ask for his support. During this interview His Excellency assured me that in addition to sponsoring the exhibition he would try to raise funds abroad. While these plans were being put into action, we decided that I should go to Narok and paint the Masai.

219

XXVI   Masai girl in seclusion during circumcision

CHAPTER II

THE MASAI

The Masai are one of the best-known peoples of Kenya partly because of their history and partly because of their interesting customs, their good looks, and their reputation as warriors[7]. They are Nilo-Hamites and some four hundred years ago they came from the north to Kenya, by way of Lake Stefanie and the south end of Lake Rudolf. Their expansion reached its peak during the beginning and middle of the last century when they roamed over some eighty thousand square miles, ranging from Lake Rudolf to the Lorian Swamp, across the Rift Valley and far into Tanganyika. In the center of this vast area is Mount Kenya whose two peaks of more than seventeen thousand feet in altitude are named after the great Masai leaders, Mbatyany and Nelion.

The life of the Masai is governed by their love for cattle – they believe that God gave them exclusive rights over all the cattle in the world. They live on the milk, blood and meat of their herds and an occasional kill of buffalo or eland (antelope) which they regard as wild cattle. In the past, to maintain and enlarge their herds, they used to spend most of their time raiding, and their highly skilled warriors were the terror of their neighbors.

They would have dominated all the other tribes had it not been for three catastrophes which finally brought them under European protection.

The first was an outbreak of rinderpest, in 1880, which reduced their stock alarmingly; then, in 1892, they were weakened by a smallpox epidemic, and finally disunity added to their misfortunes. Their great leader Mbatyany had died in about 1890. They were unable to agree upon a successor, and began to fight among themselves, with the result that they could no longer hold their enemies at bay and, but for European intervention, would have been defeated by the Kikuyu.

While the Masai were engaged in intertribal wars to decide whether Lenana or Sendeu, both sons of Mbatyany, was to be their leader, the British and the Germans defined the boundaries between Tanganyika and the East African protectorate; this cut right through Masai land and split the people in two. After 1889 the

149. Masai girl

British ruled in the East African protectorate (now known as Kenya) and by 1902 Lenana, who had vanquished Sendeu, came under the British.

In 1904 it was decided to settle the Masai living under British protection in two reservations, one in Laikipia, north of the Uganda railway, and one south of it, between Mount Suswa and the German border. But by 1911 it was thought better to unite all the Masai in the Southern Reserve and so a move was organized, which lasted for three years, by which time the tribe had been gathered together. To give

221

150.   Masai warrior (left)

151.   Masai warrior in war regalia (above)

living space to so many people, the Southern Reserve was extended to its present boundaries which run near to the Tsavo and to the west of the Mara River. It was administered from Kajiado and Narok.

I was now painting the Masai in the Narok area, where I was put under the care of a Masai Officer who guided me high up into the hills to Enjora, where, at that time, there was a large *manyata*.

The Masai build two types of kraals. One, *enkang*, consists of twenty to fifty huts, and is for married people and their families. These huts are placed inside a circular thorn fence, which also protects the livestock by night from the attacks of predators. Each family has one or two gates in the fence; the hut of the first wife is on the

222

152. Masai wearing
his busby made
of lion mane

right of the gate, that of the second wife on the left, the third wife's hut is again to the right and so on. The Masai marry as many wives as they can afford.

The second type of kraal is called *manyata*, and is inhabited by members of one age group who, after circumcision, attach the prefix *Ole* to their name, which means 'the son of', preceding the father's name, and become warriors—*il moran*. Until they marry, these young men live together with their mothers and sisters. The latter, as soon as they reach puberty, become the lovers of the *moran* (149).

These *manyata*s, in which several hundred people live in fifty to a hundred huts, are not fenced in. Each *moran* shares the hut with his entourage, but if he wants to sleep with his lover, the pair go to another hut. When his father visits his mother, the hut must be left to the parents for the duration of his stay.

I pitched my tent within a few hundred yards of the *manyata* at Enjora, and as soon as all was ready, the Masai Officer organized a Grand Parade of the *moran* from which to choose my models. Most of them were dressed in their war regalia (150, 151) with ostrich plumes framing their faces (152) or busbies, made of lion manes, on their heads. Their ocher-painted bodies were scantily covered by short skin-capes knotted over one shoulder, which was in striking contrast for their spears.

Though they were enticing models, I first painted a girl whom I saw among the crowd. I suspected that she was here only temporarily and did not want to lose her as a model. She wore a typical fringe of tiny metal chains across her eyes, as do all Nilo-Hamitic girls while undergoing the seclusion period after clitoridectomy; besides other emblems she had grass stuck into her hair, which is the Masai symbol for peace (pl. XXVI, p. 218). This reminded me of the Rendile youth who had some grass attached to his shoulder-knotted hide on the day he was circumcised. I also found a boy candidate for circumcision to pose for me in his seclusion dress (153).

During seclusion the Masai youths wear a woman's ear-rings and dress which has to be dyed black; it is knotted on the right shoulder and held in position round the waist by a string of cowrie shells. They kill small birds with blunted arrows, and arrange the feathers around their heads. They also attach two ostrich feathers behind their ears. White markings around the eyes complete the ritual emblems.

Moran are not allowed to drink intoxicating liquor or to chew tobacco, nor are they permitted to sleep with married woman (154). They may marry as soon as they have reached the senior warrior status. In the meantime they take lovers who live with them in the *manyata*, but the girls must take care not to become pregnant, or their betrothal, which the parents may have previously arranged with another man, will be broken off. If they do not like their parents' choice, the girls sometimes take advantage of this rule and see that they become pregnant by the man they love.

I painted a young mother with white markings round her eyes (155)—a sign that

153. Masai boy during circumcision

she had only a few days ago borne a child, and I saw other mothers who had just one white blotch on their foreheads for a few days following childbirth (156).

By now I had made friends with several Masai living in the *manyata*. One afternoon as I was walking close to it, I noticed a small tree, the bark of which had been peeled off in parallel strips. Since the exposed wood was still wet, this had obviously

154. Masai married woman   155. Masai married woman who has just borne a child

been done very recently. When I asked for an explanation, I was told that this tree was the one under which the elders prayed for rain. A part of the ritual was to take strips of bark off the trunk; they also buried a skin at the root of the tree, poured water over it and placed charms around it before kneeling down to pray. While we were talking the sun was getting low and soon I was asked to leave the place as the elders would be returning to pray again and no one must be present when they were so engaged.

Although the Masai, since they do not hunt for food, can be regarded as conservationists of wild life, they are great killers of lion, not only to protect their livestock but because of a tribal custom which demands the spearing of a lion as proof of manhood. This custom is now forbidden by law but is still carried out more or less secretly, indeed, the number of skins that are annually confiscated makes one wonder how lion still survive in Masai country. The same applies to the ostrich, whose feathers are used for head-dresses.

One day I talked with an elderly woman who was busy scraping the hair off an oxhide with the sharp edge of a cow's shoulder blade (157). I asked her why she

226

156.   Another Masai woman (right) just after childbirth

did not use a knife of which there were plenty to be bought at the shops in Narok —she replied that her bone was quite good enough for the purpose.

This was until recently characteristic of the Masai's attitude to life. Far too proud to work, they kept to their traditional way of life even though, since tribal wars had ceased, much of it had become meaningless, and until a short time ago they refused all Western education.

In the old days the *moran* would have spent their youth raiding and fighting, but now they had no outlet for their energy other than herding cattle or flirting or hanging about in the *manyata* until the frustration became so unbearable that they provoked a fight among themselves. Sometimes they spent a whole day beautifying each other's coiffures. No woman could have taken greater trouble than those strong young men in oiling and padding their hair with ocher, making it into tiny plaits, then setting it either loose or putting it into pigtails or large mops, which-ever fashion their rank demanded (159).

Later I painted a *moran* whose face was partly covered by a lion-mane head-dress, a trophy prized by all Masai. For some reason, possibly because of the

227

157.   Masai woman scraping hair from a skin

oppressive atmosphere which precedes the rainy season, my sitter was in such a state of tension that I found painting him difficult. Then suddenly there was a yell from the *manyata* and instantly the *moran* flung his shield and head-dress to the ground, grabbed his spear and dashed off. The shouting became deafening, so, taking my camera, I rushed to the *manyata*. Once there I realized that a real battle was going on, and that the men were throwing spears and clubbing each other over the head. I retreated at once in case my presence should encourage them to show off and fight even more fiercely, but, before leaving, I left a message for the combatants to say that I would be glad to supply dressings and medicines should any be required to deal with the results of the fight.

I did not have to wait long before the first victims arrived; one had a hole in his forehead which would have knocked out most men; another had a wound behind his ear, and several showed gashes in arms, legs, and chest which made me almost faint. I dressed these wounds as best I could with sulphanilamide, but when I suggested taking the worst cases in my car to the hospital at Narok, no one would hear of it; all preferred to walk the distance—which it would take a healthy man at least a day to cover.

The mêlée ended as quickly as it had begun. As it had put a stop to my day's painting, I washed my hair and, after setting it on rollers, went for a stroll. Soon I came upon a group of *moran*, resting under a tree and recovering from the morning's excitement (158). When they saw me, they came up, much intrigued by my hair-setting, and wanted to know all about it. Some of them understood Swahili, and so I tried to explain that this was my way of beautifying my hair-style just as theirs was to plait their hair into pigtails. This made them shake with laughter and, pulling my hair with their ocher-greased hands, they assured me it looked

228

150. Masai warrior

159. Masai warriors dressing
      their hair

like a lion's mane. I had some difficulty in freeing myself before I was plucked bald, and when I got home, smeared all over with fat and ocher, I looked like a bedraggled *moran* myself to the delight of these mischievous youngsters.

A few days later I moved my camp to Narosura some sixty miles away, where a big cattle sale was going to be held in combination with the Annual Sports. A large crowd was expected to attend both events, and I hoped I might find good models among the people. I drove there accompanied by the Masai Officer, who told me that most of the cattle going to the sale had already been to Narosura, to a previous sale which had come to an abrupt end.

At this time a simmering feud had existed between the local District Commissioner and the Masai. During long hours of bargaining about prices in the heat and dust, tension increased, and when the District Commissioner insisted on the sale of a cow which was its owner's pet, a heated argument ended with the Masai spearing the District Commissioner and killing him. The murder seemed to have been planned, for the spear used to kill him had been greased, which is only done in preparation for a killing.

The man, a member of the *laibon* clan, was hanged and his family had to pay considerable compensation to the District Commissioner's widow. After this no sale of cattle had taken place until the present one. In the hope of obliterating bitter memories, it had been arranged to hold the Annual Sports, of which the Masai are very fond, at the same time as the sale.

Narosura is located at the foot of the Loitai Plateau; here a few native shops, close to a small river, provide the neighboring Masai with essential goods. Immediately across the river an escarpment rises and leads to a plateau. This beautiful highland country overlooks the plains and reaches far into Tanganyika. The Masai *laibon* live here.

Among the Masai, Nandi, and Samburu, the *laibon* are leaders whose authority is based on mystical powers. Before Europeans came to this part of Africa it was the *laibon* who sanctioned raids and provided magical protection for the warriors. They still authorize the ceremonies connected with circumcision and age-sets; they make rain and ensure the fertility and welfare of their people and act as intermediaries between man and the other world; they are the mystical focus of all tribal activity. Since the *laibon* are not chiefs, after the Europeans came they could not be fitted into the administrative system of the country, and as it was thought desirable to control their activities—which were not always beneficial—they were confined to certain areas: the Loitai Plateau was that chosen for the Masai *laibon* and they agreed not to leave without permission.

When we reached Narosura, a huge crowd had already assembled. People continued to arrive until nightfall, and by next morning it was difficult to find a space to mark out as a sports ground. While this was being done, I strolled among

160. Masai spear-throwing

the Masai, who, tense with excitement and oblivious of the dust and of the millions of flies, chattered and laughed to the accompaniment of the noisy bleating of their cattle.

I noticed two Masai men who, though their clothing and ornaments were in no way distinctive, had such a dignified bearing that they were conspicuous wherever they went.

When I asked the Masai Officer if I could paint these men, he seemed embarrassed and told me that they were *laibon* and direct descendants of the famous Sendeu. He suggested that I should wait until the sports were over since, if the games were a success, everybody would be in high spirits and the *laibon* might be easier to persuade.

231

161. Masai high jump

We spent the day watching the men competing in throwing spears (160), hurling their athletic bodies effortlessly over the high jumps (161) and racing the long distances in record time (162). One exceptionally good looking and very tall young *moran*, Sijey Auge (163), beat the world record for a high jump with such ease that wherever he went the cheering never stopped. He accepted this with the air of a celebrity well used to ovations, and I felt very proud when later he graciously condescended to sit for his portrait.

162. Masai running a long distance race   163. Young Masai *moran* Sije Auge (opposite)

Not only were the competitions fascinating to watch, but so were the onlookers (161), who were often so carried away by their excitement that unconsciously they imitated the movements of the contestants or improvised their own jumps and dances to the encouraging shouts of their friends. By sunset everybody was settling round fires in a festive mood and long into the night we heard their laughter.

Luck was with me when the senior *laibon* Konei ole Sendeo requested a pass for a shopping visit to Narok from the Masai Officer. The Officer jokingly replied that this would be granted if he would pose for a portrait, to which the *laibon* agreed. But before I could start painting, he had first to collect his ritual garments from his home on the Loitai Plateau.

Next morning we made our way to the *manyata* of the *laibon* (164), tucked away between rocks and a patch of forest. We drove up a steep escarpment to reach the plateau. Beautiful parkland and rolling hills, on which antelope grazed peacefully next to the cattle, herded by a small toto, stretched out as far as we could see. When we arrived the *laibon's* wife invited us to come inside the hut which, like all Masai homes, was a long, low structure made of a wooden framework and plastered over with cowdung and mud. In order to enter we had almost to crawl on our knees, and it took some time before I got accustomed to the darkness inside and could see the open fireplace in the middle of the hut; around it were a few calabashes and two little wooden stools, and in the background was some sort of bedstead.

We returned to camp just before dark, having arranged with the *laibon* that he should come early next morning (pl. XXVII, p. 299). When he arrived I hardly recognized him; his eyes were circled by white paint which completely altered his expression. All my efforts to catch his likeness were defeated by his eyes which looked like two pieces of black jade set in a white frame.

Realizing that I was in difficulty, the *laibon* tried to mesmerize me, but I had experienced similar attempts in my meetings with witch doctors so I did my best to retaliate by mesmerizing the *laibon*. Soon he remarked with a smile, 'Of course you cannot paint my eyes because they are not normal eyes.' I asked him what he meant by that, to which he replied that he was not a normal human being. Finally I was satisfied with my portrait but by then I felt completely exhausted by my efforts to resist his hypnotizing stare, and I could well imagine what power he could exercise over subjects less independent than myself, and how easily they would succumb to his forceful personality.

Next I started on the picture of Sijey Auge, the high jumper; but I had to break off when I received a telegram, asking me to return to Nairobi to help with the exhibition.

In Nairobi, helped by members of the Art and Craft Society which was spon- soring the exhibition, we framed four hundred paintings. These were hung in the

234

164. *Manyata* of Masai *laibon* named Konei Ole Sendeo

Memorial Hall, which the Society had transformed into a tropical garden in which tribal shields, weapons, ornaments, and leatherwork were displayed. In order to give a lively touch to the show the Government had summoned a few Africans from various districts to attend the exhibition in their traditional costumes. The exhibition at the Memorial Hall lasted from 8 to 12 August 1951 and was later transferred to the Pumbwani Hall.

A group of African leaders were invited to the preview. After the Chief Native Commissioner's inaugural speech, which stressed the importance of this record and appealed for funds to enable its completion, we showed the guests around.

I talked for a long time to one of the African visitors and stressed that the purpose of my work was to help to preserve the knowledge of fast disappearing tribal cultures. I spoke too of my hope that it would make the people aware and proud of their traditions, and also that this record would lead others, whose help was needed in the struggle to develop the country, to a better understanding of the peoples of Kenya. Finally I appealed to our guest to use influence with the radio and press to interest the Africans in the exhibition. After he had left I learned that it was Jomo Kenyatta to whom I had been speaking.

For the next five days the hall was packed with visitors and many returned several times to study the details of the ornaments and the descriptive notes.

235

Judging by the number of visitors, the exhibition was a great success but the big donations needed for the completion of the work failed to come in.

Expecting that when it moved to the Pumbwani Hall the exhibition would evoke even more interest among Africans, the authorities took precautions to protect the paintings by a cordon, in case the visitors might become too excited when they saw their traditional tribal splendors, and guides were engaged to control the expected crowd. But during the week that the pictures were on view, only forty Africans came to see them and among these some seemed embarrassed and asked why they had been told to come. They could not recognize a two-dimensional representation of a human being, so the paintings were meaningless to them.

I was not entirely surprised, for I had often seen uneducated Africans examining my paintings upside down. They have much more response to sculpture, no doubt because it is three-dimensional and their own artistic impulse is almost always expressed in carving.

In spite of the financially disappointing outcome of the exhibition, I was determined to carry on at my own risk, and the Government assured me that they would have another try later on to raise funds.

CHAPTER 12

THE AKAMBA OF KITUI
AND THE POKOMO

When I left Nairobi I went to the Kitui district to paint the Akamba. The Kitui Akamba split off from their Machakos brothers some two hundred years ago when they moved east across the Athi River, and now wear different ornaments and have different customs. All Akamba have retained their love of hunting, as we already knew from the gangs of poachers whom George used to meet along the Tana River (which is the boundary between the Kitui district and the Northern Frontier Province). Normally the Akamba use only bows and poisoned arrows for hunting, but in the Kitui district they often chase the game with dogs as well. Totems are of great importance to the Akamba—all theirs represent wild animals, a proof of their love of hunting.

The Akamba are good wood carvers—indeed they are famous all over East Africa for their craft. I well remember when I first came to Kenya in 1937 how reluctant they still were to sell any of their exquisitely carved combs, spoons, or animal figures. Since then their skill has become commercialized, and many of their carvings are now displayed on the pavement by hotels. They are also exported, and I have found them in curio shops in London, Stockholm, and New York. Though most of these figures are no longer original in design, they are hand carved and considering the quality of the wood used and the work involved, they sell at very reasonable prices in Kenya.

Apart from wood carving the Akamba are also skilled in stone and iron crafts. They are very likable people and popular all over the country.

Their districts are run by a council of elders who are selected partly by age-grades and partly by payment. The Akamba are agriculturists, but also keep large herds which erode the country very badly, and on my drive to Kitui I noticed many bare patches in the normally scrub-covered land. On my arrival I was told that it had been arranged that I should camp at Theikuru. As this was a remote place, the D.C. insisted on sending his driver to help me across wide, sandy river-beds. The country around Theikuru is dull, monotonous, open bush in which the

165. Akamba *boma*

hamlets of the Akamba are scattered (165). While visiting one of the larger ones, I was struck by the cleanliness of the immediate surroundings. When I asked about their sanitary arrangements, I was told that human excrement was immediately buried to prevent wild animals from stepping on it, and thus accidentally getting a spiritual hold over the person involved. Women had to bury their excrements much deeper than men; I thought the reason might be that, if the woman were pregnant, she would be responsible for two lives.

166. Akamba woman sifting grain

167.   Akamba boy undergoing circumcision

This custom derives from the same fear which causes many Africans to refuse to be photographed, for they believe that the possession of even their image may give the photographer power over their spirit. But the burying of excrements is not only of ritual significance, it also has a hygienic value and prevents epidemics.

Here I met men and women who chipped their upper front teeth (incisors) into sharp points; this is done with crude iron bars with sharpened edges, used as

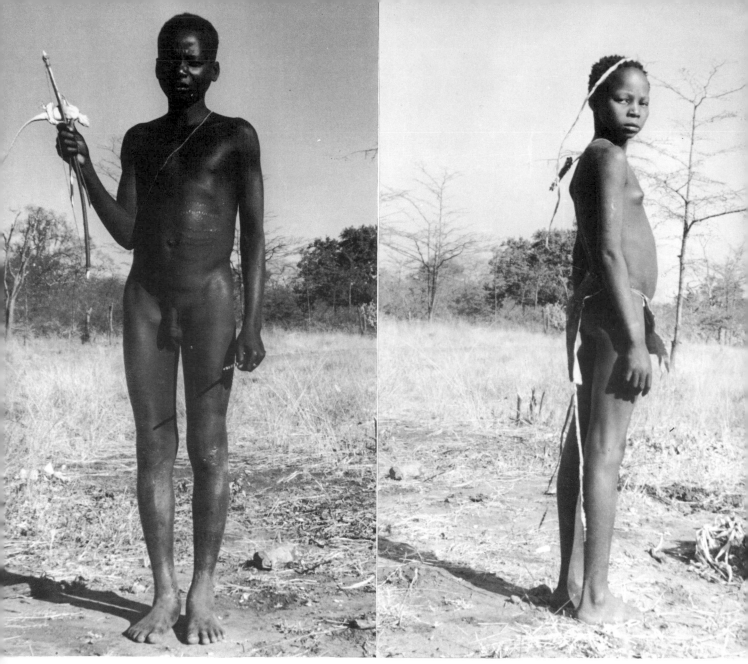

168. Akamba boy with his ritual circumcision bow and lizard

169. Akamba girl in circumcision with her ritual apron at
the back and symbolic bundle of sticks hanging from
her neck

dental tools, to chip the teeth into the desired shape purely for ornamental reasons.
When I asked what happened if the mutilated teeth decayed and fell out, I was
shown a piece of animal bone which would then be inserted into the hole to
replace the original tooth. Besides pointing their teeth, the women beautify themselves with cicatrizations over their body. For this they use the latex of the local
euphorbia; they also tattoo their cheeks by rubbing the powdered roots of plum-
bago mixed with milk into their skin which has previously been scratched.

I was lucky that the circumcision ritual had just started (167) and I was able to
get a boy (168) and girl (169) to pose for me. Here, both sexes spent their days of

240

a.

b.

170.   Akamba witch doctor sequence

c.

d.

seclusion together. One morning I noticed footmarks leading to my lavatory which had been built at some distance from my tent and was reserved for my use. I suspected the kitchen toto whom I had engaged locally, but as I had no evidence, I could not accuse him. When next day there were again fresh footmarks, I called the Askari, who had been allotted to me by the Government to act as interpreter, my boy, and the toto, and asked them if they knew who was using my lavatory? None of them would answer my question. As I was painting a witch doctor who was held in great repute among the local people. I asked him to help me find the culprit. He agreed and put on his ritual regalia and painted white and red markings on his temples and arms (he was already wearing his professional hair-style, which consisted of a narrow circle of hair around his skull and a tiny tuft at its top). Now he drew a circle of ash on the ground large enough for a man to sit inside. Along this he stuck porcupine quills at short distances between which he placed antelope horns which, I believe, are minor symbols of the feared Kithitu, a charm with great magical power which brings death to anybody who has sworn an oath by it and has broken it (170a—d). Next he ordered one of the suspects to sit in the circle, then he jumped from one porcupine quill to the next,

171. Akamba witch doctor

MUYUGO MWANZA
ANGO CHONGOMUNDU
KAMBA

172. Akamba woman witch doctor using the same instrument as the man opposite

blowing a magic horn and cracking a rope threateningly without ever hitting the man, who was anxiously following his movements. After rampaging around and making the man nervous, he clapped his hands wildly and threw charms from the antelope horns towards him. Then he entered the circle and commanded the suspect to creep forward and backward between his legs, after which he swung the man on to his shoulders and carried him, face upwards, round the circle and finally dropped him some distance away. He repeated the ritual with all the men who shared my camp.

Although this nerve-shattering treatment would have made me confess to almost anything even if I had never committed any misdeed, it did not break the resistance of the wrongdoer. So now the witch doctor lined the men up in front of him and after addressing them in dramatic words, put a little dry flour on their foreheads. Watching their expressions intently, he suddenly thundered at the kitchen toto who broke down and admitted the offence.

The whole performance was most convincing and the men walked away very subdued. Of course the witch doctor was a good psychologist and knew that from the moment he began his ritual the guilty person would have to control his emotions to a far greater extent than the other men so that his tension and his fear of the final test would cause him to perspire more freely than the others and consequently the flour on his forehead would grow wet more quickly than that on the other men. This was all the witch doctor needed to get the answer. Nevertheless, he gave the impression that all was done by magic and thus greatly increased his prestige. Instead of putting flour on the men's foreheads, he might have asked the suspects to swallow dry flour, knowing that the guilty man would have the driest throat; in this case he would watch to see who had the greatest difficulty in swallowing.

Soon afterwards I moved to Ndau, another remote place, where I was again confronted with a witch doctor. I was especially interested in one of his instruments, which is used only by the Akamba in East Africa. It is one-stringed and made of a gourd placed between a metal string and a wooden bow (171, 172). It is used by witch doctors of both sexes.

While painting him, I developed stomach-trouble and felt tempted to test his powers, so I asked him what I could do to cure it. His first question was how many male and female children my mother had had. When my reply was three daughters, he poured three pebbles from the gourd and added two more. This he went on doing until there were ten pebbles. Then he inquired if my pains were in the middle of my stomach or at the side. When I said they were in the middle, he assured me that they were due to a baby which I could not deliver, and told me that I would have far greater pain later on. (As far as my pregnancy was concerned, he was correct.) I again asked what he could do to help me, and so he added more pebbles and started beating his instrument by touching the metal string which was supported by a small wooden ridge where it touched the gourd. Finally he advised me to eat lion fat and kill a few beetles of the kind which sham death when one meets them, grind them, and then draw seven lines below my navel with this powder. This treatment would help me to give birth to a daughter

173. Akamba dance
    sequence

first and later on to boys and girls alternately. I thanked him and promised him a good present after my daughter had been born, but, as there was no lion fat available nor was I able to find the right sort of beetle, he never got his present.

After completing paintings of a circumciser, a warrior, and a woman witch doctor, I moved to my next camp at Ikutha which is on the road between Kitui and Kibwezi.

Kibwezi is a station on the Kenya-Uganda railway and on the road between Mombasa and Nairobi. It had been the starting point of the first safari I undertook in 1938 soon after my arrival in Kenya. I had joined the staff of the Coryndon Museum on a three months' expedition to the Chyulu Hills in order to explore this volcanic range which had been visited by few Europeans. We had engaged some three hundred Akamba as porters to bring us weekly provisions and to carry water to our camp, which for one month was twenty miles from the nearest spring; this spring was such a miserable trickle that to fill a four-gallon can took almost a whole day. In the circumstances, we used water with extreme economy, and even tried to add to our supply by pulling our sheets in the early morning across the wet grass to collect the dew off them. All the members of the team had been in the country for many years, and were experienced in porter safaris. We were therefore surprised that a man who had only recently arrived in Kenya obviously had more authority over the porters than any of the rest of the team. Sometimes when no one could come to an agreement with the Akamba, his mere appearance settled the argument. By chance, one day we learned that the cause of his prestige was that he was left-handed. The Akamba believe that the lion kills with its left paw, so they attributed the strength of a lion to this man, and the fact that he wore a monocle added to their respect, for they interpreted it as a sign of great wealth. As a result of his possessing these two assets, the feeling of the Akamba for him came near to worship.

246

After we completed this safari we spent a few days at Kibwezi and Ikutha where the local Africans had arranged a dance in our honor. They danced nonstop for several days and nights and none of us got any sleep.

Now on arriving at Ikutha I recalled this scene, for I could hardly get to my camp site becausing of the dancing that was going on. The Chief had summoned several hundred people to meet me and already they had begun celebrating the occasion. However, having been told that the dance was being held on Government orders, they had adjusted the style of their dancing accordingly. They were excellent mimics and it was most amusing to see their imitations of various visitors such as the D.C., white hunters, police officers and missionaries. Later they were carried away by their excitement and returned to their own uninhibited way of dancing (173a–j) their muscular bodies reeling, jumping and swinging in a whirl of ecstasy towards the girls who, quivering and writhing, provoked the young men with such natural, disarming frankness that there was nothing indecent about it. The rhythmical drumming of various bands increased the frenzy till billows of dust hid the dancers. I reflected that as long as there are dances the Africa I love so much will continue to exist.

Among all this throbbing, jerking, wriggling and shuffling crowd, my attention was caught by a solemn figure with his arms rigidly outstretched and a large wooden mortar at an almost upright angle balanced between his teeth. When he placed the mortar on the ground, I asked how he could hold such a heavy weight between his pointed teeth? He told me this was thanks to a medicine he had put on his tongue. I also learned that he was the local medicine man who specialized in snakebites and protection against lions (174). He had learned his magic from the NYAMWEZI tribe in Tanganyika with whom he had lived for six years. After his return he claimed that he could make people immune for one year against snake venom, cure them when bitten, and even revive them shortly after they had died from snakebite. He was himself of course immune to the venom and as a proof showed me many scars on his body caused by snakebites. The local Africans confirmed that his stories were true.

I had recently read a book by Carmichael about the Nyamwezi and their secret snake and porcupine society. According to this two men were sent from the United States to study the method of gaining immunity from snake venom. After living for some time among the members of this secret society, they were admitted to several stages of initiation but not to the most important ones. Their report said that carefully selected novices of the society were from the earliest age frequently inoculated with a powder made from six herbs. This was rubbed into small cuts at the elbow, wrist, knee and pelvis, in fact wherever there was little flesh between the skin and the bone. The tongue was treated similarly and then, gradually, the person became immune to snake venom except for that of the mambas.

171. Akamba medicine
man specialising in
protection against
snake bites and
lions

Another section of this secret society develops immunity against porcupines and their initiates are able to crawl into the burrows of these animals without being injured by their sharp quills.

When I asked what happened if a person got bitten by a snake and no powder was available, I was told that the medicine man would then take the skin of a lynx, the inner side of which was painted with seven black stripes made with charcoal and four red stripes made with ocher, swing it three times round the person, then ask him to sit down on it and tell him the lynx skin would prevent him from dying before the powder arrived.

This reminded me of a man who collected snake venom, and asserted that anyone bitten by a viper could recover without treatment if he had the self-control to keep absolutely still in body and serene in mind so that his circulation would not accelerate and his blood would be enabled to absorb the poison gradually.

Although I would not like to be put to the test, it sounds credible that the venom of the vipers, which is hematoxic and affects the blood by causing intravascular clotting, could be absorbed under conditions of complete physical and mental calm. On the other hand, the venom of cobras, mambas, rattlesnakes and some other snakes is neurotoxic and attacks the nerve centers and causes a quick death. The use of the lynx skin simply proved what a good psychologist the medicine man was. I was less convinced by his story that he had a powder which would stop a lion from attacking cattle, as long as this, concealed in a *dikdik* horn, was placed to the left of the entrance of the *boma*. He claimed that it would make the lion prowl around the fence but deprive him of his strength to jump over it.

I asked to be shown the six plants which made up the anti-snakebite powder, and I was able to identify them and also to get their local Kamba names:

elungu: ipomoea
mukudu: solanum
usua: asparagus
moitha: climber with large seedpod
musilinge: tree
muaa: acacia

Of the first five, the roots are used, but in the case of the acacia, the leaves. The *musilinge* and acacia trees are given a special treatment before the root of the first and the leaves of the second are used: three stones are placed under the trees and a fire lit on them, then the ashes are three times removed from between the stones and blown against the tree. It is believed that only after this rite will the root or leaves become a potent medicine.

Asparagus needs a different treatment. Having discovered it, the finder has to go to a place where two roads fork and beat the sand that lies between the fork three times with a cloth; then he takes the sand and throws it on to the root of the plant. No doubt this ritual has a psychological effect on the patient. Some Africans advised that this medicine should be mixed with honey before being applied.

I acquired some of the powder the medicine man had collected during his stay with the Nyamwezi and sent it to the laboratory of the Agricultural Department at Nairobi for analysis. According to the report, it had anti-toxic properties, but

175.   Akamba medicine man sequence

this sample was both too old and contained too much dirt for the degree of its efficacy to be determined.

As I painted the medicine man I became impressed by his sincerity and his capacities. Although some of his therapy bewildered me, there was no denying that several times I saw him lifting his mortar, which weighed thirty-four pounds, and holding the inch-wide wooden rim between his pointed teeth without using his hands to support it.

He also demonstrated his procedure for curing a sick person (175a–f). The patient is placed inside a small circle outlined with ash which is intersected with porcupine quills and gourds, containing medicines. Before the actual treatment begins, the medicine man places a wooden mortar at the opening of the circle and steps over the mortar from left to right and from right to left. Then he puts some medicine on his tongue – to give him the required strength – and lifts up the mortar and carries it around the circle. After this he kneels at the feet of the patient and sways a magic gourd inwards and outwards over the man's body. This is intended to draw out the poison. The same movements are repeated over the patient's head. The medicine man then proceeds to pretend to suck the poison from the skull,

256

chest and feet. After this he orders the patient to get up, but in fact lifts him on to his back, face towards the sky, and carries him around the circle. Finally he sets him on the mortar, which has been placed opposite the sick man's feet outside the circle.

I was very lucky to have found this medicine man for, in general, the people at Ikutha wore few traditional ornaments. Living so close to a main road and to the railway station of Kibwezi, and most of them being employed on a large sisal estate, they had been subject to a great deal of European influence and had given up their own customs. After painting a few models who had to be specially dressed for the occasion, I left the Akamba.

Kipini, thirty miles south of Lamu, was my destination. Kipini stands at the estuary where the Tana River enters the Indian Ocean. It then consisted of a few fishing huts and the office and spacious house of the D.O. From here he administered the tribes living along the lower Tana. The house had been built a good time ago when Kipini was an active port, but since then the Tana had

257

silted up the harbor and the ocean had encroached on the land and Kipini has become one of the loneliest of outposts. Two people who had been posted to it had committed suicide, and it had acquired a rather sinister reputation.

Luckily this spell had been broken by the present D.O. and his wife, a young couple who liked the isolation of Kipini and had brought a new atmosphere to the place. I spent a day with them, during which they took me a few miles north along the beach to see ruins which must have been the remains of large towns that had flourished long ago.

Unfortunately the sites were so overgrown that all we could see were fragments of wells, doors, pillars and walls, some of which were elaborately carved. Dr James Kirkman, who excavated the Gedi ruins near Malindi, had proposed to the Government that he should excavate these sites, but nothing had come of the proposal, for to collect funds for digs at so remote a place had proved impossible.

From Kipini I continued some eighty miles along the Tana to Hola where the D.O. had made arrangements for me to paint the Pokomo. I pitched my camp within a few yards of the river under some beautiful trees. As everywhere else along this river, there was a dense forest belt on the banks, and this provided shade for people and for wild animals such as elephant, buffalo and antelope. When one left this cool shelter and went further inland, one met with great heat, especially at this time of year when the rains were soon expected to break.

Hola is the center of the Pokomo; its age is attested by an abandoned mission which the Germans built there before the First World War.

I was particularly interested in the Pokomo as they were one of the groups which originated from Shungwaya north of Malindi but unlike the Nyika and Meru tribes, who had been driven away from there by the Galla about A.D. 1300, the Pokomo, led by one of their sub-tribes called BUU, had left the Coast about a hundred years earlier. I was keen to find out how much the Pokomo still had in common with either of these groups.

The most important among their institutions, but one that is rapidly dwindling in prestige, is the *Wakiju,* a secret society, which rules the people between Hola and the Coast. Its members possess great authority and are often feared, but in times of famine it is they who distribute the stored food amongst the people.

The *Wakiju* meet at the *ngaji*—a wooden drum kept in a hut supported by three poles and concealed in dense bush. By the first pole a sentry keeps guard to ensure that no unauthorized person approaches the hut. The *ngaji* is made of a hollowed tree trunk some nine feet in length; it is kept in a horizontal position. One end is covered with a tightly stretched skin through the center of which a wooden stick is inserted till it reaches a container filled with water inside the trunk.

258

176. Pokomo *ngaji*

177. Pokomo *ngaji* elder's wife, leader of a women's secret society

Whenever this stick is twirled, the end inside the drum vibrates in the water and makes a penetrating and terrifying sound. This is supposed to be the voice of a monster and is intended to frighten the non-initiated.

The Akamba have a similar drum which they call the *mabani* and the Bantu KOROKORO tribe higher up the Tana also have a drum of this type. So have the GIRYAMA and RABAI, who call their drum *muanza*. I know of no others in Kenya, but in the Congo the Pygmies have a drum, to which similar customs are attached, named the *molimo*.

At Hola the *ngaji* dignitary was a very old man and I was told that with his death the *wakiju* would die out. I painted him wearing his ritual turban with ostrich feathers attached to it; around his eyes he had white markings, and on his forehead he wore a shell. He was a nice old Pokomo and I was very glad to add his picture to my collection (176).

259

178. Pokomo boy in circumcision

I was also fortunate in getting two very old women to pose, the last represent-atives of a powerful Woman's Society, whose leaders were always chosen from among the wives of *ngaji* elders (177).

They wore, in addition to their ritual crown, bead-embroidered leather ornaments which hung from their necks and were similar to those I had found amongst the Igembe women. The traditional head-dress of the girls, of which only two could be found, were also most interesting. Their skulls had been elongated by being tightly bandaged after birth. After puberty the girls knotted the hair into horizontal lines which ran parallel over the head and ended in two little pigtails

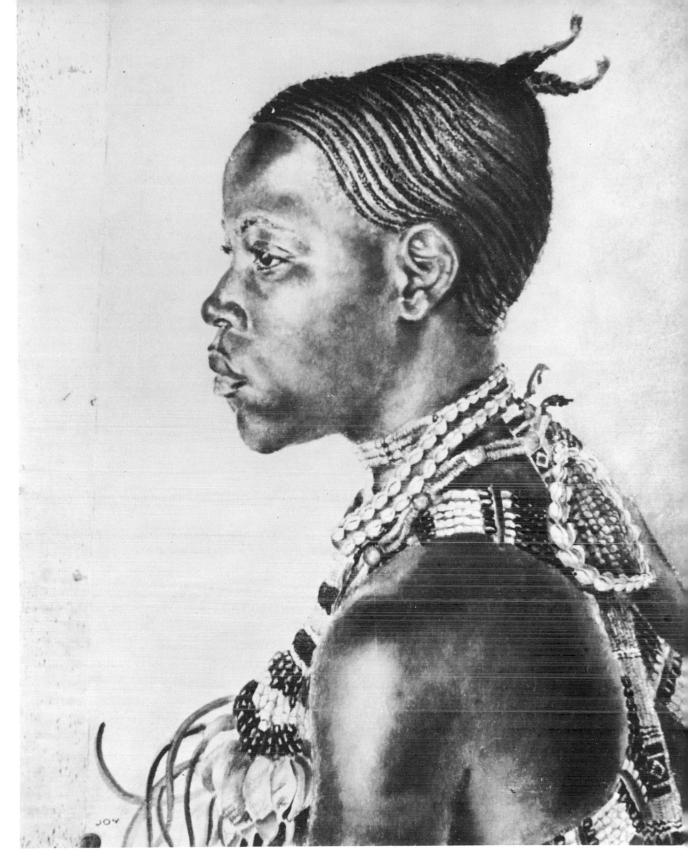

179.   Pokomo girl after puberty

at the top (179). They too wore ornaments similar to those of the Igembe women.

The Pokomo circumcise only the boys. I was able to paint a youngster during his seclusion period (178) and also the circumciser who was his guardian and tutor during this time. He wore leggings made of palm seeds, rather cumbersome to walk with but useful as rattles. During the period of seclusion he teaches the boys special songs and how to shoot with bow and arrow.

I liked the Pokomo very much, especially Kofa, the Chief. He was a born clown but nevertheless held great authority amongst his people. Another friend I made was an elderly school teacher who had worked in many parts of Kenya. His interest in the history of his people had made him visit the Nyika and Meru tribes frequently in the hope of collecting evidence of their common origin. He was a devout Christian and very sensitive. After we had got to know each other well enough for him not to regard my questions as impertinent, I asked him how many of the Africans whom we had met he believed to be truly Christians at heart and not just surface converts? He told me sadly that he only knew of two whom he considered to be true Christians.

One of the things that struck me was the number of older people among the Pokomo who suffered from a form of *filariasis elephantiasis* which mainly deformed their legs and genitals.

During the three weeks I camped at Hola the weather was oppressive, and only a few showers brought some relief. One afternoon the D.O. and an Indian veterinary officer, from Lamu, arrived and advised me to pack up and go back with them next morning to Kipini, saying that if I stayed on I might find myself marooned for many months by the rains. I thought their anxiety exaggerated, but accepted their suggestion more or less as an order. Kofa, the Chief, seemed very sorry at the abrupt ending of my stay and on my last evening there improvised a big farewell party. He told us nothing about it in advance but, while the D.O., the veterinary surgeon and I were having dinner, he suddenly arrived with a crowd of gay people who brought presents of eggs, fruit, and chickens as farewell gifts. Since such presents are usually given only when official guests arrive and not at departures, I wondered whether Kofa, fearing that we might be caught by the rains, was tactfully providing us with iron rations.

If this had been his plan it was justified, for next morning after driving a few miles, a cloudburst swamped the road and from then on the rains poured almost nonstop for days and weeks and months, causing one of the most disastrous floods Kenya has ever experienced. We, however, having no inkling of what lay ahead, were at the start only concerned with keeping our little convoy of two cars and three lorries on the road. Later, though there were several large jacks and some fifty men to push, we slithered helplessly from side to side in the mud, churning the ruts into deep puddles. With brushwood or anything we could find we tried to build a solid surface to get us over this morass. In spite of all our digging and pulling, we had covered no more than four miles by the evening and had to improvise night-quarters as best we could on a few patches of ground that rose higher than the surrounding bog. Under normal conditions the nearby groves of borassus palms and the whuffings of lions would have seemed to us an ideal setting for camping, but as we were almost eaten alive by mosquitoes we felt far from romantic.

It took us three days to go a distance which usually takes no more than three hours to cover. When finally we reached the junction where the road forks to Lamu or Kipini, we each went our separate ways. I continued to Lamu and drove ahead, as the veterinary surgeon wanted to cover the rear with all his men on the lorry so that they could help if I got stuck. In fact, his lorry overturned and landed its passengers in a swamp, and it took two days before he caught up with me.

CHAPTER 13

LAMU AND THE BAJUN ISLANDS

Lamu is on an island, and we had to telephone from Makoe for a boat to take us across the channel. When one arrives there one enters a world which stopped still when the last slave was freed. Lamu has a well-recorded history. About eight hundred years ago when the Arabs migrated along the coast, they found traces of previous inhabitants who left reminders of their civilization in ruins, tombs, and pillars; beads and fragments of Persian and Chinese porcelain can still be picked up in the sand.

Soon they made Lamu into a stronghold to which dhows sailed from Arabia and Aden, bringing the faithful to celebrate religious festivals and merchants to trade their goods. The fertile hinterland provided wealth in the form of coconut palms, mangoes, and many other agricultural products, and slaves provided the necessary labor force.

After A.D. 1498 when the Portuguese invaded East Africa, the Arabs fought against them for over three hundred years and finally conquered them. The Portuguese left a legacy in terms of impressive forts, those of Fort Jesu (at Mombasa), Siu, and Lamu. The present town of Lamu is built on ruins, buried by encroaching sand dunes, and sometimes, when the sand moves, the bones of those killed in ancient battles are exposed. After the Portuguese left, Lamu flourished again and recovered its former splendor. But with the abolishment of slavery, in spite of all the efforts which the Government made to develop the district, it decayed. Today, while less advanced but more vigorous tribes take advantage of education and develop rapidly, Lamu is still dreaming of its great past.

The old narrow streets of purdah-walled houses are crowded with men dressed in floating robes or colorful *kikois* (loincloths) who spend most of the day discussing secret transactions while sipping coffee in the streets from minute porcelain bowls. Women are rarely seen during the daytime, they only leave their purdah after sunset for a stroll in the cool evening breeze and then with their black draping *buibui* and veiled faces, they look very like walking shadows (182). Five times a day the chant of the muezzin from the minaret calls the faithful to prayer, then the streets are deserted, for all life has been swallowed up by the mosques.

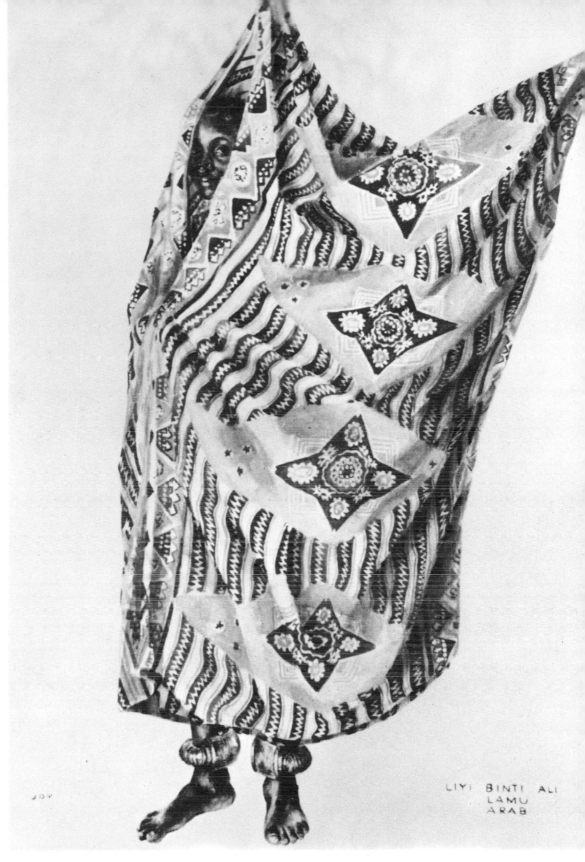

180.   Woman wearing canopy

All activity within Lamu seems to concentrate round the mosques and the large custom house. The former are the spiritual centers, while the latter is the heart of Lamu's trade. Around it a noisy bustle continues from early morning, when the first dhows arrive in the harbor, until the air gets so hot that it reduces all activity to a mere shuffle. The streets, built very narrow to provide shade, only come to life again towards sunset when dim acetylene lamps are lit in the small shops, and lights flicker on trays piled with sticky sweets, dates, spiced rice dishes and other delicacies. Outside one of these places I found an interesting notice: 'This is hygiene hotel; no spitum or other nonsense permitted.'

Only in Lamu could a D.C. have invented four rubber stamps in Swahili for minor administrative problems and used them in reply to complaints:

Shauri ya custom :   This is the affair of the Customs officer.
Shauri ya Police :   This is the affair of the police.
Shauri yako :   This is your own affair.
Shauri ya Mungu :   This is the affair of God.

The rocks on which life in Lamu is built are the D.C. and the *Liwali,* and they are rocks of reliability and efficiency supporting a very attractive but rather sleepy population of Arabs, Swahili, and BAJUN.

I knew both the District Commissioner and the *Liwali* and as soon as the motor launch landed at the jetty in front of the D.C.'s house I called on my old friends. Previously, only single men had been posted to Lamu, but the present D.C. had a wife and three children, a welcome break in the tradition for they brought a warm family atmosphere to the small white community of bachelors who lived there permanently.

Next I called on the *Liwali,* Sheikh Azan, who had been the model for my first portrait. He seemed glad to see me again, but when I warned him that I wanted to paint another portrait of him, he evaded the commitment with great tact, and considering his first experience, I could not blame him.

Meanwhile the D.C. had arranged for some prisoners to carry my kit to a camping place about a mile away from Lamu town. There were no automobiles or horses in Lamu and all transport was done by donkeys or occasionally by camels. I was installed on a Government holding ground right on the channel and only separated from the water by a promenade which ran alongside of it. I kept my stores in a small cabin used by the District Commissioner for changing before a swim, and I slept in my tent.

Besides the Arab population in and around Lamu, there are also Swahili and Bajun. I wanted to paint the former, for later on I was going to visit the Bajun, who mostly live on various islands north of Lamu. The Swahili are a mixed group of several coastal peoples united only by Islam and by their common language. Women today (180) sometimes hide themselves, in Arab fashion under a cotton

266

181. Siwa horn

182. Swahili woman wearing a *bui bui* and beating a drum

canopy supported by two sticks. In former times these were so large that as many as four women could conceal themselves in this way.

I was able to get a girl to pose for me in the traditional slave-dress—a cloth with horizontal colored stripes worn over fringed pantaloons. Today the Swahili women wear the *buibui* which they adopted from the Arabs. I was very much interested in the various instruments played by the local people. Of these the most important is the Arabic ritual *siwa* horn, of which the original instrument is carved out of an elephant tusk. I was lucky to find a model to pose with the only copy made of brass (181).

267

183. Bajun girl playing a
tambourine

Among the Swahili (as well as the Bajun) it is the women who play instruments at gatherings. I painted some blowing horns of various sizes and others beating drums (182). I also painted a young girl playing a tambourine (183) and an elderly woman using a rattle with an exquisite carved wooden frame (184). Her ear-lobes, which held the silver filigree boxes that are common amongst all these tribes, were stretched by using discs of increasing sizes carved from buffalo horn.

Little silver or gold plugs which they place in their left nostril and filigree ornaments of the same metals attached through the septum[8] are characteristic ornaments of the women of these three groups.

The rains had become increasingly violent and eventually I was forced to move from my tent into the small cabin which was already crammed full of my kit. My

268

184. Bajun woman with rattle

studio had to be installed in a rainproof house at Lamu but I got drenched walking there and back. When I went into Lamu I left my camp in charge of a not always reliable boy and Patti. She must have felt lonely during my absence for she developed the habit of coming along the promenade in the late afternoon to meet me. This entailed walking a far greater distance than I had known her to do before. Although there were no dogs in this Mohammedan town, I was worried for her safety because this was the time at which the rains usually stopped and people came out for a stroll. However, Patti had great personality and if anyone tried to be too familiar, she put him in his place; this increased her popularity and she came to no harm.

By now there were terrible floods in the hinterland and the Tana turned into a torrent several miles wide near its estuary.

Amongst the tribesmen who sought refuge in Lamu from this deluge were some Galla families. I took advantage of the opportunity to paint some of these people whose ancestors had played such a vital role in the migration of the Coastal tribes when they invaded Kenya between A.D. 1300–1400. The main bulk of these Hamites live in Ethiopia and are not a tribe, but a nation divided into a number of tribes. Many settled in the Garissa district of the Northern Frontier Province where they are also known as OROMO, which is their own name for themselves. They have a complicated age-set system from which that of the Nilo-Hamitic tribes is derived. The people I now met had lived on the south bank of the Tana since they were driven out of Kitui country by the Akamba some two hundred years ago; they were Galla who had taken to agriculture.

Except at their wedding, when they are dressed in white cotton, most of the women wear a full-length black cloth knotted over their right shoulder. I painted a girl posing in her bridal finery (185); she carried a beautiful fiber-woven container elaborately decorated with cowries and leather thongs. On the day before her wedding she would present this full of milk to the bridegroom. She also carried a wooden staff with ritual carvings similar to the one she used before circumcision.

I also painted a married woman who wore a Saka cowrie ornament on her arm, and thongs with bells attached; this signified that one of her children was under-going circumcision or getting married.

The men when young wear their long hair curled and when fighting use spears and small round shields of giraffe hide richly embossed (186). A warrior who posed for me wore a double-bladed knife-ring. Normally this would be concealed inside the palm of his hand but in an emergency he could whip it out and use it to gouge out his enemy's eyes. His spear was decorated with metal below the blade, which indicated that his status was a high one (187).

Originally I intended to stay in Lamu only long enough to paint the Arabs, but owing to the rains I had to stay on. All the hinterland was a swamp and Lamu could only be reached by sea. The mail came once a month by an ancient Italian cargo boat. So I was delighted when, at last, I received a letter from George; it had taken several weeks to arrive, and told me that he was doing control work near the Coast and intended to drive in his Land-Rover from Malindi to join me for Christmas. But I doubted if he would get through.

The D.C. from Kipini and his wife had come to join us for the holidays and on Christmas day we all went to a morning service. This was a rare treat and was only possible in this Mohammedan town because a few days earlier the Reverend Cheese had turned up unexpectedly. He was a very old man and had already

270

185.   Galla bride

186.   Galla warrior

become a legendary figure all over the country north of the Tana and into Somalia. If one can talk of living saints, he certainly was one. As far back as people could remember, he had wandered unarmed in the remotest parts of this semi-desert country, conveying less by words than by his personality the teaching of Christ. Even among people whose language he could not speak he was respected,

187. Galla warrior

welcomed, and loved. He gave away everything he possessed; in return he received enough to keep himself alive. I had heard a lot about him and his unique knowledge of tribal customs. When I met him I was deeply impressed. He was as simple as he was great.

For Christmas dinner we were all invited to the District Commissioner's house. I had already been fascinated by its classical Arab architecture, and on this night with the candlelight flickering on the carved wooden furniture and the silver ornaments shining against the well-proportioned walls, it was even more impressive. Under the spell of the setting, enhanced by the effect of champagne, I thought I must be dreaming when a soft, beautiful voice from the darkness outside started singing *Stille Nacht, Heilige Nacht*. Soon other voices joined in till a whole choir was singing. I couldn't imagine how Africans in Lamu had learned this

273

Austrian carol, then the Kipini D.C. told us that he arranged this as a Christmas surprise for me. The singers came from Ngau, a small village close to Kipini where the Germans had a mission before the First World War. Although no other trace of their influence had survived, the Africans loved this carol, which the Fathers had taught them, so much that they have gone on singing it to their children ever since, in its original language.

Next day while we were having a picnic on the beach, George passed us sailing in a dhow, his normally trimmed beard was growing all over his face and he looked as if he came straight from Arabia.

Against all advice, he had started some ten days earlier from Malindi in his Land-Rover, taking his dinghy with him. Soon the car got stuck in the mud and he had to abandon it. From then on he and his loyal boy walked, carrying the boat between them, wading through swamps and floating it behind them, or poling in it across lakes until they reached the Tana, along which they paddled to Kipini. There George found a dhow whose owner was determined to reach Lamu so that he could celebrate the feast of *Maulidi* there. And so, in spite of all obstacles, they had arrived.

George decided to add his local leave to the Christmas holidays and we determined to spend this time together visiting the islands north of Lamu. I would paint while he fished.

From Lamu the Bajun Islands are strung out to form an archipelago. Among them are Manda, Pate, Faza, and Siu, which during the zenith of Arab rule rivalled Lamu in importance.

We started off in the D.C.'s motor launch but even this sea-worthy pride of the Administration got so tossed about by the rough sea that we could not get further than Faza, the most populated of the islands.

We arrived at low tide and had to wade across a muddy lagoon to reach the spacious Arab house the ground floor of which served as the office of the local *Mudir*[9] and the upper floors as a rest-house for the D.C. and his guests. From the flat roof we looked over Faza which is a small fishing village tucked between coconut palms.

While waiting for my models to arrive, we explored the island. It is just one large coconut plantation overgrown in many places by bush, in which a few Arab, Bajun and Swahili families live in untidy huts.

In this wilderness we discovered several ruins; they were partly overgrown by vegetation but when we had cleared some of it away we saw exquisitely carved stone walls. The local Africans had made use of similar ruins to support their flimsy mud huts. It was strange to find superb carvings of floral or abstract design, probably once part of a palatial residence, inside these primitive dwellings in which the people often lived with their chickens, goats and cats.

274

In Faza we met an Arab whom we knew from our previous visits to the Coast. He was a wealthy merchant, temporarily here to marry a young local girl, an addition to his older wives. As he was an old friend of ours he invited us to his wedding, a great privilege. I had a long talk with the bride's mother, a dignified and still very attractive Arab woman. From her I learned that, though the bridegroom is not supposed to see his bride before their marriage, it can sometimes be arranged for him to have a glance at her from a distance.

For three days before the wedding her daughter had been kept at home to be beautified for the great occasion. She was massaged with fragrant oils, carefully groomed, and the palms of her hands were painted with a network-pattern. During this time she had to keep silent while all her women friends, who were helping and chattering around her, were given refreshments and generally had a good time.

On the evening preceding the wedding we heard a low singing, now and then broken by piercing shrieks. Following the sound, we saw a procession of veiled women wearing *buibuis,* swaying step by step through the village while clapping their hands and using rattles and drums to accompany their chanting. As far as I could see in the dim light, their rattles were made out of a segment of a buffalo horn. Others beat ox-horns with little sticks or shook tambourines. But the most arresting was the haunting tune of the *zomari* flute which was played by the men. The women went on chanting and swaying, and long after we had gone to bed I could hear the somber tune of the *zomari*. The party only came to an end at dawn.

The wedding had been fixed for 10 p.m. the next day, for at this hour, according to the astrologers, there was the most favorable conjunction of stars for the bridegroom. He spent all day with his future male relations, while the women put the last touches to the bride's attire. I was allowed to be present, but kept in the background. The girl was very young and exceptionally beautiful. Her delicate, pale features were enhanced by a thick coat of mascara round her eyes. Two golden coins adorned her cheeks; I was told that they were kept in position by some kind of mastic. Jasmine blossoms covered her black hair and part of her dress, and their scent mixed with the heavy perfume with which the women constantly sprayed her. While the bustle went on, she sat motionless, aloof and silent in the middle of a large bed.

Fascinated by the scene, I did not notice a girl approaching me until suddenly she lifted up my skirt and sprayed perfume under it. I was rather startled, not then knowing that this is the way to wish a woman a lucky child-birth.

During the day the bride received a present from her betrothed; this was not part of the brideprice which he had already given to her parents. If she accepted the gift, he knew that she was still willing to marry him and the wedding could then be performed without the bride being present.

275

With male relations as witnesses, the bridegroom was then seated on a chair that was slightly higher than the one opposite on which the *mullah* sat. He held the Koran in his hands while the wedding was being sealed. Immediately afterwards the men went to the house in which the bride was waiting and firing shots to announce the arrival of the bridegroom, danced the sword dance.

While all this went on outside the house, the women who were with the bride grew more and more excited. The door was still kept shut but there was much whispering behind it. Suddenly there were three knocks and immediately a curtain was drawn across the bed to hide the bride, and after this the door was opened to let the men in. They spent only a short time in the bridal room and then retired, leaving the bridegroom behind. The women, who were now very quiet, brought refreshments to the bridegroom who seated himself opposite the curtain which concealed his bride. Women oiled his head and arms, and he washed his feet. Then everyone left, except for one woman who kept discreetly behind the curtain of the bed to chaperone the bride. There was silence. At this moment the bride stretched her hand from behind the curtain and the bridegroom placed another gift in it while talking to her softly.

Then the woman in the corner gave me a signal and we left the pair alone. For the next seven days they would remain together in the house.

Of course it had been impossible to paint the bride in all her finery but I got a Swahili girl to pose for me wearing similar ornaments.

Next I painted a Bajun drummer who used by far the largest drum as well as the most peculiarly shaped one that I had seen on the Coast (188). With these models I had to be content.

After a short trip to Siu to look at the ruins of the Portuguese fort, we hired a dhow and sailed north. As we passed from the open sea and went between the islands into more sheltered creeks, the coastline varied between dark green mangrove swamps alternating with meager scrub, sand dunes and coconut plantations. We sailed past Kiwayu—one of the larger islands—and saw a few fishing villages nestling in picturesque bays. All signs of life thinned out as we got nearer to Kiunga which lies only eight miles from Ras Kiamboni at the Somali border.

We had discovered this idyllic place some years earlier when George was controlling the poaching in the Boni Forest, which stretched north of Lamu to the Somali frontier. This forest, some thirty miles wide, runs parallel to the sea. It is thickly infested by tsetse, and therefore very sparsely inhabited. Only the BONI, a primitive hunting people who were formerly serfs of the Galla and are of mixed Bantu and Arab stock, live there. Apart from some unsuccessful attempts to grow crops, they exist mostly on poaching. Their bows and arrows are by far the largest in Kenya.

276

188. Bajun drummer

As we had found it impossible to get porters and no pack animals would survive the tsetse, we had to take our lorry on this safari although there were no tracks and we often had to cut our way through thick bush. Game was abundant in the forest and we passed many fresh water pools, covered with blue and white waterlilies as large as soup plates. It was a real paradise except for the tsetse flies which guarded it in their millions. As we came nearer to the Coast, we found extensive dams several hundred yards in diameter; they looked as though they had been built a very long time ago. Nearer to the sea we saw ruins of oblong shape with arabic ornaments carved on the stones and one pillar about fifteen feet high with a phallus at the top: a fertility emblem. Most of the ruins were so overgrown that we could see only fragments of them. When we finally reached the Coast, to our surprise, we found a large double-storied stone house towering over the small fishing village of Kiunga. The people came rushing to greet us and by their behavior we could see that they were not used to visitors. The headman of the village offered us the use of the top floor of the house, which had been built about 1880 by the Imperial British East African Company. They had hoped to establish a base here for trade with Khartoum. The project had not succeeded and since then the ground floor of the house had been used as an office by the *Mudir* who dealt with the minor problems of the district (these he reported to Lamu, from where Kiunga was administered) while the top floor was reserved for occasional official visitors; it contained a table, a sideboard and a few chairs.

The only way of reaching this last outpost of the British Administration along the Kenya coast was by the route we had taken on our first visit through the fly-infested forest, or by sea. In rough weather the sea route could be very dangerous as several wrecks thrown up against the sharp coral reef proved. We therefore understood why few people visited Kiunga, but in spite of the risks involved we had often spent our local leave there for it was a perfect place for fishing and skin diving. In the course of our visits we had made some real friends amongst the local people, in particular Dilimua bin Lali who took us out fishing. He was an old Bajun. His skin was very loose and he had a habit of lifting it up into folds to show how empty his stomach was; this was by way of encouraging us to catch some fish. Besides ourselves and our fishing tackle, he would squeeze several of his grandchildren into his tiny boat to look after his paraphernalia for deep-sea fishing: tins with hairy hermit crabs for bait, and cooking utensils for roasting crayfish. As long as we were in shallow water Dilimua punted the boat along with a mangrove pole. When he could no longer reach the bottom, he transformed the pole into a mast, with his loincloth as sail. While his grandchildren acted as crew, Dilimua sat at the prow, facing the sea singing happily about all the fish we would catch with our wonderful harpoon guns. He took us not only to the coral reef but also to small coral islands which when the tide is low look like mushrooms

189. Boni hunter

owing to the erosion of their base; islands where we could find a small, green cray-fish which is more delicious than the larger species of the reef. Sometimes we climbed to the top of these mushroom-shaped islands which are used as grazing ground for fattening sheep; they have the advantage that there is no need for a herdsman. On one of the larger of the islands Dilimua showed us ancient, stone-heaped graves where we found small, conical-shaped earthen containers with impressed ornamentations and elaborate handles; he could not tell us who had made the graves or the purpose of the containers.

279

Now, as we drew anchor at Kiunga, our old friend came rushing along ahead of the rest of the crowd; he was as pleased to see us as we were to see him and he put himself at our disposal. He soon found that it was easier to take us out fishing than to find models for me because in this remote spot the Mohammedans refused to be painted. But when he realised how distressed I was at the lack of sitters, he obligingly persuaded his family to pose for me, so I started with his granddaughter as she sat piercing tiny holes in cowries and stringing the shells on a thread.

The women and children collect the cowries at low tide and these, together with the sale of fish, provide the local population with most of their income. Only the men fish. I painted one of Dilimua's sons with all his tackle; he had a black line drawn above the left eyebrow, which was characteristic of the Bajun men of his people. After a lot of trouble we found a sword and shield similar to the ones the Arabs use, and so I was able to add a warrior to my collection.

I had better luck with the Boni. One day some of George's Game Scouts who patrolled the area turned up with several Boni poachers (189). They provided excellent models, for they were wearing the traditional outfit of this people. When a few days later some of their relatives appeared, I painted a young girl (190) whose hair was plaited in exactly the same fashion as that of the Pokomo girls; I thought this interesting since it might provide a link between these people.

Then I painted a woman dressed for a wedding; it struck me that she carried a ceremonial carved stick such as I had found amongst the Galla women. Both tribes also use the word *kaniki* for the black cloth worn by women. Later, a witch doctor sat for me; he had white markings round his eyes and was equipped with a gourd containing his charms; he held an axe.

One day George discovered fossilized giant clams some four miles inland. As I was anxious to see them, I went next afternoon with a gun bearer and, after walking for about one hour through thick bush, found the clams embedded in coral rock which must, in prehistoric time, have been at the bottom of the sea. There were several complete pairs close to each other, but only their undulated openings some three feet long were visible. Knowing how rare those prehistoric clams are, we started to break one loose so that we could take it to the Nairobi Museum. In my excitement I forgot about the time and only thought about going home when it became too dark for digging. As we walked silently along a narrow path, I suddenly felt a warm breath, heard a low growl, a shot, and then a crashing in the bush. The presence of mind of the gun bearer had saved us from a lion whose pugmarks we were able to trace next morning.

The following day Dilimua suggested that I take a little time off painting and make a trip across the border into Somaliland to look at some ruins. He had

190. *Boni girl*

obtained an invitation from the headman of Ras Kiamboni and, as no one here bothered about passports, we set off. Sailing in Dilimua's boat, we passed the small fishing village of Shiakani, halfway to the Somali border and, through our field glasses, saw two ruins with pillars; after a short distance we came to the border, which was marked by a shoulder-high stone. Another few miles' sailing around small islands brought us to Ras Kiamboni. Its name is an ambitious one for such a tiny fishing village littered with bleached and smelly fish-bones. The whole population came to welcome us. Our visit was a great excitement for these lonely people

281

and the headman invited us to his home, a four-walled mud building roofed with palm-leaves. Inside were three chairs and a small round table: it was evidently used as office, dining room and sitting room. A curtain divided it into two and on the far side I saw a rough bed. While an Askari, wearing white shorts and a white shirt with the badge of Somalia stitched on, offered us hot tea and hard boiled eggs, we talked in Swahili. After the preliminary exchange of courtesies we asked the headman if we could see the ruins of which Dilimua had told us. They were within a mile of the village but only after convincing him that our interest was not political did he agree to guide us there. We walked across the sands, followed by the population of Ras Kiamboni, who were as excited as we were. We passed several wells and a few coconut palms in whose shade camels ruminated, and then we reached a slight rise in the ground at which point thick bush closed in.

Here we saw strange ruins standing within a few hundred yards of each other. Rectangular in shape, the longer walls were about thirty feet long and built of grey stone (191). They were only about six feet high and richly carved with Arabic designs such as one sees on many mosques, and the upper edges were cut into rounded sections. Most of these ruins had a thin pillar about twenty-four feet high at the narrow front which faced the sea, on the top of which a phallus was carved. A few of these pillars had fragments of porcelain plates stuck into depressions obviously made to hold them. We recognized the plates as belonging to the Ming dynasty. Though they were close to the top of the pillars, most of them had been chipped out a long time ago. I wanted to trace the reliefs on the plates and, to the great amusement of our audience, climbed a pillar. After a lot of effort, I managed to trace a peacock and a beautiful floral design.

Two of the ruins, instead of having a pillar, had two large round slabs which faced the sea. There was no indication that these walls had ever been covered by a roof and we assumed that they were tombs, of the type known as 'pillar tombs'.

There were eight ruins in all; but if one adds to these two at Shiakani, two near Kiunga and one at Malindi, we had now seen a total of thirteen. Who built them, and when? What struck us most was the odd combination of phallic emblems symbolizing fertility and the structure and carvings which were of Arab design. One theory is that these 'tombs' or 'worshipping places' were made by Arabs who, disapproving of Islam, migrated to the south where their culture had been influenced by the local religion and its fertility cult. The Ming plates were probably bartered from the Chinese who traded along the East African shores in those days but these theories will remain unproved until research can reveal the history of these ruins. Meanwhile all we can do is to try to preserve them.

Close by were ruins of a mosque, the foundations of several houses, and a number of Mohammedan graves.

191. Ruins of Ras Kiamboni

On our return to Ras Kiamboni, I went to see a woman in her home. The one-roomed mud building was crowded with veiled women and children; all wanted to touch my blond hair and my clothes. They seemed as much intrigued by my lipstick as I was by their kohl-painted eyes. The only unexpected objects I noticed in the crudely furnished room were drawings in red and blue pencil pinned on the wall, which depicted original conceptions of boats, fish, coconut palms, the moon, stars, and shells, obviously done by a child. When the artist's mother saw that I was interested in them, she tore off a few drawings and gave them to me.

Soon afterwards we were due to leave Kiunga. George was to go to Isiolo and I to paint the tribes south of Lamu. When the news of our departure got round, the whole of Kiunga, prompted by Dilimua, prepared a farewell party.

There was a full moon; the shadows of the feathery palm fronds patterned the sand between the village huts where the people strolled about in their best clothes. They were all in good spirits, for two giant turtles had been caught that morning and these were going to provide a fine addition to the feast. Before we were allowed to join the official party, Dilimua, looking very unfamiliar in the shirt which he wore on these occasions, ushered us into his home. Here his entire family, down to the last of his grandchildren, were present. All watched eagerly while Dilimua's wife gave me a string of tiny, snow-white cowries of the finest quality which they had themselves collected. This was the very best present these people could give me. Dilimua then offered George a home-made cake to take

283

with him for his journey. When I shook his hands I felt a lump in my throat and was glad we were interrupted by the sound of the *zomari* flute and the tinkling of tambourines, inviting us to join the crowd outside.

The people had already fused into a solid mass of bodies swaying to the rhythm of the booming horns and clapping hands. Although it was more of a shuffle than a dance, it seemed appropriate to the soft air and leisurely life which these Mohammedans led. Their subdued chanting was like a background swell, pierced now and then by the high-pitched screams of women. There was no climax to the dance, but the party went on until the moonlight waned and the new day began, and we had to say good-bye.

It was three months since I had arrived in Lamu, but the country had only just dried up sufficiently to make a safari by car possible. Before leaving the district I wanted to add a few more Galla to my record, so I again camped close to Kipini. Here I found a girl who was willing to pose for me in ornaments worn before circumcision, and also two warriors, one young and one old.

CHAPTER 14

IN KAYA COUNTRY

Next on my list were the Sanye. They lived in the hinterland of Malindi where the D.C. arranged for me to camp at Adu right in the open forest which is typical of this country.

Together with the Dorobo of the General Mathews Range, the Sanye are the earliest of the inhabitants of Kenya. They are primitive hunters who formerly associated with the Galla, and they still speak the same language.

When I arrived the headman welcomed me with a group of people performing a dance (192). It was a strangely controlled affair and differed from the dances I had previously seen among Mohammedans in that the young men formed a group opposite to that of the girls. They advanced either in a closed line towards each other, or stepped forward singly to clap hands. I chose as my model a youth with black markings on his face, a bead ornament on his head, and a copper chain with cowries and beads round his neck.

Among the six Sanye I painted was an elder with an unusual ornament made of six metal plates which hung from his neck, some at the front and some at the back. He also wore a rare two bladed brass finger-knife which I had so far only found among the Galla. An elderly woman indicated that her child was undergoing circumcision by wearing an ornament *(saka)* on her arm similar to that of Galla women (193); another carried a carved ceremonial stick like those used by the Galla, the Boni and the Borana women.

While visiting the nearby village of Marafa, I was told by the local Africans of a spirit that lived in the cliffs close to it and that anyone to whom it appeared in the form of a bright light became ill. Extensive swamps in the vicinity suggest that this evil spirit is some phosphorescent phenomenon, but to the Sanye it is the *Sheitani* (devil).

One day as I walked through the forest I found a little shrine, round which were scattered a few chicken bones; inside I saw a small wooden board with two cups, a bottle of oil, and some frankincense. It was a low simple construction consisting of a grass roof resting on a few poles, to one of which a white cloth was tied. I was told that this little shrine belonged to the neighboring Giryama. If

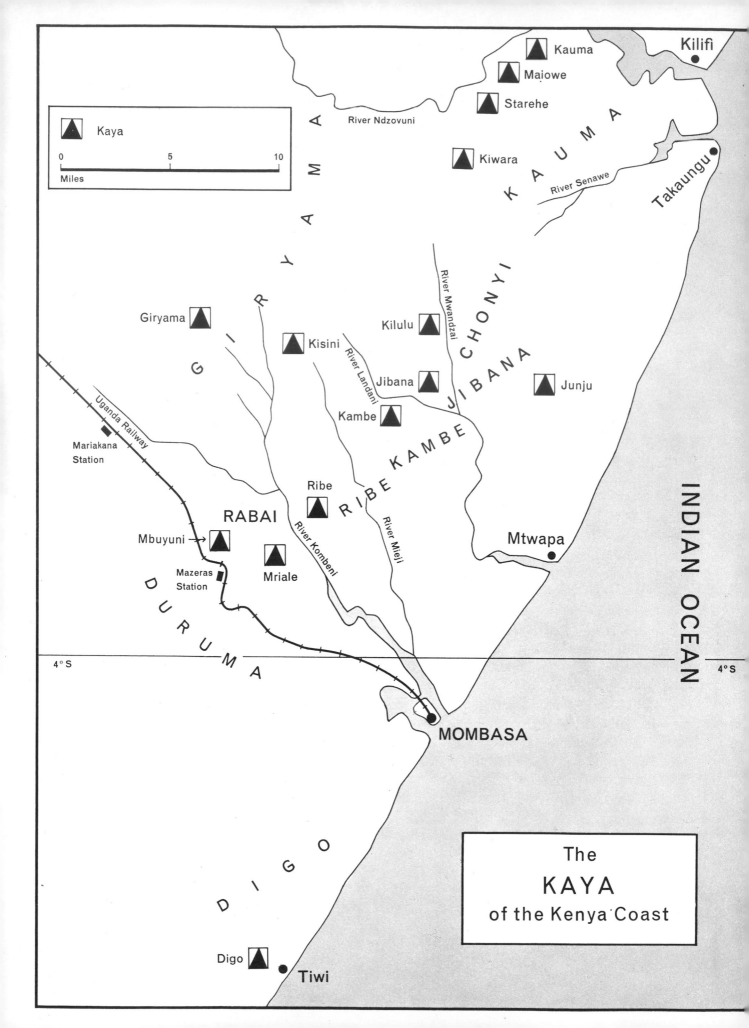

The
KAYA
of the Kenya Coast

192. Sanye dance

the people wanted rain, a rainmaker would come and sacrifice a chicken or a goat and give half to *Mungo* (God) while beating a buffalo horn and praying for rain; then he would tie a white cloth to the roof and leave it there until his prayer was answered.

This was my introduction to the Giryama, one of the peoples belonging to the Nyika group whom I had been asked to paint.

Nyika is the Swahili term for bush country and is also used to describe the people living near the Coast between Malindi and the Tanganyika border, including the major tribes: the DIGO, Duruma, Giryama and Rabai, and the minor ones: the KAUMA, CHONYI, JIBANA, RIBE and KAMBE. All have migrated from Shungwaya, which is an area north of the mouth of the River Tana from where, as I have described earlier, the Meru and the Pokomo moved to their present locations. I was interested in finding out more about the *kaya* ceremonies common to all these tribes, and the differing rituals and costumes connected with it amongst each tribe.

The *kaya* itself may be described as a fortified sanctuary, a refuge in time of war. With a view to defence, it is usually situated on top of a hill in dense forest and consists of a well-stockaded clearing. Later it developed into a sacred place,

287

193. Sanye elderly woman

a burial ground for important male members of the tribe and in rare cases for female witch doctors. In the middle of the clearing are the tribal shrine and a few huts occupied by the elders who invoke the Deity in times of famine, drought, or other disasters. During the ceremonies they wear a special dress, and no one is allowed to enter the *kaya*. Surrounding the huts are the graves of important people, those who had worn armlets of polished buffalo horn—called *luvoo*—as a sign of their status. These graves were marked by beautifully carved wooden posts about three feet high and a foot wide; they were effigies of the human figure all facing sunrise. The anatomy was symbolized in geometrical designs made up of little incised triangles, filled with red ocher, white ash or charcoal, all of these

288

194. *Kaya Fungo* effigies

mixed with the latex of euphorbia to a texture which hardens like enamel.

Around the center of the *kaya* is a clearing protected by a palisade in which, in the old days, the tribesmen took refuge in time of war, and where their council house and huts were built. This stockade is surrounded by thick forest and is accessible only by a narrow path leading from the base of the hill to the center of the *kaya*. At its entrance one often sees a little shrine such as the one I had found, containing bowls with offerings of oil or maize flour *(posho)*. The path is easy for bow-men to defend and is also guarded by three gates, next to which offering bowls are inserted in the ground. At some *kayas* one has to take off one's hat and shoes when entering the second gate, and when coming after dark one was obliged to blow out the light upon arriving at the third gate.

Before I started painting the Giryama, I visited their *kaya* which is the best known and the easiest of access. It is about a mile in diameter and is unusual in that it is not on a hill. The Giryama call it *kaya Fungo* (194), as it is supposed to have been founded by the grandfather of the hero Fungo, who lived five generations ago and whose grave is known to be here.

It had been very dry lately, and I was advised to be discreet in case the elders might be praying for rain in the *kaya*. After walking along a well-trodden path through the forest and passing three gates which had fallen down, my guide and

195. Giryama elders at shrine

I arrived at a large, overgrown clearing where we saw several huts and wooden head-posts in fairly good condition. In the center was a tidier clearing about twenty yards in diameter; in it we saw a large fig tree and one grass hut *(nyumba tutu)* about three feet high. This, the guide told me, was the *moro* or shrine where the sacrificial ceremonies are held and which no one, except the Kambi elders, is allowed to enter.

Now I saw the Kambi elders kneeling at the root of the fig tree, praying and chanting and burning frankincense. After a while they moved to the shrine (195) and repeated their prayers. I watched them for some time and then withdrew so as not to disturb them by my presence. I hoped their prayers would be granted soon as the country certainly needed rain. The rites last for four days; on the first a chicken or goat is sacrificed and prayers held in the morning and evening. On the following days frankincense is offered with two prayers on the second and third days, but only one prayer on the fourth day.

At the *kaya Fungo* there are five elders—the *Atumia Akambi*. The most important among them is called *Viza* (196) and at great ceremonies he wears a cylindrical head-dress of ostrich feather. The four lesser elders are called *kulombe* (197); they indicate their rank by attaching a cow-tail set upright to their foreheads. All elders carry the ceremonial double-forked staff and wear the buffalo armlet *(luvoo)*. The Kambi elders live in the *kaya* and are provided with food by their sons.

After the death of a Kambi elder, the others select a successor from the next age-grade *(nyeve)*, irrespective of his means or standing. Before he is allowed to

290

196. Giryama *Viza*

wear the ceremonial cow-tail, he is initiated into their secrets for at least eighteen months.

The Giryama differ from other Nyika tribes in that they not only erect head-posts within the *kaya*, but every man who has worn a buffalo armlet is buried near his home and there a grass-roofed shrine is built which contains his grave-pole *(kigangu)* (198). Should the family move, the original *kigangu* is left behind but a simplified replica is put up near the new home; it is called *kibao* (199). Should

291

197. Giryama *kulombe*

the family get into trouble and need help from the spirits of the departed, low wooden stumps are placed in a line right and left of the *kibao;* they represent effigies of women and children. These are called *koma* and are draped with dark blue and white strips of cloth around their imaginary necks and waists.

I started painting the Giryama at Kanoneni in the northern part of their country. Here the land is broken by dry riverbeds, but towards Kilifi, where the Administration Headquarters of the tribes is situated, it gradually changes into parkland. Wherever I went in the bush I found abandoned *kigangu*s. It gave one a strange feeling to see the people irrigating their patches of maize, millet or

292

198. Giryama *kigangu*

199. Giryama *kibao* and *koma*

beans close to these sentinels of the dead, their bleached wood often covered with lichen. I tried to get permission to remove one of the effigies to take to the Nairobi Museum, but in the end had to be satisfied with having a replica made. The fact that so many grave-poles had only recently been erected proves that this custom is still practiced here. Almost every homestead had its *kibao*; many of them had only been recently put up. Little shrines are very common all over the country and are used by witch doctors when praying for rain or for the recovery of sick people.

Though many of the Giryama are still pagans or Mohammedans, since the first missions in East Africa were built along the Coast in 1844, many have adopted Christianity. Nearly all, whatever their religion, seem to believe in magic. I was told, for instance, that the safest way to cross a crocodile-infested river was to put magic medicine into the water; when this had been done no one was allowed to collect water in pots which had been put over their kitchen fire, as dirt was believed to attract the crocodiles. If one observed this precaution I was assured that one would not be eaten. And even if, through ignorance, a stranger trans-

200　Giryama rain
maker

gressed the rule, no harm would befall him, but it would come to the first person who came after him.

The Giryama circumcise only boys and do this at any age. Immediately after the operation two charms are attached to a string previously dipped into a magic fluid; this they wear around the waist until the wound is healed.

Both sexes remove the two lower middle incisors, and for aesthetic effect, chip the corners off the upper incisors.

My first model was a snake doctor (201), and next I had a wizard to pose for me. His task was to creep at night into his victim's hut and by blowing his magic powder, often made from datura, on to the sleeper either to make him ill or to kill him. I sketched him in the costume he wears when going to a dance.

201. Giryama snake
      doctor

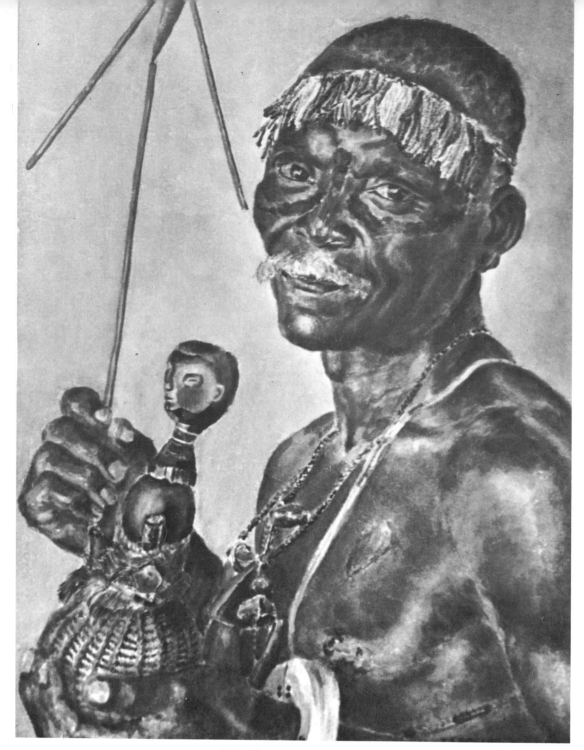

202.   Giryama witch doctor

I also painted a rainmaker (200) whose special emblems were the buffalo horn and a long fly-whisk which he uses as a divining rod. Up to seven assistants might be needed to help him at his prayers, each one beating a buffalo horn.

Here again I met with the little horn oracle. A witch doctor (202) claimed that he was able to tell the outcome of a war or of any other important event by balan-

203. Chonyi *kaya* effigy   204. Chonyi *kaya* effigy

cing the horns; if the construction collapsed, the outcome would be bad, if they remained steady, this denoted victory.

I painted nineteen Giryama, all picturesquely dressed, but it was often difficult to find the grass skirts which men and women used to wear, but which had now been replaced by cotton kilts.

I was unable to obtain evidence of the sacred drum *(muanza)* which the Giryama use in the same way that the Pokomo use the *ngaji*. All my inquiries drew a blank; but I learned that the sound produced by it resembled a hyena's howl. The hyena is regarded as sacred by this people.

Having completed my pictures of the Giryama, I went on to paint the Chonyi. The campsite chosen for me was on a hilltop, one amongst many, overlooking beautiful country. On one of these little hills was the *kaya* which I visited the next day with an old man as guide.

We climbed along a steep and narrow path which led through virgin forest, in which we were often held up by a network of lianas twisting across the thick undergrowth, and came upon the remains of two gates. Soon after we passed between two large trees, which had evidently been used as posts for the third gate, we reached the top of the hill and entered a small overgrown plateau with a few coconut palms standing up from the bush. The stillness was only broken by the eerie cry of a hornbill which seemed to be making a protest at our intrusion.

A few effigies barely visible in the high grass were partly destroyed by termites or so weather-beaten that the split poles overgrown with soft-colored fungi looked more like ghosts guarding the secrets of the past. As I walked among them I felt as if I were committing a sacrilege. While exploring the *kaya* I discovered an exquisitely carved head with so sensitive an expression that it seemed almost alive (203). In another effigy a comb personified the head, while other grave-poles indicated the human anatomy by geometrical designs (204). Unfortunately my guide could not remember anything about the people they represented who had lived long ago. When it got dark, I left the place reluctantly and was so haunted by its atmosphere that next day I returned and painted some of these beautiful effigies which belonged to a cult already extinct and the last evidence of which termites would soon erase forever. The Chonyi call the effigies, at the *kaya*, *kibao*.

In camp I painted the leading *kaya* elder who was called *Mwyambura*. During the rites which lasted three days he had to wear a solid crown made of earth woven into his hair, to which three split palm leaves, resembling feathers, were attached (205). His assistant, another elder called *Mwezi*, was distinguished by a cylindrical head-dress made of ostrich feathers. Both elders carried the double-forked staff and the *luvoo;* the latter they wore only on ceremonial occasions. A Chonyi widow indicates her state of mourning by wearing a roll of white cotton across her breast until it is worn out (206).

I also painted a witch doctor with an elaborately carved staff and ornamented gourd containing many charms and medicines, the potency of which was reinforced by many cowries attached to his head-dress of ostrich feathers. He wore a thick

298

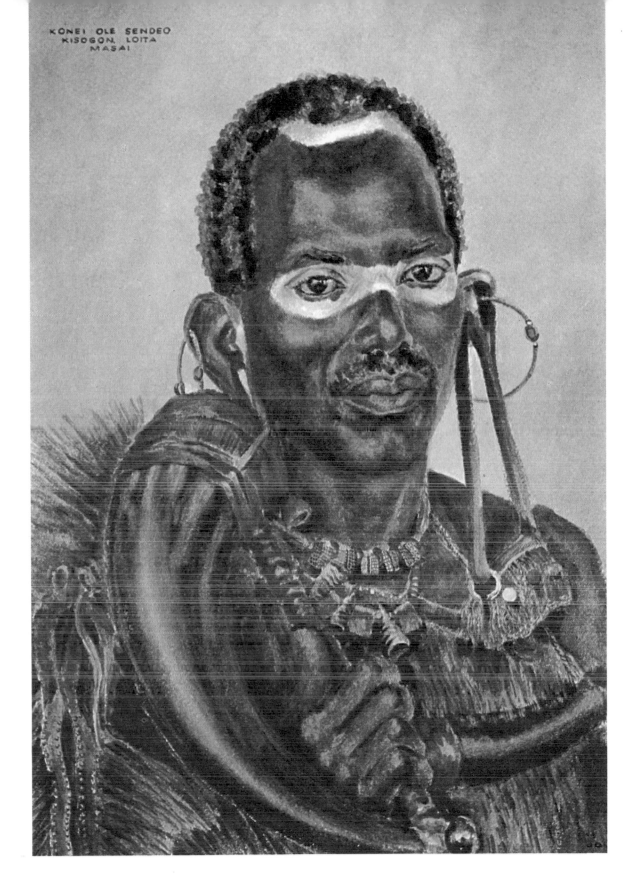

KONEI OLE SENDEO
KISOGON, LOITA
MASAI

205. Chonyi *Mwyambura*
elder

bracelet of ivory cut from an elephant tusk (pl. XXVIII, p. 300). Another elder whom I portrayed in his ceremonial costume had three of these prized bracelets; I thought he probably wore them to show off his wealth.

The Chonyi circumcise only the men, but the cycle was not on, so I could not paint a candidate.

XXVIII   Chonyi witch doctor

206. Chonyi widow

207. Jibana *kaya* effigy

Close to the Conyi live the Jibana, a smaller group whose *kaya* is on top of a hill
so steep that my guide warned me, 'it is as if one would climb a coconut.' After we
had reached the well-concealed entrance to the path and had clambered from rock
to rock almost vertically, I agreed. We passed two gates before we arrived breathless
at the top. Though the rites were still performed here, the place, with its tumble-
down huts between coconut palms and chopped-up copra, looked very untidy. In
the midst of this disorder were many recently carved grave-poles showing natural-
istic representations of the human face, their expressions varying from sadness,
humor, dignity and terror to the grotesque (207). Only a few, which were obviously

303

older, were similar to the poles at Chonyi. No one could remember the people who were buried by them. Close to the entrance of the *kaya* was a wooden stump, resembling the grave of a woman witch doctor.

The ceremonies here were performed by three elders of equal rank, called *Bari,* each of whom wore a cylindrical head-dress of ostrich plumes. The rites lasted two days, on the first of which a sheep or chicken was sacrificed.

After painting a few of the effigies, I went on to Rabai, about ten miles northwest of Mombasa from which the tribe of this name is administered. Here is the oldest mission station in East Africa; it was founded by Krapf in 1844. Perhaps because of this I could find no suitable models among the large crowd waiting at my arrival. After impressing upon the Chief and the headman that I needed their help to get people wearing traditional ornaments and not khaki, I visited the *kaya.* In the old days there had been five *kaya*s, which had been shared with the RURUMA, a small tribe related to the Rabai. The one I visited was on top of a steep hill and no longer in use. There was a small shrine at its entrance, but no trace of the huts which must have housed the elders. The Rabai have never used carved grave-poles; they bury the men near their homes and put up little tree stumps bearing blue and white cotton strips around their imaginary waists. These stumps are called *koma* and are left to stand until the weather destroys them, after which they are not renewed. Small stone slabs, sometimes with cotton tied around, or a little wooden stump close by, are put up for the women. In spite of the fact that the people had adopted modern clothes, I saw these traditional stones and stumps all over the area.

Here four elders were in charge of the *kaya;* the most important was called *Mutumia Wa Kaya.* He wore a head-dress of an ornamental leather frame some two inches wide, which went all round his face and to which a frame of ostrich feathers was attached (208). He had as well a fine cape of sable antelope including the mane which hung around his shoulders, the forked staff and *luvoo* he shared with his three assistants. These elders attached a row of ostrich feathers which stuck out at right angles to their heads, and made them look as if they were carrying a feathered basin. The *Mutumia Wa Kaya* was a very old man, and I was most grateful to him for agreeing to pose for me, the more so because with him this office would probably die out. On the other hand, proof of how tradition can survive in spite of the progress of civilization was shown in the method by which the women prepared flour (209). Though mills provided every shop in this area with flour, the women preferred to make their own using a very old Swahili method. First they pounded the corn in wooden mortars and then ground it between two rotating round stones.

One afternoon I heard the sound of a party, and was told this was being held so that the witch doctor would be able to drive the devil out of a young mother whose milk had stopped for three days. I went to the scene and saw the young woman

304

208. Rabai *kaya* elder

wearing a new white cotton garment; a cloth was wrapped in turban fashion round her head, to the right and left in which two coconut leaves cut to resemble feathers had been inserted. While the dance went on she was held by two other women, but as soon as the dancing stopped, the witch doctor took her and a chicken, which her husband had provided, some distance away. Here they killed the fowl and put it on a fire.

209 Rabai women grinding flour

Then the woman, bareheaded and covered from her breasts to her knees with a white cloth, sat down. The witch doctor painted little white markings over her chest in parallel lines. After this he scratched the skin with a knife until it bled slightly, and then rubbed a black medicine into the wounds. Later I saw him pour another medicine prepared from leaves soaked in water into his hands; he made the woman drink twice from it; with what remained he cleaned the white markings and the black medicine from the wounds. She then exposed her breasts and I saw that she had placed a little stick with charms attached horizontally across her bosom. Now she stood up and the witch doctor hoisted her on to his shoulders with her face turned towards the sky and jerked her twice. Then he carried her on his back, this time face downwards, to the fire where the chicken was cooking. As soon as he had passed it, he dropped the woman and sent her home. Finally he inspected the intestines of the chicken and ate part of them, leaving the rest of the fowl for a future meal. When I asked what would happen if this treatment failed, I was told that after two days the ritual would be repeated. Should this too produce no result the trouble would then be regarded as the will of God.

210. Rabai
bride

Like the Giryama, the Rabai men and women remove both lower middle incisors and chip the corners off the top incisors. Something else which both peoples have in common is the sacred drum.

I painted a charming bride (210) holding a bowl in which, on her wedding day, she would offer milk to her bridegroom. Then I went on to visit the Ribe.

The Ribe were the first and the least numerous of the Nyika peoples to settle in this area; they number only a few hundred. Their *kaya*, which is the smallest of all the local *kayas*, lies hidden in thick forest on top of a hill. It was abandoned long ago except for a shrine at its entrance in which I noticed a bowl filled with oil. A few effigies stood in the bush looking forlorn and seemed not only older than any I had seen before, but also more abstract in design. Among the few which had not been destroyed by white ants, I found one in which the ribs and pelvis were shaped into quadrangular blocks, while the head was symbolized by a rhomboidal comb. In another the ribs were represented by horizontal lines, and the face by vertical lines. In strange contrast was a simple round pole with a strikingly impressive head, naturalistically carved.

As far as I could discover, the Ribe had only one elder responsible for their *kaya* rites; his only emblem apart from the forked staff and *luvoo* was a woman's necklace (211).

Many children wore owl's talons around their wrists or ankles; these, I was told, were charms to protect them against evil.

At Ribe is the second-oldest Church Missionary Society mission in East Africa; it was founded in 1862 by New and Wakefield. I visited the old graveyard close to the present mission, and as I read the dates 1863 and 1864 on the tombstones of women and children, I was vividly reminded of what havoc malaria played with these pioneers who hardly knew about quinine, and had no prophylactic medicines with which to fight the disease.

The Kambi live within a few miles of the Ribe. To my surprise they still actively performed the *kaya* ceremonies. Again I had to climb a steep hill and walk through two gates to approach the *kaya*, and I had to take off my hat and shoes. We passed several shrines with offering bowls (213). When we reached the top we came to a large clearing where coconut palms gave shade to numerous huts: the largest (215), which had no walls but only poles supporting the roof, was the dining hall for the *kaya* elders (212). There were four of them. The leader *(Gohu)* wore an ostrich head-dress similar to his Giryama colleague, and his three helpers *(Bora)* had to carry an extremely heavy crown made of earth woven into their hair. I was told

308

211. Ribe *kaya* elder

it took six days to mould it into the shape of a sugarloaf, about one foot high, after which a few ostrich feathers were added to the top, and the crown and the upper part of the elders' bodies were painted with ocher and dotted with white and black spots. For six further days they had to bear this enormous weight, and I thought how uncomfortable their nights must have been. They also had to conceal their faces behind a mask made of thorns which must have been as unpleasant to wear as it was to look at.

I was shown the ceremonial drum (214), which was a replica of the one I had painted when I was with the Bajun. They are the only remaining specimens on the Kenya Coast. The elders agreed to pose for a photograph with the drum provided complete silence was observed while the drum was being handled. Scattered between the huts and palms were many effigies, two of them showing fragments of arms.

213   Kambe shrine with offering bowl   214.   Kambe elders with ceremonial drum

215.   Kambe *kaya* dining hut

To complete my record of the smaller Nyika tribes, I visited the Kauma, who have four *kayas*, two of them north of the Sabaki River, and two on Giryama territory. I went to one of the latter, which was on ground that was level with the surrounding country, and was hidden in a bushy forest. First we entered a small opening and after passing a little shrine, I saw a few recent, crudely carved effigies and one older one of more abstract design (216). Continuing, we came to a second gate where I had to leave my shoes and hat before entering the *kaya*. This was such a wide, open place that I could not see its boundary. It was sown with maize and thickly populated. Among the maize I found two old effigies and was told that they were the only remaining ones, the rest having been destroyed by white ants.

The *kaya* Kauma has four elders equal in rank called *Gohu*, who on ceremonial days wear the same head-dress as the leading elder of the *kaya Fungo*. Among the Kauma only the *kaya* elders are allowed to wear a *luvoo*, and when they do so they have to wear an earthen cone like that of the Kambe elders, and a thorn mask, and also paint their bodies.

They circumcise the boys from the age of seven to twelve in small groups. After the operation they live in the forest where they are looked after by their fathers. During this time they tie a string with charms attached to it around their waists until their wounds are healed. During their seclusion they shoot little birds with bow and arrow, a custom I had up to now known to be practiced only by Nilo-Hamites.

The mourning period for Kauma widows is one year, during which time they have to let their hair grow, and drape a piece of cotton crosswise over their breasts.

The next tribe on my list was the Duruma who live on either side of the railway close to Mombasa which they supply with milk and vegetables. They were living here in 1594 when the Portuguese invaded East Africa; though they have been for so long under European influence, most of them are still pagans.

They were administered from Kwale in the Shimba Hills south of Mombasa. As I drove up into this beautiful range through open forest glades and parkland, I had a superb view of the coastal belt and also got a few glimpses of the sable antelope which is found in Kenya only in the Shimba Hills. Kwale is an attractive Administration Center, surrounded by woods and small rivulets, and has a pleasant climate. I was therefore sorry when I learned that my first campsite in this district was to be on the foothills in hot and dull country. But when on my arrival there I saw, among the crowd from which I was to choose my models, two men with wooden masks (217), I was very happy, for these were not only the first wooden masks I had come across, but as far as I know, the only ones found in Kenya. They belonged to a pair of slave-catchers. One of the men was disguised as a woman. He

312

216. *Kaya* Kauma effigy   217. Duruma men with masks

wore feminine ornaments such as ankle bells, a string of beads around the loins, a woman's basket and a mask on which the soft, round features of a woman were carved. Thus disguised, he hoped to be mistaken for a woman, and thereby find it easier to catch one. His partner was out to deceive men. He wore a mask carved in a square, strong shape to which a false beard was attached to stress his masculine nature. To trick his victims, he carried powder in a gourd, which was supposed to make him invisible, and was further fortified with charms to protect himself against sorcery and snakebites.

My next model arrived on stilts (218). He was a witch doctor on his way to a dance. I was most excited for this confirmed what Professor K. G. Lindblom had written in *The Use of Stilts*[10] : 'Due importance should be attached to the circumstance that the occurrence of stilts in Africa closely coincides with the occurrence of

313

218. Duruma man on stilts

masks and more or less secret societies.' But judging by the sensation they aroused among the crowd and the man's clumsy use of them, stilts were obviously nowadays an unfamiliar sight.

To give the poor witch doctor a rest during our session, I suggested that he should sometimes sit down; but as the stilts were lashed by fiber to his legs and could not be removed easily, each time he had to be helped on to a chair by the onlookers which caused much amusement. Patti, who always kept close while I worked, was fascinated. She explored the strange-looking objects, clambered up and down the stilts, nestled in the rustling grass skirt, and chewed at the fiber. As the witch doctor could not move without support from his helpers, he was, to the delight of our audience, quite defenseless against Patti's antics.

314

219. Duruma witch doctor

My next sitter was another witch doctor of unusual caliber (219). Among the paraphernalia he carried was a wooden staff, the top of which bore carvings of a man and a woman. The woman was depicted in full detail, but the man's anatomy was incomplete. When I asked why this was, he seemed astonished and pointing to the carving of the man, imitated its glance and assumed an expression of arrogance which obviously represented his attitude towards women. Then he turned to the

315

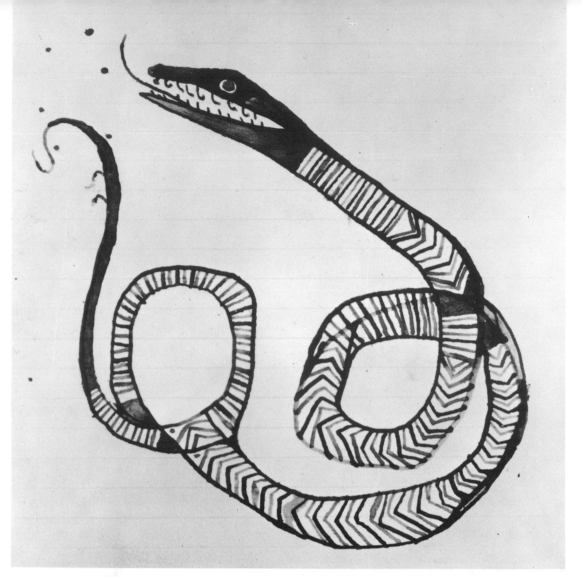

Paintings of Luhani   Fig. 3   Coiled python

woman's figure and stared vacantly ahead. I think he wished to make the point that the difference between the intelligence of a man and the stupidity of a woman was so outstandingly shown in her expression that any variations in anatomy were not worth recording.

He was a very amusing person and held in high esteem among the people. When I asked some questions relating to his professional secrets, he invited me to his home. Here he pulled from underneath a palm fiber mat which served him as a bed, a few sheets of paper on which he had drawn the spirits of various illnesses in blue and red ink, the only colors he could buy in the local shop. One represented the spirit of the 'trembling illness', obviously malaria, which made people shake from a high temperature; another depicted a coiled python, the spirit of snakebite. The fact that in his picture of the snake he had reproduced its rudimentary legs was a credit to his powers of observation, but he had had more difficulty in coping with the intertwining coils (fig. 3). He also drew a table but, as he knew nothing about perspective, the legs stuck out horizontally (fig. 5).

316

MJITA   BEKOBE
DZIVANI.   GANDINI
    DURUMA

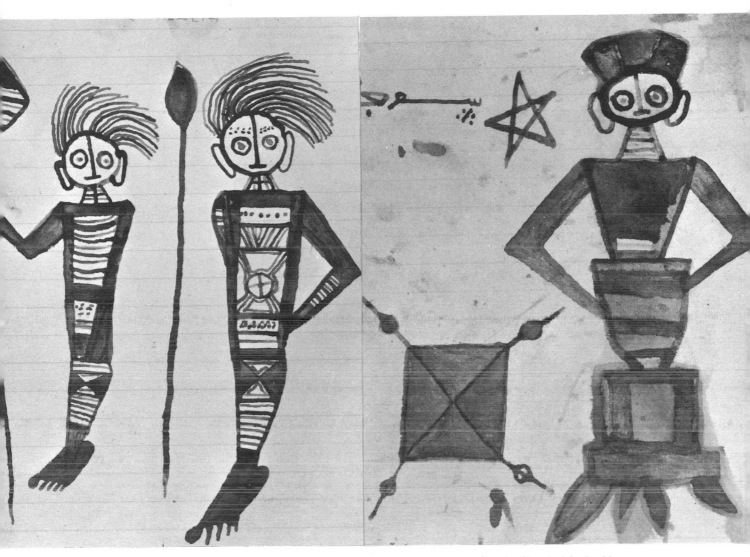

Fig. 4 Spirit of trembling illness   Fig. 5 Spirit of Leika Mungo

As I looked at more of his demons, I was fascinated by the way in which the witch doctor handled the perspective of the human figure. He achieved this by drawing the head and the extremities in profile and viewing the rest of the body from the front, as in Egyptian art, which he could not have seen. His geometric designs, intended to represent the body's bone structure, corresponded with the older effigies I had found at the *kaya* Chonyi (fig. 4).

The witch doctor believed that a person could not be cured by just giving him medicine, but that the patient had to keep a picture of the spirit of the illness under his head while sleeping to make it drive the devil out of his body. Judging by the

319

220. Duruma woman witch doctor

state of his drawings, this was a popular cure and it was with much difficulty that I persuaded him to sell me a few of his 'spirits'.

Professional etiquette did not bother him, and he had no scruples in competing with a specialist for snakebites who was my next model. When curing patients this witch doctor also consulted a spirit and carried the image of one in the form of a carved wooden doll. In addition he had a large assortment of charms such as bells, horns of various sizes, cow-tails, and a gourd filled with pebbles. He wore a mask of animal skin with the hair partly scraped off and little horns attached (pl. XXIX, p. 317).

Finally a woman witch doctor came to be painted; she was loaded with charms and cowries (220). These women are considered to be as powerful as their male colleagues and the people are in awe of them.

320

221. Duruma *kaya* Gandini gravestones

Meanwhile, I was determined to see the *kaya,* but for this I had to move my camp to Gandini on top of a hill from which I had a splendid view over Mombasa and Port Reitz, only a few miles distant. I was warmly welcomed by the Chief, who looked impressive in his colorful loincloth and long scarf flung in traditional fashion over one shoulder, but when I inquired about the *kaya* he was evasive. I was told that up to now no white person had seen it and of course this made me all the more eager to go there. During several days I made diplomatic approaches till at last the elders agreed to guide me to the *kaya.*

We walked a long way through beautiful parkland until we came to a wooded hill. Here we had great difficulty in finding the entrance to the path which suggested that the *kaya* was not often used. Climbing up the steep hill, we were just able to detect the remains of two gates in the dense undergrowth before we reached the *kaya* itself. In the center was a large, square clearing with a pole in the middle. This was the shrine, *Moroni,* where on ceremonial occasions castor oil was sprinkled on the ground and a black chicken or black goat sacrificed. The

321

people came here to pray for rain and hold a ritual dance. The three elders who perform the rites are called *Kambi* and wear a head-dress with ostrich feathers at the front and a skin of sable antelope or giraffe with the mane used as a middle ridge over the back.

The Duruma have never made effigies and indicate a grave either by a wooden pole with simple cuttings or by head-stones on to which they tie blue or white cotton; these are called *koma*. I noticed a stone dressed like a doll with a tiny woman's skirt and bead embroideries, on the grave of a woman witch doctor. Some of the head-stones were sheltered under grass roofs which had only recently been put up (221).

The Duruma, like most of the Nyika tribes, remove the two lower middle incisors and chip off the corners of the top incisors for ornamental reasons. They circumcise the boys before the age of eight years, performing the operation inside the hut without ritual and with no seclusion period following.

I painted a witch doctor whose emblems were a tiny tuft of hair at the top of his shaved skull and a ceremonial staff together with his paraphernalia of cowrie-decorated charms and a crude knife.

After having completed ten paintings, five of which were of witch doctors, I left the Duruma and moved to Vanga close to the border between Kenya and Tanganyika. It is a small village on the sea, where a *Mudir* looks after the population of Arab, Swahili, Digo, SHIRAZI and SEGEJU.

The present *Mudir* was the son of Sheikh Azan; we soon became good friends. We often walked together in the late afternoons and discussed local problems or the difficulties in reconciling old Arab customs with modern education, especially where girls are concerned. Although the *Mudir* had a great respect for the traditional views and habits of his father, he wanted to give his family a liberal education and life and was often criticized by conservative-minded neighbors. He showed me with pride the irrigation schemes he had established at the creeks to improve the oldfashioned methods of cultivating rice and other crops. As we walked along the beach we watched fishermen bringing in their catch in outrigger vessels which were as old as skilled navigation itself and common to primitive people from Melanesia to Africa. We walked on to ruins which recalled the time when Arab rule was at its zenith and which were now only inhabited by ghosts familiar to everyone in the area.

I was fascinated to see how the people here accepted civilization while retaining their deep-rooted ancient belief in spirits.

On one of my walks I passed an old Arab house almost overgrown by bush and got a glimpse of one of the most beautiful women I have ever seen. I wanted to paint her but her husband would not hear of her leaving the house and it was only through the intervention of the *Mudir* that I was eventually allowed to bring

222. Digo witch
doctor

323

my kit along and paint her in purdah. Sitting face to face with this enchanting woman, draped in soft carmine-colored silk, I felt very remote from the tension which was now gripping Kenya, as the first rumors of the Mau Mau rebellion started. Here at Vanga life went on as usual.

My purpose in coming here had been to paint the Digo and Segeju, whose history is closely linked. The first mention of the Segeju at Malindi dates from 1571; their habits were then described as similar to those of the Masai.

I was therefore much interested to see a witch doctor arrive to be painted who not only carried a Masai spear but wore a grass roll dipped in red ocher which fell from his forehead to the nape of his neck (pl. XXX, p. 318). This emblem, I was told, originated at the time when Segeju tribesmen sold ivory to the Masai and often came in contact with their warriors. Believing that their superior strength came from their hair, they hoped to transmit this power to the witch doctors by an imitation of the Masai hairstyle. Besides this symbolic roll, the witch doctor wore a cloak richly embroidered with beads and seeds and edged with the white hair of a Colobus monkey. A similar cloak was worn by a witch doctor of the Shirazi, a small tribe of whose origin little is known except that they may have migrated from Persia.

The Digo are one of the most important of the Nyika group. They inhabit most of the area between the coast-land south of Mombasa to Tanga in Tanganyika. Although they are very numerous, I was only able to get two people to pose for me, one a hunter and the other a witch doctor. The witch doctor wore bead ornaments of three different colors. Half the masking fringe on his head-dress has to be of white beads. The little bead-decorated leather bag on his chest is a charm, while the carved stopper on his gourd represents the devil. He plays a large rattle (222).

The Digo have several *kaya*s which are no longer used. Before leaving Vanga I visited the nearest which is at Lunga on the border; then I moved north to Tiwi where I visited another and I also looked at the *kaya* Pungu near Mombasa. In none of these were there any traces of huts, and I was told that the elders here never lived in the *kaya*, and that to-day when they pray for rain, they wear no ritual dress. Important people are buried near a tree within the *kaya* and the head of the grave is indicated by a stone; sometimes this is sheltered by a grass roof supported by six poles. I saw a few of these. Like the Segeju, the Digo circumcise both sexes.

With the Digo I had completed my record of the Nyika peoples and my study of the *kaya* and of the effigies. All my inquiries as to the origin of these grave-posts brought me no clue about the cult. I knew that grave-posts of the same kind exist in Burma, for I had seen five in the British Museum. They were similar in shape, but the designs represented records such as the number of enemies that the deceased had killed, or how many wives he had owned.

I have also seen an Arab grave-pole in the Musée de l'Homme in Paris, which had similar designs but no indication of human anatomy nor any head.

Geographically, the nearest grave-posts are in Ethiopia where the Konso, who are of Galla stock, have almost identical grave-posts which they combine with a phallic cult. If it was the Galla who introduced effigies into Kenya and if the Nyika adopted them as a result of their contact with the Galla, why, I wonder, do only a few tribes make them and why are there no effigies further inland among tribes such as the Somali, Gabra and Rendile with whom the Galla have also had relations? Is it possible that it was not the Galla but the people who arrived by outrigger vessels from Asia who brought the effigies to Africa?

CHAPTER 15

THE TEITA AND THE TAVETA

My next assignment was with the Teita people. The Teita derive their collective name from the hills near Voi[11] on which the bulk of them, some forty thousand[12], settled under the name of DABIDA. Another section numbering four thousand occupy the nearby Sagalla Range, while a third section numbering nine hundred inhabit the isolated region round Mount Kasigao. All these Bantu are administered from Voi. The country is hot, and grey bush covers sandy plains from which the hills rise abruptly to an average of three thousand feet, the highest peak reaches seven thousand feet.

I called on the D.C. who advised me to begin by painting the Dabida. So I drove off along a very steep, eroded road, and promptly blew out a tire. Soon afterwards I had two punctures at a place where the road, barely wide enough to hold one car, was hugging the mountainside and topping precipices. Several times I had to stop to let the engine cool which gave me time to look at the sheer cliffs which rose at such precarious angles to sugarloafed peaks that I had the impression they might topple over at any moment, and were only kept in position by the vegetation which struggled across their walls of stone. At last I reached the top where narrow valleys broadened into a broken plateau. Here I found the Administration Post of Wundanyi. The D.O. and I selected a campsite near the football ground. Though they live isolated from the rest of the world, the Dabida are one of the most industrious and mechanically minded people I have ever met, and they grow such fine crops on these forbiddingly steep slopes that their vegetables are in great demand along the Coast.

Because they are so progressive, it is difficult to find traditional costumes, and while waiting I explored the countryside and called on the missions, hoping to find photographs of traditional ornaments.

I went first to Wusi, where the C.M.S. mission dates from 1900. The guide took me along a narrow mountain path winding its way through a wall of thick vegetation intertwined with lianas until we came to the edge of a cliff with a drop of some three thousand feet. The guide told me that in the old days criminals were taken to this spot, tied in a sack, and thrown down into the abyss. Theft was one of the crimes punished in this way and, as a consequence, is to-day very rare among the Teita; for every child knows about the bones at the foot of the cliff.

When we arrived at the mission, which is run by two women, I was shown around the premises and introduced to bright-eyed girl students in spotless uniforms, but when I asked about traditional customs or photographs, I was referred to a clergyman who ran another mission nearby. Having been longer in the district than any other white person, it was said he would be bound to know about old traditions. I called on him but found him uncommunicative. Later I learned that he had only recently been in trouble, and though exonerated, since his trial viewed any visitor with suspicion.

Though since 1883 various missions had been trying to convert the local Africans, only one fifth of the population was Christian. The rest were pagan, who believed in a supreme God, and also in the power of the dead. Any disaster was attributed to a curse, to a fetish, or to the angry spirit of a recently deceased member of the family. If the latter was considered responsible, the skull of the deceased had to be exhumed and placed next to other exhumed skulls in the shelter of an overhanging rock. Here, in time of trouble, the elders sacrificed a cow or sheep with ceremonies to which neither women nor young men were admitted.

I was anxious to see the place and was guided to a well-concealed rock in the forest where several skulls grinned at me from a ledge. I noticed that their teeth —so far as they were still in position—were of a natural shape, while the present fashion demanded the chipping of the upper four incisors in both sexes.

I inquired about funeral rites and was told that after death the body was washed, and that in the old days it was buried in an upright position facing sunrise; the head was covered with only one foot of earth and its position marked with the main stone (ingo) of the first wife's three cooking stones. These also supported the center pole of the hut. After the burial the mourners went to a river where the women bathed separately from the men while close relatives, who remained inside the hut, were washed by friends. The widow had to cut her hair and remove all ornaments and remain alone for one year, after which the elders selected a new husband for her. She could exert no influence over their choice. The body of a deceased husband remained interred six months or up to two years, after which time the skull was dug up and placed next to other skulls of members of the family.

If a man was killed in battle or died while on safari, his head was cut off, taken home to be buried, and later exhumed. If there was no time to do this, a tuft of his hair was cut off, taken home, and fixed to the head of a sheep which was killed, and its skull buried and later dug up and added to the human skulls along the rock.

223. Teita girl in *kuaika* seclusion   224. Teita Figi elder

The Dabida circumcise the boys between the ages of seven and twelve, and the girls a few weeks after birth.

When the girl comes of age, at about fourteen years, she is kept for one year in seclusion in her mother's hut and no one is allowed to see her. During this time she is supposed to be reborn and is not allowed to talk to men, but only to female relations. She covers her eyes *(mingugu)* and when leaving the hut, which she is only permitted to do after 8 p.m., she has to wear a cylindrical grass head-dress *(kirembo)* and anyone meeting her must turn away (223). During this seclusion *(kuaika)* the mother instructs her daughter about marriage and certain rites which the girl must not disclose to anyone; if she does, she may not get married.

After circumcision boys also undergo an additional initiation which falls into two sections. The first, *kuaika,* lasts four days during which they live secluded in the forest. This period is followed by six days called *kiruguru.* The first day is the most important; the candidate is oiled and painted, has to have a special hair-style, and must wear the ornaments of a woman.

328

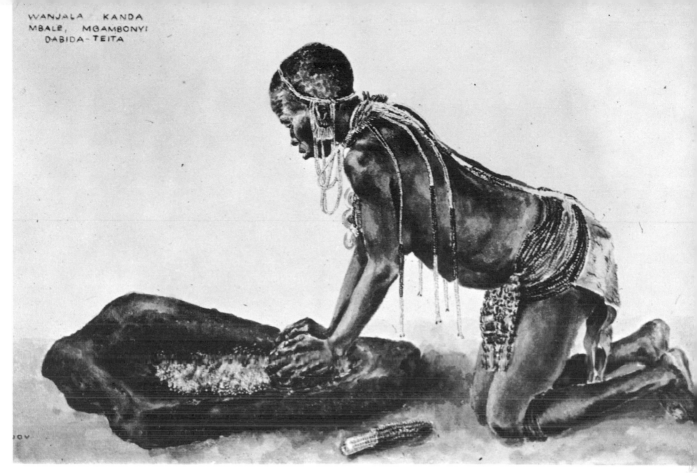

225. Teita woman grinding flour

The Chief was very helpful in arranging for a youth and a girl to pose for me in these costumes, and also persuaded a *Figi* elder to sit for me (224).

The *Figi* belong to a powerful secret society consisting of five orders; as their priesthood is hereditary, they must be married and have at least one son. Their ceremonies are performed at a sacred place and are intended to defend the people from sorcerers, the cattle from wild animals, and the land from enemies. For the last purpose they use two medicines *(ngingu* and *mafindiko)* which are believed to stop the enemy from crossing the border. Such protected places still exist in the district, and unauthorized people, and women in particular, may not enter them. Should the attack be made by night, the next morning the enemy will be found close to the boundary line and will be killed. If the medicine fails, this is attributed to the misdemeanor of a man within the village who has to be found and punished.

I was interested to see that the traditional dress of the Teita women was similar to that of the Luo and Maragoli who live so far away. I painted a woman, wearing the two small aprons, who was grinding flour between two stones (225), a method even more primitive than the one I had recorded among the Rabai.

In spite of the Chief's support, it was difficult to find traditional ornaments or co-operation amongst the local Africans.

While I was waiting for new models, I went with Maina, my new Kikuyu cook, for long walks in the hills. I enjoyed his company, though our topics of conversation

329

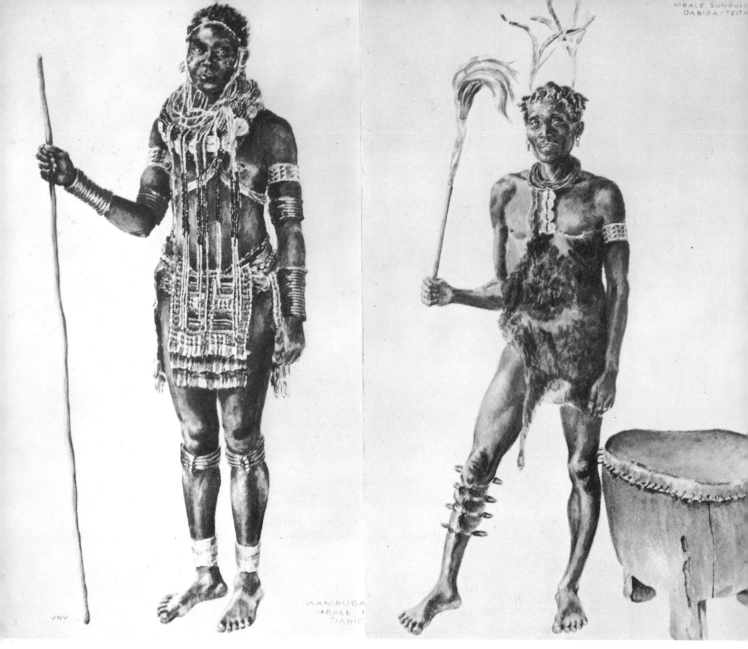

226. Teita bride   227. Teita youth attending a dance

were very limited, and he could not understand why I walked when I had a car. Walking made him feel he was losing face before all the people we passed; most of them were busy piling fruit and vegetables into lorries to be sold in the market in Mombasa, or were treading sewing machines turning out masses of khaki shorts, or converting old tires into sandals.

One day we walked up the Wueru Mountain, the highest peak of the Teita Hills. Struggling across clinging creepers, twisting roots and rocks, we finally reached the summit from where we had such a colossal view that everything around seemed dwarfed. We gazed over a boundless plain—all details veiled by its vastness. The sun was low and turned the haze into a deep indigo almost too intense in contrast to the orange sky in which the snowy outline of Mount

330

Kilimanjaro appeared as though floating in space. Maina and I sat silent, overpowered by the immenseness and stillness around us.

I wondered what Maina was thinking? He was part of the Africa I loved so deeply; he belonged to it just as the lion does. Did this grandiose spectacle before us affect him as it did me? I, the foreign intruder in his country, was so stirred that it almost hurt. But Maina was burning with ambition, wanted to know all about the Western world, its factories and large cities and hoped one day to have a car and earn a lot of money.

I wanted to walk and leave the car behind, wanted to learn about the law of nature and attune my life to it and forget about man-made values. Maina wanted to start on a journey from which I wanted to return. Was it a mere coincidence that we two, both loving and belonging to Africa in different ways, sat here together? Perhaps we could help each other?

On our return I found a girl (225) waiting for me who was prepared to pose for me as a bride. While I was painting her, she told me that, had she really just been married, she would have had to undergo a ten-day ritual during which she would have been kidnapped by the bridegroom and three of his relatives. Then there would have been exchanges of presents and food until on the eighth day her woman relatives would have anointed the pair with oil and red earth and the couple would have shaved off some of each other's hair and buried it between the hearthstones. The following day she would have been shown the patch of land she would have to cultivate and from which she would have to bring a load of sugar cane. Next, a bundle of firewood would have been put on her head as a sign that she was now allowed to greet her mother-in-law. To complete the marriage ceremonies she would have had to take some cooked bananas to her family and return with a load of fresh ones to her new home. Of course, no girl could get married unless she had been initiated.

I completed my record of the Teita by painting a youth attending a dance (227), an occasion for which he would wear a number of metal bells of Masai design tied to his shin (they were a relic from the time when the two tribes intermarried); a warrior carrying not only a bow and arrow but also a spear (230), an elder playing a flute made from an antelope horn, and finally a hunter (229) who carried poisoned arrows and a bow with which the Teita used to kill elephant, rhino and lion before Game Laws prohibited poaching.

After a month's stay among the Teita I went to Kasigao. To reach this small village nestling at the foot of the imposing mountain, after which the tribe is named, I had to go down nearly to sea level, drive through hot, arid thornbush country and cross many sandy riverbeds all of which were dry. The Chief

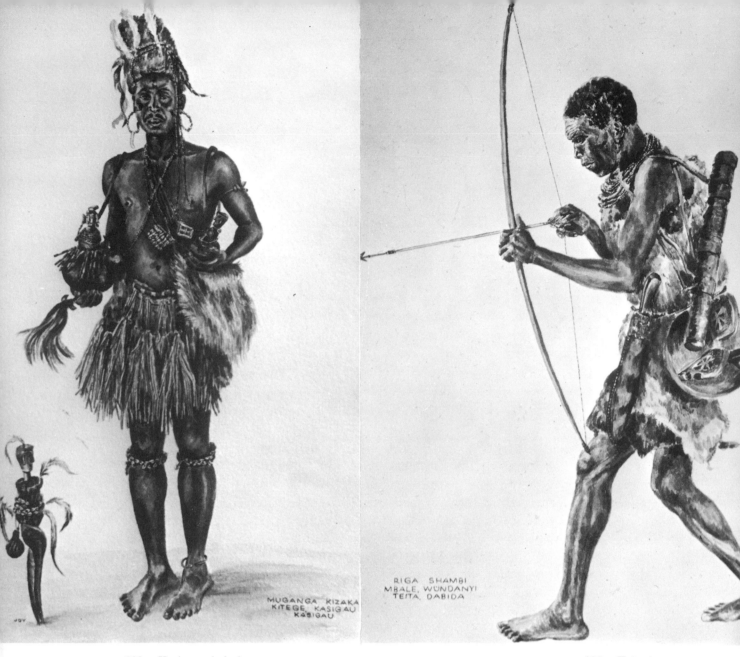

MUGANGA KIZAKA
KITEGE KASIGAU
KASIGAU

RIGA SHAMBI
MBALE, WUNDANYI
TEITA, DABIDA

228.   Kasigao witch doctor   229.   Teita hunter

welcomed me with the gift of a chicken, and helped me to select a campsite close
to the village as it was not safe to camp further into the bush because of elephant.
That there were many of them in the area was evident from the spoors we had
seen along the road.

Next day I woke up with a severe attack of malaria and was ill for a week.
Patti too went sick with a stomach infection, and the two of us gave the dresser
at the little dispensary a busy time.

While I was ill the Chief looked for models for me, and when I recovered I
found a bride waiting to be painted (233). Unlike her counterpart in the Teita
Hills, she had no fineries except for a bead necklace, nor had she to undergo

230. Teita warrior

such complicated rites before she was allowed to start her married life. All that was needed was for her to stay two days in the hut, and on the third day to walk with a bundle of firewood on her head through the village with her mother following close behind.

The circumcision rites too were different from the Dabida's; both sexes are operated on as infants. Later, the boys are initiated into *kuaika*. They are kept

333

MBORAMBAHA LEMEREI
MBOGHONI TAVETA
TAVETA

231.   Taveta girl during seclusion   232.   Taveta woman whose daughter is in circumcision

for four days in a hut where a tutor teaches them the code of behavior. This follows the *kiruguru* period, which lasts five days during which time the boys wear women's ornaments and attend a big party. These rituals signify their entry into manhood. The girls undergo a four-day seclusion during *kuaika* at which time their mothers keep them in their huts while teaching them their future obligations.

The exhumation of skulls and other customs of the *Figi* were similar to those of the Dabida, except that here a widow was confined to her hut for three days and had to sit with her arms crossed and her ears tied together with a string across her neck. After I had painted a woman in this pose, a bride, and a girl during and after *kuaika*, I ran out of models.

334

233. Kasigao bride

Taveta was my next destination, but before I left for it I painted a witch doctor who had a finer collection of charms and wooden carved stoppers on his gourds, depicting various spirits, than I had seen before (228).

With the exception of the Akamba, wood-carving in East Africa seems restricted to people living near the Coast, and most of their carvings have to do with witchcraft. Wooden masks had been to my knowledge used only among the Makonde tribe who live along the Ruvuma River on the border between Tanganyika and Portuguese East Africa, but to these I could now add the two masks I had found among the Duruma.

I was very keen on painting the TAVETA who are a mixture of Bantu and Nilo-Hamites, and are made up of the Akamba, Masai and Teita who live in Kenya, and the ZIGUA, SAMBAA, GWENO, and CHAGGA who live in Tanganyika. The Taveta speak a language of the same type as the Teita and the Pokomo, but practice Masai circumcision rites and have Masai-type names. They developed into a tribe during the seventeenth century.

Driving along the main road close to the base of Kilimanjaro, whose ice-covered dome was hidden behind clouds during the hot hours, I passed through miles of sisal and pineapple plantations. When I finally arrived at Taveta it was afternoon, the place seemed deserted, and I had great difficulty in finding someone to show me a suitable campsite. After some hours of search, I chose an abandoned car dump several miles from the *boma* at the edge of a forest. It had a water supply and the advantage of being on dry ground while all around were swamps.

Next morning I called on the D.O. who introduced me to the Chief and assigned a couple of Askaris to look after me. Then I returned to camp and waited for models to arrive. As I walked late one afternoon along a narrow path through the magnificent forest, I heard a tinkling sound and after a few moments saw a woman accompanied by a hooded figure. In the fading light I could just see below the covering cloth the legs of a girl ornamented with several strings of cowries. Guessing that the girl was in seclusion (231), I stopped the mother (232) and tried in my best Swahili to persuade her to let me see the girl. After a long discussion she agreed to consult the Chief and guided me through the dark forest to his home, which was much further away than I had anticipated from her explanation. The Chief confirmed that the girl was in a state of seclusion and, after reassuring himself as to my discretion, not only talked the mother round to letting me see the girl, but cajoled her into promising to allow me to paint her the next day.

When she arrived I was fascinated to see that, like the Teita women, she wore thick layers of beads arranged crosswise over her breast, and that her cowrie-

234. Taveta young
pregnant woman

embroidered skirt was Kamba fashion, while the rest of her ornaments followed the Masai tradition.

After completing her picture, several days passed without any new models turning up. My inquiries received evasive replies from the Chief, and the Askaris behaved rather insolently. I visited the market hoping to find a model there; we were close to Lake Jipe and as the local people are fond of fish there were a great many kinds for sale, together with fishing tackle and nets.

I was struck by the sight of a young, pregnant woman who not only had her hair longer than any of the other women I could see around, but also wore an unusual bead necklace from which thin metal chains fell over her body to her knees (234). I persuaded her to sit for me.

337

One afternoon I walked with Maina a long way across swampy plains until we came to a small hamlet where I noticed a woman who was wearing ornaments that evidently had some symbolic significance. I could only just get a glimpse of her under many metal chains. I made inquiries and was told that she had married recently, and was still wearing her bridal costume (pl. XXXI, p. 339). I found the ritual here almost identical with the seclusion rites of the Tigania, Teita, and Imenti girls who undergo a state of rebirth during this period; their eyes are kept covered and they make a pretence of helplessness by appearing to be unable to walk without help. In addition to all these women, showing the phases between initiation and child-bearing, I was able to paint a few before circumcision.

Up to now I had had to find all the models myself, as neither the Chief nor the Askaris made any efforts to co-operate; indeed they behaved in such a strange and offensive manner that I finally complained to the D.O. who was embarrassed but appeared unable to do anything about it.

Christmas was approaching but far from being in a festive mood, I was very depressed by the atmosphere I sensed around me. Even Maina arrived one morning with several new cooking pots already packed up, and asked to be dismissed. I talked him into staying on and gave him the day off to celebrate Christmas. As soon as he had gone the Askaris bolted so I was left alone in the camp. Since someone had to guard the place, I refused an invitation to share a Christmas meal with the D.O. Sitting in this untidy spot at the edge of a forest, miles away from the nearest European, with only Patti for company, I felt rather miserable. I might have felt much more uneasy had I realized in what dangerous surroundings I was; though I knew that the Mau Mau revolt had broken out I did not know that some of the rebels were now hiding at Taveta.

To make up for my lonely Christmas, the D.O. next day sent two new Askaris to guard the camp and invited me to come with him and his wife for a picnic to Lake Chala. This is a deep crater lake at the lower slope of Kilimanjaro, well concealed in the forest. According to a Taveta legend a whole tribe was drowned in its waters and it is haunted. No one will go near the place after dark for fear of the spirits of the *Wazigua*. A long time ago they had come from the Pare Hills in Tanganyika and, after settling at Chala, angered God, who made the earth sink under them and filled the hole with water.

The crater walls are almost vertical and we had to cling to lianas which we used as ropes on our way down. As we sat at the lake side, I recalled the story of three friends who once went out for a swim here. Having almost reached the middle of the lake, they noticed a log that had not been there before. As they turned back the log followed and steadily gained on them until, perspiring with fear though the water was icy, they just reached the bank before the crocodile caught up with them. Nobody had ever heard of crocodiles inhabiting Lake Chala,

JOY

NAYA SAGARU
ABORI, TAVETA
TAVETA

235. Taveta skulls

and we wondered how the croc reached it, for the nearest river infested with them is far away and it seemed incredible that a crocodile could have covered all that distance overland.

On our return to Taveta I remarked on the unusual number and tameness of the ground hornbills in the area—they look rather like black turkeys—and I was told that this bird is the totem of the tribe.

I also learned that the Taveta exhume the skulls of their dead, although their burial rites do not otherwise correspond to those of the Teita. In the old days the Taveta used to bury their men in a sitting position with the left arm resting on the knee and supporting the head. An important person was interred at the door of his first wife's hut, others were buried inside the hut. Women were buried near the door of their hut in an upright position with the right arm resting on the knee. People without children were put into a pit and left to the hyenas. One year after a death had occurred, a kid was sacrificed and all male relatives of the deceased person were invited to the feast. While the ceremonial *merigu* drum was beating, they had to place the bones of the kid under a *dracaena* tree—the spiritual home of the ancestors—and sprinkle earth from the grave of the deceased over the bones which symbolized the remains of the founder of the family.

Before the feast started, the skull of the deceased had to be exhumed and hung on a branch of a tree which after a few days was removed, placed in an earthen pot, and either buried or left above ground. After some negotiating I was taken into the forest and shown several earthen pots containing old and partly broken skulls under a large sacred tree (235).

341

236. Taveta dressed for Izumu feast

Luckily my visit coincided with the circumcision cycle of the boys and I was able to find a youngster willing to pose for me (pl. XXXII, p. 340). His initiation costume was typical of the Nilo-Hamites, but in addition he carried a bow on which riddles were incised in the bark. To solve these was part of the initiation test. Although there are similar carved initiation sticks among the Kamba and Chagga, only the Taveta use bows with such carvings and I was delighted to add this to my record[13].

342

The Chief had promised to summon a man who owned one of the rare costumes worn at the *izumu* feast. But the days went by and he did not arrive. The new Askaris had also deserted me and I was left without help.

Not willing to accept defeat, I went off to find the *izumu* model and walked towards his home at Mata, but it took longer than I expected and on my way back through the forest night fell. I don't know why I was so frightened, for I have often walked alone in the dark, but I was so scared that when I saw a tiny light approaching I was very relieved. It turned out to be a bicycle on which a man was pedalling in the opposite direction to that in which I was going. When we met he advised me not to walk alone and not only volunteered to escort me home but offered to find the man with the *izumu* costume for me.

I was most grateful; when the model came I found that the *izumu* costume was an interesting combination of Masai and Bantu ornaments (236).

The Taveta are certainly fascinating people with interesting traditional costumes, and it was very frustrating that it was so difficult to find sitters.

CHAPTER 16

WITH THE SAMBURU ON THE LOROGI PLATEAU

I left Taveta and drove towards Nairobi. On my way I stopped for a short time in the Kajiado district to add a few more Masai pictures to my record amongst which was one of a young mother with white spots on her forehead which indicated her state. Although I camped in a remote place, I became aware of the tension which was gripping the country. Later, when I arrived in the capital, I was alarmed when I saw everybody with revolvers stuck into their belts and the headlines of the papers carrying accounts of Mau Mau murders.

George had come to Nairobi to plan our overseas leave which was due within a few weeks. By now I had completed my paintings of the most important tribes except for the Borana and Samburu. I delivered my pictures and all were accepted; we then left Africa.

When I returned from Europe I found the country in a state of great unrest, so I decided to paint the Samburu at their center Maralal which is on the Lorogi plateau bordering the Northern Frontier District to the west; this was one of the few areas in which it was still safe to camp.

The Samburu are a people of the Masai group and have similar customs; but certain sections differ in that they eat game. Samburu country is well populated with wild animals and therefore attracts many tourists, but poaching is a menace in these areas.

The road from Isiolo via Nanyuki and Rumuruti climbed steadily to a plateau which was covered with bush and, higher up, with cedar forest. The *boma* of Maralal is most attractively situated among trees; it consists of the Administration building and a few cedar-log houses where the Government Officials and their families lived. In a glade a short distance away was a line of African shops including a well-stocked store owned by Cardovillis, a Greek, who was a great character.

The D.O. put me up for the night, and sitting by the crackling fire in his drawing room, we discussed plans for my stay. He suggested that I camp high up in the forest at Losuk where there was a spring to which the Samburu took their

344

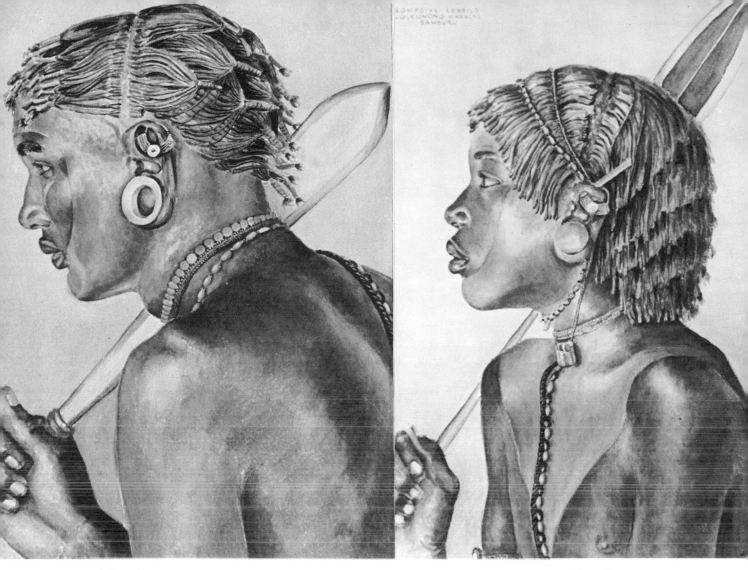

237a. *Sakara oirena*

237. Samburu Moran hairstyles

237b. *Sakara olaa*

stock for watering and where I would have excellent opportunities for choosing models. Before starting off in the morning he introduced me to a few chiefs who seemed interested in my paintings, and promised their help.

The track wound through dense forest up some seven thousand feet to Losuk. Here I met a friend from the Agriculture Department, who provided me with men to cut a clearing for my camp, and helped me choose a site where we would be safe from elephants. Judging by their droppings, there were a great many around. It was a beautiful spot overlooking the spring and a small valley, and was sheltered by trees which would not only protect us from the wind, but which were also close enough for us to climb up them if an elephant became too familiar. The first small herd arrived before dark and since they were very inquisitive, I thought it better to sleep with Patti inside my car until they got used to our presence. After some anxious hours watching the giants from far too close for my liking, I fell asleep, only to be woken up by the chatter of equally inquisitive Samburu who had surrounded the car and were peeping at me, giggling and watching

345

237c. *Ilmasi wala*   237d. *Ilmasi wala*

every move I made. They were mainly *moran*, their status being shown by their different hairstyles. They provided me with a splendid lot of models (237a–g).

I started with a youngster whose ocher-greased hair was rather short and could only be twisted into tiny plaits which were divided by a parting across the middle of the skull. This style was called *sakara oirena*. Next in rank was a *moran* with his plaited hair hanging loose to his neck, a style known as *sakara olaa*, then came the *ilmasi wala* style, in which the hair falls halfway down the back, and the front section is twisted into pigtails over the forehead. Another version of the same style is achieved by letting the front hair fall evenly distributed across the forehead over an ocher-dyed piece of cloth used as padding.

Another model wore his hair in two pointed pigtails of considerable length, a style known as *ilmasi opiaya*.

All these hair-dos needed elaborate care. In order to protect their long plaits when going on safari, the *moran* tie them into a bun at the neck called the *ilmasi*

346

237e. *Ilmasi opiaya*

237f. *Ilmasi wochiko*

wochiko style. Important elders fashioned their hair in a cap called *mikuri*.

These *morans* were splendid fellows and we had great fun together while I painted them. They boasted that one of their tests of courage was fixing a sandal on to a rhino's horn. I was tactful enough not to ask if the rhino was asleep. They told me (not knowing that I was the wife of a Game Warden) how they disguised a donkey as an orynx antelope by tying a skin mask resembling it with two long sticks in lieu of horns to his head, after which, bending low to hide themselves, they walked in so close to these elusive orynx that they were able to shoot them with an arrow. Every *moran* carried a wooden club and spear, but none possessed a shield. I inquired why this was so and was told that there were hardly any left in the district. When after a lot of trouble one was produced, I was surprised to find it similar to the type used by the neighboring Suk and Turkana. This was astonishing as most of the Samburu ornaments and customs are similar to the Masai's, including the circumcision rites.

347

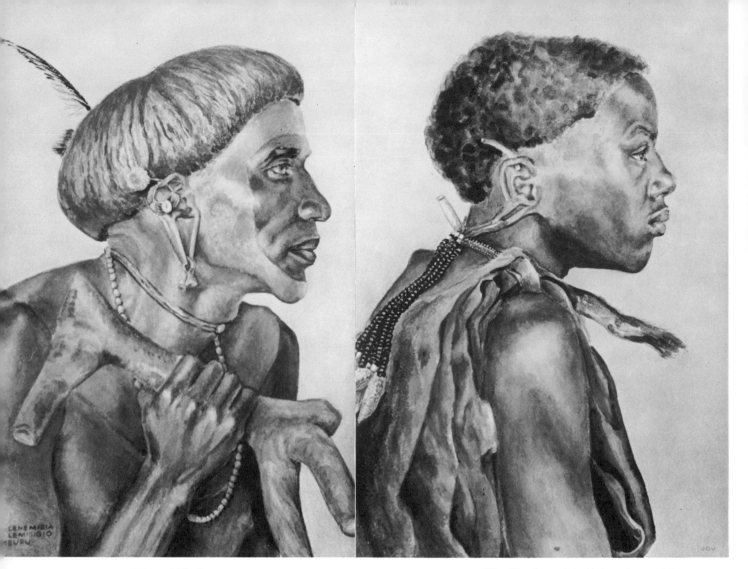

237g. *Mikuri*   238. Samburu boy before circumcision

Unfortunately the initiation cycle was not due for several weeks, but I was told that three months before the ceremony the candidates wear a black-dyed hide cover, smear their hair and skin with charcoal and wear a special ornament of blue beads and beetle-wings hanging down the spine which has to be tied by sheepskin straps to their ears. During this period the youngsters keep themselves apart, and I was very lucky that the brother of my cook, who was from Maralal, agreed to sit for me while he was in that stage (238).

It was not easy to find women willing to pose for a picture, but with the help of the Chief I painted one who had recently married; she wore ornaments which signified the transition between being no longer a virgin but not yet having borne a child (240). She had pronounced Mongolian features which I had also noticed among some of the Rendile women, and I wondered where this characteristic had originated.

Another interesting model was a woman who was sterile (239). This was indicated by her neatly trimmed, black-dyed hair. To remedy this condition, a

348

239. Samburu woman unable to bear children

240. Samburu woman recently married

bull had been sacrificed and a strap had been cut from the hide with a slit in the middle so that she could pull it over her head, the ends, decorated with cowries, hung over her breast and back. Finally the elders had spat on her; this is a blessing intended to make her fruitful[14]. Until she bore a child, she was called a *namayama*.

While I painted these women, several of their relatives and friends sat around watching us, among them a mother with a tiny baby. They attracted my attention as the child kept quite still, lying all the time on its stomach and this did not seem natural. It was wrapped in a filthy rag covered with flies which also clustered round its eyes so that it could barely open them. I picked up my Optrex bottle to wash away the filth, but at the mere sight of it the mother screamed and tried to run off. Only by using a lot of patience could I convince her that no harm would result, then she allowed me to treat the child, which accepted my ministrations placidly while its mother yelled blue murder. After I had done the best I could, the mother calmed down and lifted the rag to chase the flies away. Now it was my turn to scream with horror for, where the baby's buttocks should have been, I saw a hole of raw flesh filled with wriggling maggots and flies. While she put the rag back over this shocking sight, she calmly explained that a few weeks ago the child had fallen into an open fire and burned itself, and assured me that nothing could be done but wait until the flesh healed. When I suggested taking her and the baby to the local hospital, she stared at me in terror; she plainly thought I meant to kill the child and, before anybody could stop her, she ran screaming away with it.

I camped for a month in this place which I had come to love in spite of the almost daily rain and the fact that the climate at this altitude is virtually arctic. The Samburu are a charming people, and I made several friends among them who showed their affection by bringing me presents of milk and eggs.

The elephant were the only trouble-makers and we all suffered our share of their depredations. They often used their trunks to pull off the door-logs from the well so as to get at the water more comfortably than by sucking it from the spring, and no matter how cunningly the Samburu secured the logs, the elephant were still more cunning in removing them again. Finally the weather got so bad that I had to return to Isiolo.

241.   Termite air-funnel

CHAPTER 17

THE GADAMOJI CEREMONIES
OF THE BORANA

At Isiolo I learned that the Borana along the Ethiopian border were celebrating *gadamoji*, their initiation cycle; I had been waiting for seven years for this occasion. The final ceremonies at Marsabit were not due till 1955, but the Borana section near Moyale had started their ritual earlier, and I persuaded the P.C. to let me go there.

He was rather reluctant to let me start off as Moyale is some three hundred and fifty miles to the north and the road crossed very difficult country. Luck, however, was with me for an Indian trader's lorry was leaving next morning for Moyale and with it following behind my car it was considered reasonable to let me go off with Maina and Patti. For the first hundred and thirty miles all went well; then we reached sandy ground and in my efforts to keep the car on the road, I bent the steering rod. We had no tools with which to straighten it, but after waiting for the lorry, which never came, we finally managed to bend it into position.

We spent the night in the car near the Uaso Nyiro River, kept awake by swarms of mosquitoes. The next morning we cautiously drove on to Wajir where we arrived in the afternoon. We stopped there just long enough to get the rod repaired and then, as the Indian trader's lorry still did not turn up, drove on alone across sandy plains covered with scrub. There were no landmarks except for many termite air-funnels which rise to a height of up to fifteen feet (241). Since these had been bent by the prevailing east wind, they gave a sense of direction.

Eventually we entered more hilly country and finally climbed a steep escarpment leading up to the Ethiopian highlands, and arrived at lunch-time at Moyale which is half in Kenya and half across the border.

The Kenya *boma* was laid out in a typically British way with well-kept lawns around the office and flower beds in the residential quarters. I called on the D.O. in charge, and he told me that the *gadamoji* ceremonies were taking place some distance across the border, and that it might be very difficult if not impossible to

351

242. Borana woman grinding flour

go there and paint the people. Instead, he very kindly offered to ask permission from his Ethiopian counterpart for some of the *gadamoji* to come into Kenya to be painted. He also introduced me to Chief Hunti, and asked him to help me. Finally he offered me a spacious guest-house some distance away where I would have privacy while painting the people in their initiation stages.

As soon as I had settled in, I went for a walk along a path patterned with lion pugmarks. I met a few Borana, riding their typical, sturdy ponies, their manes blowing about in a wind so sharp that it almost took my breath away.

The Borana are a section of the Galla who not so long ago inhabited the Horn of Africa and form a large percentage of the population of Ethiopia. They speak the Galla language and number about two million. At the beginning of the century, some one hundred and fifty thousand moved into Kenya and settled along the border and round Marsabit. They have retained their original customs with the exception of some forty-five thousand who moved south into the Isiolo district and were converted to Islam.

During the several days it took me to find models, I made friends with Chief Hunti who lived at the foot of the escarpment. I had a steep walk downhill through thick forest to reach his big *manyata* where I was always welcomed with milk or eggs. Hunti was a charmer, a good horseman, and very popular. He introduced me to his large family, and while I watched the women coping with the children, of which all Borana are very fond, or grinding flour by rotating two stones against each other (242), Hunti talked about his people and their customs.

352

The Borana are pagans who believe in a supreme God, *Waka*. The intermediary between him and the people is a ritual expert, the *Qallu,* who is believed to be in constant communication with the deity. Next in rank is the *Abagada* who, in turn, has lesser dignitaries under him. The most important custom of the Borana is *gadamoji,* the initiation cycle which lasts eight years. This is based on the division of the tribe into five *luba:*

LUBA		FATHERS	SONS
a.	*Bulle Dabassa* – Initiation cycle during the years:	1–8	40–48
b.	*Arero Godu*	8–16	48–56
c.	*Liban Kuse*	16–24	56–64
d.	*Guyo Boru*	24–32	64–72
e.	*Aga Adi*	32–40	72–80

From this table it can be seen that every son belongs to the same *luba* as his father with four initiation cycles of eight years each separating the generations, so that a period of forty years elapses between the initiation of father and son. Every *gadamoji* candidate has to sacrifice three animals: a bull when he moves into the *gadamoji boma* on *bararti* day; shortly afterwards he has to kill a sheep on *elejesa* day, and during the final *jilla* ceremony, when his hair is shaved on *huffat* day, another bull is killed. If the candidate cannot produce these animals, he has to wait for his next turn or, as an alternative, can change his *luba* for the one which starts the soonest, but he will then be called a *gultu* and have to build his hut on the left side of the elders belonging to this *luba.*

Girls can be circumcised at any time, without any ceremony being held; sons are only circumcised during the last year of their fathers' *gadamoji* period. As a consequence of these rules it often happens that the men are grown up and even married before they can be circumcised. They are then called *raba,* and any sons born to them are known as *daballe.* In the old days all children of uncircumcised fathers had to be abandoned except for the first son who could be reared but had to wear a girl's dress and hairstyle. The unfortunate children (called *chirwani*) who were abandoned were in fact usually rescued by relatives or people of a different tribe who returned them to their parents in exchange for livestock after their fathers were circumcised. The *daballe* wear a crown of cowrie shells from the moment of their birth for nearly one year. Their hair is not shaved until their grandfather becomes a *gadamoji* and consequently their father can be circumcised. Then the cowrie crown is added to their mother's *kalo* (a ritual ornament) and the shaven hair of the *daballe* is placed on a cow which from then onward is the property of the child and called *handura.* For the next eight years the child is known as *gamme,* after which he will be shaved during the next *gadamoji* ceremony and is then called a *kusa.*

At the beginning of the *gadamoji* cycle, eight men from the same *luba* tie a lump of resin *(kumbi)* into their loincloth and carry it for the next seven years. They and their families stay together for this period and live under strict rules. For instance they are not allowed to kill, and instead of a spear they carry a wooden staff *(ororo)* which eventually will be placed on their graves. They have to ignore any insult; they use special expressions for certain words like meat or spear which are said to belong to a ritual language. They have to observe a special diet. They live abstemiously and are supposedly in contact with the deity.

Every initiated Borana must have killed a man or a dangerous animal, and he must also have fathered a son. A thin plait of hair at the crown of his head, called *gutu,* is a sign that he has accomplished all this.

During the *gadamoji* period the candidates do not shave their hair. At the beginning of the eighth year they unravel the *gutu* and interweave all their hair with fiber, shaping it into a kind of halo known as *guduru.* To this they add a phallic emblem, the *kalacha,* originally made from iron ore but recently from aluminium which is obtained by melting down cooking pots or scrap metal. The *kalacha* is attached to a boss *(halko)* made in the old days from a special shell from across the border, but now from ivory. The *halko* is the most sacred object and must never be touched. The *kalacha* is traditionally supplied by the neighboring Konso who live in Ethiopia. These people are well liked by the Borana, who call them *dirri* which means clean people, who have no inferior classes such as slaves.

One morning several old *gadamoji* whom the D.O. had invited to come over to Kenya, arrived. Their natural dignity was enhanced by their age. It must have been an ordeal for them to come here, but they never lost their composure.

With them arrived their families, wearing interesting ornaments. All these people were anxious to return as soon as possible to the *gadamoji boma* which was a long way off, so I had to content myself with taking photographs of them, except for one *gadamoji* who agreed to stay behind so that I could paint him (243).

I wondered how I could get more of these people to pose for me but saw no hope till one evening I was invited to a party at the boundary commission which was at the time resurveying the frontier between Kenya and Ethiopia. Since the commission had to work closely with Ethiopian officials, some of them were at the party. One was a Senior Official who had travelled extensively in Europe and collected antiques. He wore a well-cut suit and had the manners of a man of the world. When I told him about my problem he invited me to his home at Moyale in Ethiopia to discuss the possibility of persuading some of the *gadamoji* to pose for me and next day he kindly sent an escort to guide me across the border. After crossing a small gully which separated Kenya from Ethiopian Moyale, we walked uphill along the only road which is lined with whitewashed mudhouses

243. Borana *gadamoji* elder

typical of all Northern Frontier Province villages. We stopped at the top of the road and from a modest house which looked like all the others my host emerged to welcome me, and then ushered me into his one-room home. He offered me the only chair; it stood next to a small table. He himself sat on his low bed from which he had first removed a bundle of clothing wrapped in a cotton cloth with the four ends tied together. This must have contained his wardrobe for there was no other furniture.

After suggesting various ways of persuading the *gadamoji* to pose for my record, he advised me to call on the D.O. whose office was further down the road and looked just like all the other houses.

I knocked at the door and the D.O. appeared, looking rather startled. After I had introduced myself, he produced two chairs, placed them outside the door,

355

244. The very old mother of a *gadamoji* elder

245. Wife of *gadamoji* wearing her *habba*

and we sat down and discussed the purpose of my visit. He too promised me his help, with the result that during the next few days several of the people I wanted to paint arrived. Among them was a very old woman, mother of a *gada-moji* elder (244), the young wife of a *raba* with her *daballe* baby clinging to her back (246), the mother of a *daballe* during the period in which she wears the *kalo* (247), and a father also wearing a *kalo* as he does on the day his son is named. The man's appearance reminded me of an incident which happened some years ago in Marsabit. One morning I had heard singing far away mingled with the jingle of bells. Soon the sound came nearer and I saw a man running downhill toward our camp, wearing a cowrie-decorated strap across his body with little bells made

356

246. Mother of a *daballe* wearing the *guluma* and carrying her baby   247. Mother of a *daballe* wearing the *kalo* after *komitsha*

from the tops of gourds attached to it. He seemed very happy and, waving his arms at us, rushed on, inviting everybody he passed to come to the feast and rejoice at the naming of his son.

Much as I appreciated the opportunity to paint these interesting people, I was disappointed that I could not visit their *gadamoji boma*, but this proved impossible.

However, I made the best of my stay and explored the Burji village adjoining Kenya Moyale. The BURJI are a people of non-Galla stock who speak a language related to Konso. As these two tribes live in close contact with each other, I found it interesting to watch the Burji spinning (248) and weaving (249), a craft I had never seen the Borana practice. I saw small groups of Burji men talking together

248. Burji man spinning

while spinning cotton on little spindles (248). Others sat under the eaves of the grass roofs of the mud huts weaving the smooth thread into ribbons about three inches wide (249) which later were stitched together to make cloth. The looms were primitive wooden affairs set in the ground; a hole was dug underneath which made a space for the weaver's feet and enabled him to pedal the warp and thus operate woof and shuttle.

I remembered that some of the tribes we visited in the Cameroons on a trip through Central Africa used identical weaving methods, and I wondered why the art of weaving is mostly confined to people living north of the equator, for there is hardly any evidence of indigenous weaving south of it. I liked Moyale, the Borana, and the invigorating highland atmosphere, and so was sorry when I ran out of models and had no excuse to prolong my stay.

Again the problem of finding an escort for my return journey arose. No vehicle was scheduled to go to Isiolo for some time, but I thought that since I had managed to come here without any help from the Indian lorry, I might risk going back unescorted.

249. Burji man weaving

In the event, we ran into difficulties for, after driving some time and reaching the middle of nowhere, a spring broke. Maina and I spent hours before we succeeded in changing it. Later we took the wrong turn at a crossroads and arrived very late at Wajir and had to spend the night there.

Next day we started off early for Isiolo. All went well until the late afternoon when the car stopped, and nothing we could do would start it again. It was obvious that we should now have to spend the night on the road and I felt uneasy as we were in an area where Mau Mau gangs often crossed from the Jombeni Hills into the Northern Frontier Province, and they were known to have many hide-outs in the nearby extinct volcanoes.

So when, towards midnight, we saw the headlights of a car and our faithful driver Ibrahim appeared, I was immensely relieved. The D.C. at Wajir had sent a radio message announcing our arrival there and when we had failed to turn up at Isiolo, George had sent out a rescue party. Ibrahim traced the trouble to the petrol filter, and after repairing it, we drove safely home.

In July 1955 George and I were at the south end of Lake Rudolf and explored South Island which had only once been visited by the ill-fated Fuchs expedition in 1934. After we had returned safely we heard that the Borana at Marsabit were preparing for the final *gadamoji jilla*. Having previously obtained permission from the P.C. to paint the people there it now only remained to pack my kit and drive

359

the one hundred and sixty miles to Marsabit. As the track lay across forbidding lava escarpments, eroded ravines, and ninety miles of the Chalbi Desert where mirages were apt to lead one astray, George lent me Ibrahim. The D.C. at Marsabit made all the necessary arrangements for me to paint the *gadamoji* and I received further help from Dabasso Wabera, a local Borana who had studied anthropology at London University and was very knowledgeable about the history of his people. Through his influence I made friends with one of the *gadamoji* elders and his family who all agreed to pose for me and finally invited me to attend the *jilla* ceremony which was to take place on the 22nd of July. I realized what a great privilege this was as very few Europeans had witnessed this ceremony.

On my walks with Dabasso after the painting sessions he told me of the difference between the *kalacha* emblem used by his people and that of the Ethiopian tribe who, on ceremonial occasions, wear the genitals of the enemies they have killed as trophies. He told me that this type of mutilation was still a common practice in Ethiopia.

Dabasso also told me of the snake worship which was still practiced more particularly by two sections of his people. The Sabo kill all snakes except the puff adder, while the Gona kill puff adders but no other snakes. When one of these groups wishes to kill a reptile which is taboo to them, they call on the other group to do the job.

The Sabo and Gona are each ruled by a *quallu*. The two *quallus* co-operate in general and particularly during the *jilla* ceremony when a large snake is worshipped. This takes place every fourth year at Sumburi in Ethiopia. The Borana dig a hole in the ground and fill it with camel's milk. Then they sacrifice a young camel and offer the fat of its stomach mixed with the milk to the snake.

The same ritual is also practiced among the Gara section of the Gabra tribe who, approximately every fourth year, offer prayers to a puff adder at Furolli near the Huri Hills.

One day Dabasso introduced me to his two wives and his children. Although we had no way of talking to each other, they soon lost their shyness and later visited me every day. We became great friends.

The Borana may marry as many wives as they can afford. The girls marry when they are about sixteen; they must be virgins. A Borana who seduces a girl becomes an outcast. When I asked Dabasso if this custom was still respected, he assured me that a man known to be a seducer is not allowed to sit on a chair, sleep on a bed, or drink from a bowl, nor can he enter through the front gate of a cattle *boma*. He is called *chabama* and he will never find a wife.

Dabasso was a charming man, dedicated to his people and to his country. In 1963 he was appointed as the first African District Commissioner to Isiolo. At that time the Northern Frontier Province was a cause of dispute between the

360

250. *Dobu*
251. *Fudu*

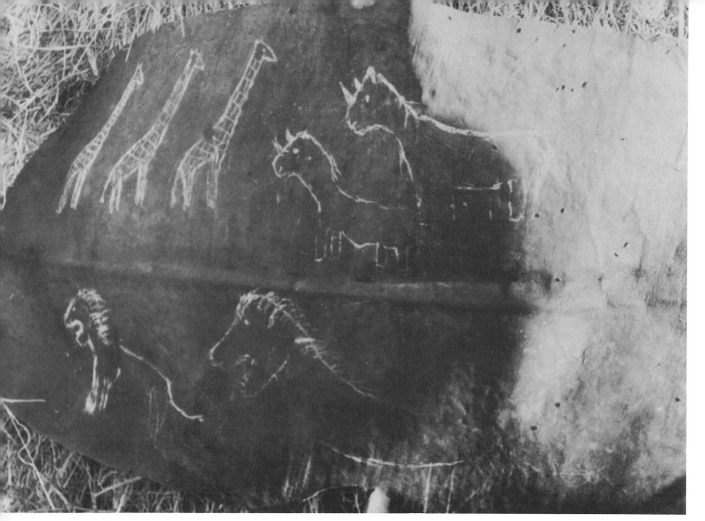

252.   Drawings of animal trophies on cow hides

Somali, who claimed the province for their republic, and the Kenya government, who refused to give it up. Dabasso upheld the government view, which coincided with his own. His life was several times threatened and eventually he was brutally assassinated by Somalis. But when I was in Marsabit all this was in the future and the people's only concern was with the great *gadamoji* celebration, the *jilla*, which was due to take place in two days' time.

With the permission of the *gadamoji* and the D.C. I moved my tent close to the *gadamoji boma*, which had only just been completed in time for the ceremony. It was situated a few miles away from the Marsabit *boma*, at the top of an open ridge close to the forest's edge. From it one had a magnificent view of the Kaisut Desert far below and of the slopes of Marsabit Mountain. Close to the *boma* I noticed several *gadamoji* elders sitting silently under a croton bush. This, I was told, was the holy tree under which the elders prepare themselves by prayers for the final ceremony.

The *boma* was laid out in the usual circular shape, but had one unusual feature; the huts were only built along one half of the circle, and although the Borana are pagans, all the huts faced Mecca. They were protected by two parallel thorn fences which left a walking space between the front of the huts and the inner fence

362

253. Borana shield attached above the door of the hut (beside his head)

that protected the cattle by night. Each hut faced an opening in this inner fence leading into the cattle *boma* and there were corresponding openings in the opposite half of the circle which could be closed with branches. Next to the inner openings along the hutless semicircle stood low containers, the *dohu* (250); they were made of cowdung. On the outer side of the fence were solid heaps of cowdung called *fodu* (251).

The following day I watched the people fixing one or two large hides to the front of their huts, on which the outlines of giraffe, lion, elephant and man had been painted, also dots and rings in red or white, representing smaller animals such as antelope (252). These recorded the dangerous beasts and human enemies which the *gadamoji* had killed. Finally a shield was attached above the door which was of the small round type that the Galla and Somali use (253). I painted a hut with a unique display of 'trophies' while all around me the women rushed about, preparing food for the feast and impregnating their hide dresses with oil and aromatic herbs to make them soft and scented for the *jilla*.

Next morning all the *gadamoji* again assembled under the holy tree for prayer. I walked around the *boma*, watching the children being groomed and the women tidying up the place; early in the afternoon the elders returned to their huts.

363

254. Borana *gadamoji* and wife shaving their son

255. Borana elder collecting *koti* branches

256. Borana elders decorating their door with *koti* branches

During all this time I had kept close to my Borana friends, for if not, those who did not know me might well have objected to my taking photographs. Watching from some distance, for I felt it well to make myself as unobtrusive as possible, I saw the *gadamoji* and his wife shaving the hair off the head of their small son who would be initiated in forty years' time (254). The *daballe* were also being shaved by their parents.

Later in the afternoon I followed my friend who went with the rest of the elders to the forest where they collected branches from the *koti* tree *(rubia)* (255). With these they decorated the doors of their homes (256) and also fixed a branch to the center pole inside the hut to which, I was told, a container with milk would be fastened tomorrow.

By then it was late afternoon, the *boma* was humming with talk and activity, and little groups stood round the fires or were dancing in slow movements. At

365

257. Borana *gadamoji* sacrificing bull

sunset the D.O. and the local missionary arrived to camp nearby and watch the *jilla*. I asked the missionary, who had been in the region for many years, what happened at a Borana wedding. He replied that he never attended pagan ceremonies and therefore could not answer my question.

It had now become dark and a chilly wind was blowing round the mountain side, making the fires flicker irregularly and throw moving shadows of the crowd. The singing and dancing had become vigorous; it had a catching rhythm, enhanced by the tinkling of bells and of ornaments with which the women made up for their lack of instruments. Strangely enough, the more excited people grew, the more controlled their movements became. It was well after midnight when the dancers retired into their huts, from which the sound of singing continued all through the night. We too went to bed, but I went on listening to the muffled singing. There was much liveliness and warmth in the songs, which related the legends of the past and the various achievements of the elders. Other songs told about cattle going to a waterhole and being stampeded by lions; some about the tedious bucketing of water from deep wells.

At dawn I heard the people leave their huts, and I followed the *gadamoji* to the lower entrance of the *boma,* where they joined their leading elder for the ceremonial

366

sacrifice of a bull (257). The animal stood quietly, its legs hobbled, while the elder anointed its head and spine with fat. The expression of the *gadamoji* was that of serene meditation; and, far more than any words could have done, the utter silence enhanced the impressiveness of the ritual.

At this moment the first rays of the sun lit up the sky and relieved the tension but did not diminish the intense devotion with which each *gadamoji* in turn touched the head and backbone of the bull with his small *diri* stick, repeating the prayer in which he asked for children, rain and good grazing. Finally the elder cut the throat of the bull.

I now followed my friend, who, like the rest of the *gadamoji*, returned to his hut to sacrifice his own bull. He had to make the initial cut at the throat himself, but whenever the elder was not skilled enough to kill the bull properly, a Somali professional stood by to complete the job.

My friend needed no such help; as soon as the animal was dead, he cut a narrow strip of skin (258) from near the navel and tied it round his left wrist.

Watching from a distance, I then saw him move nearer to his hut where his wife and little son were waiting. Sitting down on a small stool, he carefully untied his *kalacha* and placed it above the forehead of the child, who from that moment became a *komitsha* (259).

258.   Borana *gadamoji* cutting a wrist strap from a sacrificed animal

259.   Borana *gadamoji* placing *kalacha* on his son's head

Now the *gadamoji* was ready to have his *guduru* shaved. Bending his head low over an outspread hide, he waited for his wife to begin cutting the hair off. This was one of the most important moments in the lives of both and their faces were grave. Starting with the fluffy hair near the temples, she shaved the halo off with great care all in one piece (260); this requires a skill which few women have. After she had washed her husband's head with milk he covered it with a cloth and rushed inside the hut as if ashamed to be seen in this state.

Meanwhile his wife collected the hair from the hide and carefully mixed it in a container with milk and a special grass. During the entire ceremony her face never lost its serene expression. Now, with great dignity, she and the little *komitsha* carried the container to their cattle (261), and I saw her resting it for a brief moment on one of the finest cows (262). I was too far away to see if this ritual gesture was accompanied by prayer. Both then carried the container to their *dobu* in which they buried it very solemnly. After carefully closing the opening with cowdung and covering the *dobu* with branches so that no cattle could get near it (263), she joined her husband inside the hut which he would not be allowed to leave for the next three days.

368

While all this went on, the sacrificed bull had been cut up and certain parts of the meat had been fixed to the shield above the door. The rest, including the intestines, was covered with the animal's hide and remained on the spot for the time being.

Next I noticed the *komitshas* and the daughters of the *gadamoji* standing in a group a short distance from the *boma*. They were motionless and silent and were obviously praying. After a while they walked in solemn procession (264) through the opening between the *fodu* and *dobu*, the boys wearing for this day only their fathers' *kalacho* and *lichowhip* (265). It was a moving sight to watch this group of children proceeding with bent heads and at a slow pace toward the lower end of the huts where they stopped in front of the first one. They called three times and were answered from inside by the *gadamoji*. Then the *komitshas* fastened a wooden bell to the door and as many of them as the small hut could hold went inside. As soon as they had disappeared, we heard the tense voices of the *gadamoji* and his wife telling the *komitshas* of the heroic deeds in the life of the *gadamoji*, realistically recalling the killing of dangerous animals and the slaying of enemies. The listening crowd outside the hut were soon infected by the excitement of the tale and started to fight and eventually some men threw fits.

While the shouting people were carrying the unconscious men away, the *komitshas* emerged from the hut with the milk container that had been fastened to the center pale and carried it close to the remains of the sacrificed bull.

260. Borana *gadamoji's* wife shaving her husband's head

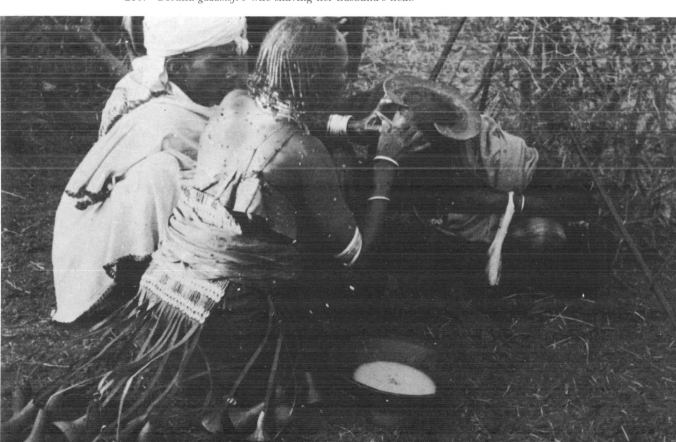

261.   Borana *gadamoji's* wife carrying container

262.   *Gadamoji's* wife resting container on cow

263.   *Gadamoji's* wife burying *guduru* in *dobu*

264. Borana children's *komitsha*

Here they sat down in a circle around the bucket and, beginning with the youngest among them, a tiny tot hardly able to walk, each took a sip of the milk from a large wooden spoon (266). As soon as everybody had had his share, they moved over to the bull's remains and lifted the covering skin with their staffs (267).

Before the meat was divided, a soothsayer investigated the intestines to read from them the family's fate (268). When he had finished looking into the future, the *komitshas* and girls returned to the open field for prayer, repeating the ceremony from hut to hut. This took up the whole day. By then, though I was only a passive onlooker, I was utterly exhausted.

After the *komitshas* had completed their last round they proceeded to the place where the first bull had been killed at sunrise. The skins of all the sacrificed animals were cut into narrow strips and distributed among the people.

While the men were thus occupied, the women gathered in groups talking and singing. That night again the dancing continued till dawn, though less vigorously than on the previous night.

I left next morning, deeply impressed by what I had seen. When I returned a few days later, I found the *boma* abandoned for the Borana had gone back to

265. *Komitshas* wearing their fathers' apparel for one day   266. *Komitshas* sipping milk from the ritual spoon

their distant *manyata*s leaving the *fodu* and *dobu* to the elements, until a new cycle should bring them back.

On my return to camp I struggled up through thorny bush and rocks to the summit of a small hill where I sat, listening to the wind and looking at the mysterious forest of Marsabit immediately below me and across to the surrounding desert which extended far into the distance.

It was all immense, timeless and beautiful. Suddenly there was a rustle of twigs and a greater kudu looked straight at me with its large, soft eyes and I hardly dared to breathe for fear of frightening away this magnificent antelope. We gazed at each other for so long that the barrier which usually separates man and animal seemed to break down. Finally, after nibbling at some leaves, the greater kudu walked off, carefully groping for footholds across the rocks. I listened until the sound of his hoofs ebbed away, and again I was alone in the stillness.

By now the sun was sinking and the sky, which had been scarlet with flashes of bright yellow and streaks of warm purple, slowly faded to cooler shades of indigo and grey and finally subsided into darkness.

373

267. Borana *komitshas* lifting skin of sacrificed bull

How deeply I loved Kenya, its mountains, lakes and plains; its animals, flowers and people. I realized how fortunate I was to be living in this fascinating country while many of the traditional customs of its peoples were still practiced. However inevitable the toll of progressive civilization may be, all who love Kenya must work together to preserve its unique natural resources and to record, at least in writing and pictures, the tradition of its people. For it is from this tradition that the Kenyans derive their integrity and the strength they need to keep those assets of their country which mean so much to everyone who has known them.

374

268   Soothsayer reading future of the family from the bull's intestines

EPILOGUE

by G. W. B. Huntingford, B.Sc., D.Litt.

The land now called Kenya lies roughly between latitude 4° north and 4° south, and between longitude 34° and 41° east; it is crossed by the equator, and the Great Rift Valley runs through it from north to south. Although the total area of Kenya is about twenty-two thousand square miles, a great deal of it consists of desert shrub country, where conditions are almost those of the desert; yet even here nomadic pastoral tribes manage to eke out a hard life. In the south-western quarter of the country, between the two lakes, Victoria and Rudolf, and extending eastwards beyond Mount Kenya, is a highland zone, where much of the land is over six thousand feet above sea level, and in places rises to over nine thousand feet. This part is mainly parkland, with patches of evergreen forest, plenty of rivers, and a rainfall of between forty and seventy inches a year. At the northern corners of this zone stand, like sentinels, the two great extinct volcanoes Kenya and Elgon, while away to the south is Kilimanjaro, the third great mountain of East Africa and the 'Mountain of the Moon' of the Greek geographers. East of this zone is a belt of thorn-bush country, at a lower altitude, with a lower rainfall and less inviting for human occupation, though it is nevertheless occupied by nomadic peoples. Along the coast is a strip about thirty miles wide where are to be found patches of tropical forest and, mainly close to the shore, plantations of coconuts. As the land rises away from the shore it gets drier, and about thirty miles inland degenerates into a waterless thorn-bush type of country which finally merges into the desert shrub zone that comes down from the north.

In the history of East Africa there are three dominant factors. The first is its isolation, due to the fact that there was no outlet from the north end of the Red Sea till the Suez Canal was made. This kept Europeans, ancient and modern, out of the area till the nineteenth century;[1] and though there was much traffic to the coast from Arabia, India and Indonesia throughout the centuries, none of this succeeded in penetrating the interior. The main reason why nobody reached the interior was the presence of a wide strip of waterless and uninhabited thorn-bush country which lay inland, and constituted the second factor. It was only in comparatively recent times that the Arab and Swahili traders began to penetrate inland, and then they went south of Kilimanjaro, turning northwards through the Rift Valley. The third factor is this Rift Valley, a great depression, in some places wide and shallow, in others deep and spectacular, and associated with difficult and mountainous country. The presence of the Rift in Kenya seems to have acted in some way as a dike dividing the eastern and western Bantu, though this division was maintained and intensified after the seventeenth century by the Masai, another important factor in Kenya's history, whose territory (even if sparsely inhabited) lay across the Rift Valley from Lake Rudolf in the north to beyond Kilimanjaro in the south. The Masai formed a tough barrier to the trading caravans from the coast.

In such a land, which ranges from low-altitude and almost waterless scrub to high-altitude and well watered pasture and forest, the main occupations of the people have been influenced by the kind of country in which they lived. Agriculture has been possible only in the equatorial parkland zone, part of the thorn-bush zone, and at the coast. Elsewhere, cattle, camels, sheep, goats, and donkeys form the chief wealth and occupation of the people, though of course cattle, goats and sheep occur in large numbers in the parkland zone. In pre-European days the main crops were maize, millet, eleusine *(wimbi)*, sweet potatoes, peas, beans, pumpkins, bananas, tobacco, and, at the coast, sugar. Coconuts, brought over by the Indonesians, seem to have grown at the coast since the first century A.D.

The present African population belongs to four different major ethnic groups, all comparatively recent immigrants: the evidence indicates that none of them entered what is now Kenya before the eleventh century A.D. (if as early) and many of them much later. They were preceded, however, by others who have now nearly all vanished. There were the people of the Stone Age, who have left their stone tools behind them, but cannot at present be correlated with any of the existing peoples, though survivors of some Stone Age groups may have mingled with the newcomers and been absorbed by them. There were also the people who made the ruined stone dwellings that are to be seen in parts of western Kenya, before the coming of the Nandi and Masai; their culture has been called Azanian and, whatever they may have been, they were distinct from the more primitive Stone Age people. Then there are the hunting people commonly known as Wandorobo—they call themselves Okiek—who, though grouped linguistically with the Nandi, were here before they or any of the present inhabitants arrived. The Wandorobo live in the highland forests, but there are other surviving hunters called Ariangulu, Sanye and Boni who live in the thorn-bush and the desert west of the coast forest strip. Yet other hunters, who have not survived, were the Gumba of Kikuyu tradition and the Wasi of the coast. In older days, too, there was a scatter of bushmen throughout Eastern Africa, whose strain has entered into the physical make-up of many tribes, though the only bushmen now surviving in East Africa are the Hadz of northern Tanganyika.

The existing people belong to four groups, three ethnic divisions known as Hamitic, Nilotic, and Nilo-Hamitic, and a fourth grouping known as Bantu, which is linguistic, there being no such thing as a Bantu 'race' or Bantu 'culture'.

The first of these groups lives in the northern and eastern borderland of Kenya – the Northern and Coast Provinces, where are the Hamitic peoples represented by the Galla, Somali, and Rendile. These Hamites belong to a large family which long ago came from southern Arabia into Ethiopia and the Horn of Africa in successive waves of immigration which developed into (1) the Agaw and Sidama peoples of central and south-west Ethiopia, (2) the Galla, (3) the Somali and Danakil. It is only the Galla and Somali who have come as far south as Kenya, and even then it is only a very small fraction of them who live here, the rest being in Ethiopia and Somaliland[2].

The Galla were originally settled in northern Somaliland, and were gradually driven out by the Somali, who came over from Arabia in ever-increasing numbers during a period of migration which ended perhaps about the eighth century A.D. As they expanded the Galla were forced eastwards and southwards, but mainly southwards. Some Galla settled in the highlands of eastern Ethiopia (the Harar region) while the main body moved southwards, and sometime between A.D. 1200 and 1500 split into two bodies. The larger of these turned west, and about 1522 entered Ethiopia from the neighborhood of Lake Rudolf, and spread over a vast area of Ethiopia, having by 1570 got well into the heart of the Ethiopian kingdom. The smaller body continued southwards and between 1300 and 1500 settled in the Tana Valley, where they came up against the north-eastern Bantu tribal groups now distinguished as Pokomo and Nyika. These southern Galla have been separated from their relations in Ethiopia so long that many of their institutions have changed. The Galla are divided traditionally into two main groups, the Bareituma and the Borana, corresponding roughly to the eastern or agricultural Galla, and the western or pastoral Galla. The name Borana, however, became attached particularly to the pastoral Galla of southern Ethiopia, whose territory extends into the northern part of Kenya, and for this reason it is customary to say that the Galla of the Northern Province are Borana, whilst those of the Coast Province are simply Galla.

The Rendile, who number perhaps six thousand, are another Hamitic people of whom very little is known. They live near Marsabit and speak a language related to Somali rather than to Galla.

The Somali people consists of two parts, the 'noble' or free Somali, and the Sab. The 'noble' Somali, who claim descent from a man named Somali, are divided into four large groupings (confederacies or 'tribal families') called Darod, Dir, Is'hak, and Hawiya; and the Sab, said to be descended from an Arab called Sab who was

379

expelled from Arabia because he refused to pay tithes, are divided into two group-ings called Digil and Rahanwein. At a higher level of genealogical fancy, however, Somali and Sab are called brothers, the sons of Hill, a man of the lineage of the prophet Mohammed. Each of these groupings is divided into a number of tribes. Most of them are pastoral nomads, the camel being the most important animal in the north, with cattle in the east and south among the Hawiya, Digil, and Rahanwein; it is here also that agriculture is mainly found, though there is a little cultivation in the north, and in some parts a primitive wooden plough is used.

The 'noble' Somali groupings also claim descent from Arab sheiks who settled in Somaliland at various times, mostly after the Hejira (A.D. 622), but although there was undoubtedly a wave of immigration about this time caused by persecu-tion in Arabia, the Somali are not 'Arabs' in the usual sense of the word.

Living among the Somali, but not of them, are several outcaste groups known collectively as Sab[3], that are attached to 'noble' tribes for whom they perform certain duties in return for payment and land; formerly they were not allowed to marry Somali, to own any livestock but sheep and donkeys, or to claim compensa-tion for homicide from Somali. They are of the same category as the Watta of Ethiopia (found among the Galla) and the Dorobo of Kenya (who however are not 'servile') in that they are the remains of the earlier inhabitants of the region. The most important of these groups in Somaliland are the Tumal, who are smiths and makers of charms and amulets; the Yibir, who are hunters, leather workers and magicians; and the Midgan, who are also hunters and leather workers as well as surgeons and circumcisers—Midgan men circumcise Somali boys, and Midgan women perform the operation of infibulation on Somali girls.

The Somali now living in Kenya belong to the Aulyehan, Marehan, Mahamud Zubeir, and Talamuge of the Darod confederacy, and the Murillo, Ajuran, and Digodia of the Hawiya confederacy. These seem to have begun to cross the Juba about a hundred and forty years ago, and had reached Wajir by 1906, and eventu-ally the entire eastern edge of Kenya was occupied by them.

The second group of people, the Nilotic, is represented in Kenya by the Luo, a collection of tribes speaking a language akin to that of the Acholi of Uganda and Shilluk of the Sudan. They live on both sides of the Kavirondo Gulf, and on the south extend well into Tanganyika. They came into Kenya from the south-west side of Mount Elgon, led by two brothers named Adhola and Owiny, who quarrel-led and separated, Adhola and his followers remaining near Elgon, where they form the Jopadhola near Tororo. Owiny with his followers went southwards, probably across the corner of the lake, to Kavirondo Gulf, where they arrived perhaps early in the eighteenth century.

380

The third group is formed by a wide belt of Nilo-Hamites, who extend from the Sudan frontier down into Tanganyika, and consist of the Turkana in the north, near Lake Rudolf; the Suk; the Kalenjin (the Nandi-Kipsikis group) and the Masai in the south. The Turkana came in from north-eastern Uganda, probably not very long ago. The Masai and Nandi came from the region north of Lake Rudolf and began to enter Kenya perhaps between the fourteenth and fifteenth centuries, the Nandi coming to their present home about 1600, and the Masai reaching Ngong near Nairobi a little later. The Suk consist of a union of two separate peoples, who when first seen by Europeans were in process of fusion and integration. The core of the tribe is the Hill Suk, 'the corn people', who are agricultural and use a system of irrigation, though they keep cattle; the other element in it is the Plains Suk, who are pastoral. The Hill Suk, forming about a third of the tribe, are of Nandi stock, and in dress and appearance are probably what the Nandi looked like a hundred years ago. The Plains Suk on the other hand are of Karamojong stock, forced out of the area north and north-east of Elgon by the Turkana. Fusion between the two elements is complete as regards language, since the people of the Plains have adopted the Nandi-type language of the Hill Suk; but in certain other respects, notably age-sets, integration is not complete. Grouped with the Nilo-Hamites because they all speak dialects of Nandi are some twelve hordes of Wandorobo (Okiek) living in contact with the Nandi, Kipsikis, Masai and Kikuyu; they are primarily hunters, originally without cattle or cultivation[4].

The fourth group consists of the Bantu-speaking peoples, who are found in three separated blocks: (1) the western or Luhya, sandwiched in between the Nilotic Luo and the Nilo-Hamites to the north-west of Lake Victoria; (2) the eastern or Nyika, along the coast, with the Teita and Taveta inland towards Kilimanjaro; and (3) the central, round and to the south of Mount Kenya, comprising the Meru, Embu, Chuka, Tharaka, Kamba, Kikuyu, and other smaller tribes.

The Luhya (who with the Luo used to be known as Kavirondo) came mostly from Uganda. One Luhya tribe, the Tiriki, seems to have begun to enter Kenya about the middle of the fifteenth century, while the Hanga may have come about 1600; the rest seem to have come during the seventeenth and eighteenth centuries, some even as late as the early nineteenth century. Others again came northwards from the direction of Usukuma in Tanganyika, probably after the arrival of the Luo, and so perhaps about the middle of the eighteenth century; these are the Gusii (Kisii) of south Nyanza and the Ragoli or Logoli (Maragoli) of north Nyanza[5].

The ancestors of the eastern Bantu came from an early dispersal center on the Teita Hills near Kilimanjaro, where the Teita now live, and went eastwards to a district on the coast called Shungwaya, which was somewhere between the rivers Tana and Juba. They had not been there very long before they were displaced by a southward movement of the Galla into the area, as a result of which part of them retreated up the Tana and settled along its banks, becoming the Pokomo. Others went further inland, and eventually reached the region of Mount Kenya; these developed into the Chuka, Meru, and Kikuyu; others crossed the Athi River and became the Kamba. There is some difficulty in dating these movements, because we do not know for certain when the Galla arrived, though it was some time between 1300 and 1500. What does seem fairly clear, however, is that the Chuka, Embu, and Ndio were the first to develop into tribes in their present home, and that the Meru and Kikuyu did not reach their present homes till much later, the Meru perhaps about 1750, while the Kikuyu may not have reached the Kiambu district (near Nairobi) till about 1800. Not all of the Shungwaya people left the coast, for the remainder went southwards, crossed the Sabaki, and developed into the group which became known to the Swahili as WaNyika, 'the people of the bush', and includes the Giryama, Digo, Duruma, and a number of smaller tribes. The ancestors of the Teita, who seem to have been part of the group which became the Giryama, may have begun to move into the Teita Hills during the seventeenth century. To the west of the Teita are the Taveta, a Bantu-speaking tribe which seems to have been formed in the seventeenth century by a settlement of Kamba hunters who were joined by the Masai and by Bantu elements from the Pare Hills and the slopes of Kilimanjaro.

One tribe in the eastern area, now classed as Nyika, the Segeju, presents something of a problem. Appearing in Portuguese records of the sixteenth and seventeenth centuries as 'Mosseguejos', they now live on the coast on both sides of the Kenya-Tanganyika frontier. By tradition they came from Shungwaya with the Digo, but a part of them is said to have originated in the Hadramaut. Though now thoroughly Bantuized, it is said by some that the famous coast hero Liongo Fumo was a Segeju.

In most of these Kenya tribes, the tribal spirit was, and to a large extent still is, an important element in the solidarity of each society. A tribe is a group united by the possession of a tribal name in which the members take a pride, of a language, and of tribal territory, as well as a tribal character that differentiates it from other tribes. This tribal feeling has been intensified by the fact that before the establishment of the British administration the tribes of Kenya had no chiefs. With one exception they were controlled by local councils of elders combined with an institution called age-sets in the Nilo-Hamitic tribes and some others which initiated them; something will be said about this institution later on. In many tribes, especially the Nilo-Hamitic pastoralists and some of the Bantu, there were not even villages, merely groups of scattered homesteads combined into units each with a name and a local council. The one tribe which did have a chief was the North Nyanza tribe called Hanga, whose ruler was a 'divine king' who in former times was put to death, like the ruler of the Nkole tribe of Uganda, when his bodily powers failed. This form of kingship had ceased to exist before 1883, when Thomson met their chief Mumia; but there is evidence that it did exist and that it had connections with western Uganda.

The result of a chiefless society is that there is only one class in a tribe, for though the social standing and importance of individuals can vary according to wealth in cattle or crops, all men are socially equal, and there is no division, for instance, into 'nobles' and 'serfs' as there used to be among peoples like the Nkole and Ruanda; with the disappearance of the 'divine king' from the Hanga, all traces of a similar division seem to have disappeared also. In chiefless societies the elders and warriors form the two most important sections of the community, each in their own sphere; but there is no class-distinction between them, and the leader of a council, whether he acquires his position by acquiescence as among the Nandi, or by election as among the Kakumega, does not rank socially higher than any other elder.

Some of the peoples of Kenya commonly regarded as 'tribes' are in fact tribal groups consisting of a number of named and often independent tribal units. The Galla and Somali, both consisting of more than a hundred distinct tribes, are in fact tribal groups on a large scale; and on a smaller scale the Luo, for whom Hobley, in 1902, gave a list of seventeen tribes, also qualify for this term, though their tribes were much more integrated than those of the Galla or Somali. Till the middle of the nineteenth century the Masai consisted of seven separate tribes each with its own name, but all acknowledging the name 'Masai'. The Bantu Kavirondo, on the other hand, formerly had no collective name but a little before 1939 they coined for themselves the name Luhya, which with the plural prefix aba-, means something like 'fellow-tribesmen'. The Nandi speaking group likewise had no collective name, but within the last few years the Nandi and Kipsikis have adopted for themselves and certain other tribes of the group the name Kalenjin, a Kipsikis word meaning 'I tell you', because they say 'this is a word frequently used in the course of conversation'.

II

In the life of most Kenya tribes, the initiation of the individual—his passage from boyhood to manhood—is a matter of supreme importance and is accompanied by elaborate ritual. All the Kenya tribes practice male circumcision, with the exception of the Luo, Turkana, some of the Plains Suk, and part of the Pokomo; and some have also female circumcision[6]. In place of circumcision, the Luo remove four of the lower incisor teeth; the Turkana and Plains Suk have no form of mutilation. Among the Turkana an ox or goat (according to whether the boy is an eldest or second son) is speared and the contents of its stomach are rubbed over the boy's body; the main feature in the Plains Suk ritual seems to be the plastering of the hair with mud.

Though circumcision, or a substitute ritual, is the essential act of initiation, it occupies only a small part of the time devoted to the complicated set of ritual performances which make up the process of initiation, and initiates may be secluded from the rest of the tribe for anything up to five months, as among the Nandi; though in some cases it is much shorter, it may be much longer, up to two years in the case of the Tigania. In this book Mrs Adamson describes the circumcision of the Borana and Kipsikis (whose custom is very like that of the Nandi; the Masai practice also is not unlike that of the Nandi, though it is completed in a shorter time). Both boys and girls are normally circumcised between the ages of twelve and eighteen and after the operation they are subjected to a period of training and discipline, often severe, so that they may become good and useful members of their tribe.

Seclusion after circumcision involves the wearing of special dress, which some-times takes the form of masks which cover the head and shoulders, and are intended to protect the newly initiated from harmful spiritual influences to which at this time of transition they are especially susceptible. Among the Nandi group and some of the Luhya (Kakumega, Tiriki) the boys' mask consists of a grass head-piece which extends over the shoulders; Nandi girls wear a pointed leather hood with two eye-holes. At a certain stage in the Nandi and Masai seclusion period initiates wear clothing of the opposite sex.

Initiation of men, whatever form it may take, is usually connected in East Africa with some kind of institutionalized age-grouping, which may consist of (a) 'age-sets', in which all the people initiated during the same period form a group, which in some cases is an important and essential element in tribal organization; (b) 'age-grades' or stages through which each set of initiates passes in succession; (c) a combination of both age-sets and age-grades. The essential difference between a set and a grade is that a man is either born into a set, or enters it at initiation, remaining a member of it all his life, while the grade is a temporary stage through which he passes during a fixed and limited period of time. Where the combination of set and grade occurs, every set passes through all the grades one after the other, but always retaining its own identity.

The most comprehensive form of age-grouping in East Africa is that of the Galla of Ethiopia, from whom the age-set system spread to other peoples of East

Africa. It consists of an age-set system working within a framework of grades. The males of each Galla tribe were comprised within ten sets called *luba*, which were linked in pairs and ran in two half-cycles of five; the sons of members of the first half-cycle belonged to the set of the second half-cycle which was linked with that of their fathers. Once a man has entered a set he remains in it all his life. During the first forty years of their lives men passed, as members of their sets, through a series of five grades, called *gada*[7], in which they remained for eight years. In the fourth grade they formed the tribal government; one of their number was elected *Abba Boku* (father or possessor of a sceptre) or *Hayu*, and he was the tribal ruler for eight years. At the age of forty they ceased to belong to a grade, but were still members of their set.

The Pokomo of the River Tana have a system of sets and grades which seems to have some relation to those of the Galla, though much modified. Boys in each tribe are circumcised between the ages of six and eighteen, and after circumcision they enter the young men's house, *gane*, and constitute a *luba* or age-set, remaining in the *gane* for about fifteen years. During this time the set is divided into two sections corresponding to the two sections of the tribe and called *honge* and *vibara*; a chief (with the Galla title *hayu*) is chosen from each section, the senior chief belonging alternately to *honge* and *vibara*. In addition to the *luba* are five grades through which every man passes in succession, the first being entered soon after birth, and the second and third before marriage. There is a fee and ceremony for entry into each grade. The last two are the highest, and the *hayu* belong to the most senior.

Other kinds of age-set are not accompanied by institutionalized age-grades. In the Nandi type, a man is born into a set, of which there are seven which succeed each other in a recurring cycle of a hundred and five years; he remains a member of the set all his life. The situation is that at any time, one set is that of the warriors (Nandi *murenet* circumcised man) and is in power for fifteen years; two sets contain the small boys and initiates; and the remaining elders of various ages. At the end of their fifteen year period the warriors hand over power to the set below theirs which has now completed the period during which its members were circumcised. The effect is that each set moves up one place, the small boys becoming initiates, the initiates warriors, and the warriors elders, while the set of the oldest men passes out of existence (all its members being now dead) but immediately begins life again as the new set of small boys. The timing of the circumcision is done by means of alternate flowerings of a bush called *setiot* (*Mimulopsis* sp.) which flowers at intervals of seven to eight years.

Since fifteen years is a long time for a man to be an active warrior, the Nandi have devised a method of solving the difficulty by having an overlap: when a man has completed his circumcision ceremonies, he is allowed to become, unofficially, a junior warrior, though his set does not become the official warrior set till the appointed time comes. The Masai do it differently. Their sets have lost their cyclic character, and the names do not recur regularly. A set is formed, and there are in fact two sets always in existence, a senior set called 'the right hand circumcision' and a junior set called the 'left hand circumcision', the two forming one generation. Each set goes through the same sequence of ceremonies, including a period of three to four years during which all the boys are circumcised, but the formation of the left hand set begins six or seven years after the formation of the right hand set, and since both sets cease to be warriors at the same time, the length of a left hand set is about seven years shorter than that of a right hand set; the left hand is in consequence considered slightly inferior to the right hand[8].

The Suk system consists of (a) the Nandi type of age-set, brought in by the Hill Suk, and (b) the 'color' grouping derived from the Karamojong or a similar source. The first is similar to the Nandi, and is based on circumcision; the second is called *sapana*. This latter seems to have been introduced about 1870, and the two types have not become integrated; if a man goes through the circumcision he may then go through the *sapana* cycle, after which he may marry. The most noticeable external feature is the plastering of the hair with mud; after the *sapana* the young men are initiated into color-groups called *munyan* of which there are two to each *sapana* set.

The Kikuyu have a system of age-sets based on circumcision which takes place every year. An age-set, *rika*, consists of all the boys circumcised during the year; and these sets are grouped into larger sets, also called *rika*, which correspond roughly to the warrior-sets of the Masai and Nandi. Each of the larger sets is in power for a period of twenty to thirty years, and is brought to an end by a handing-over ceremony. In addition to the sets, there are institutionalized grades, which are called *kiama* ('council'). The first is the *kiama kia kamatimo*, with several sub-grades, the first of which a married warrior may join after the birth of his first child, on payment of a fee of one goat to the elders. The other sub-grades are then entered by paying more goats. The second grade is called *kiama kia athamaki*, with three sub-grades, the first of which may be entered when a man's first child is circumcised, likewise on payment of a goat. The senior sub-grade contains the senior elders who form the *ndundu* or inner council.

Here we are getting away from the Hamitic pattern; in other Bantu tribes, like the Isukha, the system is much simpler. The Isukha circumcise boys at intervals of two to five years, and those who are circumcised during the same period form an age-set, *elikhula*, which is given a name when it is formed. The name is generally taken from some current event; but there is no such thing as a specific warrior-set or warrior-period. This kind of set is in fact to a large extent functionless, for beyond acting as a means of linking in a social bond a group of people, it has no

386

part in the political life of the tribe, and not a very strong part in the social life. It is one of those elements borrowed for reasons of prestige which have not affected tribal structure and could have been dropped at any time without injuring it.

All the types which we have been describing are associated with female circumcision, except in the case of the Isukha; and in some tribes there are separate age-sets for women, though these have not the same importance as the men's sets; female age-sets occur among the Pokomo, Kikuyu, and Kamba, but not among the Nandi, Masai, or Isukha.

III

The village, that is a more or less compact group of homesteads occupied by unrelated families, scarcely exists in Kenya. The nearest to it is probably found among the Pokomo, who live in groups of from ten to fifty huts stretched along the banks of the Tana River, or the Nyika, who formerly lived in fortified centers called *kaya*. The *kaya* were built on hills, usually in dense forest, and in them were not only the dwelling-huts of anything up to six hundred inhabitants, but the tribal and clan council-houses; where they survive, the *kaya* are now used only as tribal meeting places. Pastoral peoples tend to live dispersed over the country, but the Masai live in large kraals which are of two kinds: (1) the elders' kraal, *enkang*, where the older men live with the women, children and cattle in fenced compounds holding from twenty to fifty huts, each family having its own gate; (2) the warriors' kraal, *manyata*, an unfenced collection of many huts where the warrior company of a district lives. Both types are very widely spaced, and the warriors' kraals are strategically placed. The Luhya lived in groups of huts surrounded by a mud wall with a gateway, though in some parts there was only a thorn fence; the Luo hut-groups are not real villages, but are occupied by elementary or joint families, surrounded by thick euphorbia hedges, and formerly by mud or even stone walls. The Teita have scattered compounds containing two or three homesteads, with larger clusters of homesteads in some places. The Kikuyu have scattered joint family homesteads, while the Kamba have similar units fenced and grouped in 'parishes'. The Dorobo used to live in small clearings deep in the forest, each containing three or four huts, which were out of sight and sound of others, but grouped in clan areas which formed the political unit.

Other tribes lived in scattered homesteads which were the home of a single elementary family—a man, his wife or wives, children and cattle. The Nandi and Kipsikis are a good example of this type, a homestead consisting of the living hut or huts, bachelor's hut, granary and cattle-fold. These are scattered apparently haphazard over the country, but actually forming units containing twenty to a hundred homesteads which constitute a *koret* or 'parish' with its own council of

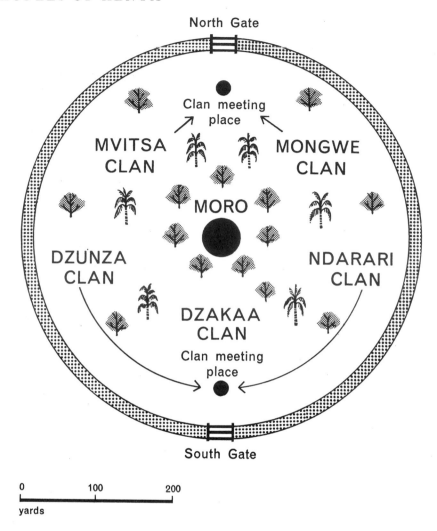

North Gate

Clan meeting
place

MVITSA
CLAN

MONGWE
CLAN

MORO

DZUNZA
CLAN

NDARARI
CLAN

DZAKAA
CLAN

Clan meeting
place

South Gate

0   100   200

yards

elders. The Plains Suk live in structures so flimsy that they can hardly be called huts—rough temporary shelters for a man and his wife and children; the huts of the Hill Suk are more substantial and grouped in 'parishes' like those of the Nandi. The Turkana, too, live in the very roughest kind of structure set up in an enclosure, where a man lives with his wives, each having her own hut or rather shelter and gate.

Associated with the dwellings are the councils of elders which formerly controlled most of the tribes of Kenya, whether they were district-, village-, or clan-councils, and mostly they met in the open. The meeting place was usually a permanent site, and the council often sat under a shady tree; one council place in Nandi forty years ago was marked by a line of six wild fig trees called *choruet* by the Nandi. Even the more advanced Galla met in the open, but they put a hedge or fence round the parliament ground, and in this enclosure lived the magistrates, the *abba boku* or *hayu*, the leader, and the *dori* and *raba*, assessors and judges, whose camps were set about a mile apart. In this enclosure, called *chaffe* or *tarre*, the assemblies were held. It is only among the Nyika that a building is found, and this is the council-house in the fortified *kaya* which has already been mentioned. The *kaya* is a circular clearing in the forest, surrounded by a strong palisade, and entered by two, three or four gates, even the path leading up to it being fenced on each side with poles. Inside were the huts grouped by clans, with the tribal council-house, *moro*, in the center, and the clan council-houses and the shrine containing the tribal emblems (friction and percussion drums, rain-charm, and war-charm) round about it. The area enclosed is often extensive, and part of it was usually cultivated; the *kaya* Kauma was about five hundred yards across from gate to gate, and the *kaya* Duruma at Mtswaraka contained about eight acres, with room for five hundred people in its council-house. Outside each gate there were three others closed by heavy wooden doors; the *kaya* Duruma had two gates outside each of its two entrances.

The Nyika are also the only people in Kenya who set up carved wooden memorials *(vigango)* to the dead. These consist of narrow squared wooden posts carved with various patterns, some terminating in roughly-shaped human heads. These *vigango* are found not only where people are buried near their homes, but also inside the *kaya*, where important people are buried. The Duruma, Giryama, Kauma, Jibana, Chonyi, Kambe, Ribe, and Rabai set up these memorials. The nearest African parallel to these are the carved wooden figures set up by the Konso, a Negro tribe with a megalithic cult in southern Ethiopia; their figures however are much more elaborate than those of the Nyika.

NOTES

1. Where the name of a tribe is written in small capitals it is being mentioned for the first time.
2. (p. 46) Originally a defended place. It is now used to describe an administrative post, as well as any enclosed African habitation.
3. (p. 82) Terms used by the Masai: *manyata* is the warriors camp; *enkang* the fenced enclosure where the elders, women and cattle live.
4. (p. 89) *Journal of the Royal Anthropological Institute*, January–June, 1912, vol. 17, 'The Tharaka'.
5. (p. 144) An account of the Dorobo by G. W. B. Huntingford, 'Social Institutions of the Dorobo' is published in *Anthropos*, vol. XLVI, 1951. He mentions that the Dorobo of Mukogodo do not appear to be true Dorobo in an article in the *Journal of the Royal Anthropological Institute*, 59, 1929, p. 335.
6. (p. 195) I asked the cook of the Park Warden here who is an old Kipsikis for the explanation: *tilet* is a stick which is given to male and female when they are circumcised. This signifies they have been circumcised but have not yet passed out of their initiation period. The stick is used instead of any spear, tool, weapon whilst they are recovering.

   The ceremony of the cutting of the stick takes place at the passing out. After this the girls may take up their tools for cultivating crops and the boys may take their spears, axes, or whatever other implement they may use.
7. (p. 220) For studies on the Masai, by Thomson, Merker, Hollis, Sandford, Huntingford and Fosbroke, see bibliography.
8. (p. 268) Cartilage division between nostrils.
9. (p. 274) Equivalent to a D.O.
10. (p. 313) *The Use of Stilts in Africa and America*, p. 25 (Riksmuseets Etnografiska Avdelning, Stockholm, 1927).
11. (p. 326) The Teita Hills were a dispersal area for nearly all the Kenya tribes whose migrations are described by A. H. J. Prins in *The Coastal Tribes of the North Eastern Bantu*, and by Huntingford in *History and Archaeology in Africa* (School of Oriental-African Studies, University of London, 1955).
12. (p. 326) Census of 1952.
13. (p. 342) Taveta references: A. C. [Sir Claud] Hollis: *Journal of African Society* 1901. Gerhard Lindblom: *Carved Initiation Sticks and Bows from Taveta Kenya Colony* (Stratens Etnografiska Museum Stockholm, 1950).
14. (p. 349) Spitting is of great importance and a sign of blessing among many tribes.

1. (p. 377) This does not mean that no Europeans ever came to the coast, for the Portuguese, coming from the south on their way to India, were here from 1500 to 1700; but their 'occupation' had a very small effect on the African peoples.

2. (p. 379) The total Galla population in Ethiopia may be about two and a half million, and there are a few thousand of them in Kenya. The Somali number perhaps two and a half million, and there may be some seventy thousand of them in Kenya.

3. (p. 380) These Sab are not the same people as those previously mentioned. The word Sab means 'people' but has come to have the significance 'unclean' or 'outcaste'. The Somali do not count the outcaste groups as Somali, some of them do not recognise even the Digil and Rahanwein as Somali, and apply the term 'Sab' to all these groups.

4. (p. 381) The tribes of the Nilo-Hamitic group are these:
   MASAI: *Northern:* Il-Uasin-Gishu*; Il-Aikipyak (Laikipia)*; Samburu.
         Central: Il-Kinopop (Kinangop)*; Il-Kaputie; I-Loitai (Loita).
         Southern: Il-Kisongo (in Tanganyika).
   Those marked * no longer exist.
   NANDI: *Northern:* Kony; Pok; Sapei; Sapaut (on Elgon).
         Eastern: Keyo (Elgeyo); Tuken (Kamasya).
         Southern: Nandi; Kipsikis; Terik.
   SUK: Pokoöt (Suk); Endo; Marakwet.
   TURKANA.

5. (p. 381) The tribes of this group are these:
   Northern: Abakukusu (Mitosh); AbaTatsoni.
   Eastern: AbaNyala (Kabarasi); AbaKakelelwa, who are of Nilotic origin; AbaTsotso; AbaIsukha and AbaIdakho, who together are known as Kakumega; AbaTiriki; AbaRagoli.
   Central: AbaHanga (Wanga, Kawanga); AbaMarama; AbaKisa; AbaNyore or AbaNyole.
   Western: AbaKhaiyo; AbaMarachi; AbaSamia; AbaNyara or AbaNyala.
   Southern: (not reckoned as Luhya): AbaGusii.

6. (p. 384) Tribes which practice or have practiced female circumcision (clitoridectomy) are the Borana, Galla, Somali, Rendile, Masai, Kalenjin, Hill Suk, the Central Kenya Bantu (Meru, Kikuyu, Kamba, etc.), Teita, Taveta, Digo, and Segeju.

7. (p. 385) The following are typical names of *gada*-grades (which varied from group to group) occurring among the Ethiopian Galla; it will be noted that the fourth set is divided into two four-year periods. Entry into all but the first two is by means of ceremonies.

		Ages:		
I.	DOBOLLE	1- 8	Small children.
II.	FOLLE	8-16	Boys.
III.	QONDALA	16-24	'Strong young men'; may marry, but not have children.
IV.	DORI	24-28	Governing grade.
	LUBA	28-32	Circumcision.
V.	YUBA	32-40	Advisory grade; no executive functions. After 40 there are no more grades.

The Southern Borana system differs considerably from that of the rest of the Galla.
A man remains in each of these grades for 8 years. But the *luba*-sets are different, for a man is born into a *luba* and remains in it all his life. The following is a typical Ethiopian Galla *luba* system:

392

| Half-cycle i. (fathers): | 1. Melbah | 2. Mudana | 3. Kilole | 4. Bifole | 5. Mesle |
| Half-cycle ii. (sons): | 6. Harmufa | 7. Robale | 8. Birmaje | 9. Mul'ata | 10. Horata |

After Horata the cycle started again with Melbah.

8. (p. 386) The order of the Nandi age-sets from 1923 to 1938 was: Juma (small boys), Maina (initiates), Nyongi (warriors), Kimnyike, Kaplelach, Kipkoimet, Sawe (the last four elders). In 1938 the order changed, and Sawe became the small boys' set. In the past, the circumcision period began some two years after the handing-over of power, and lasted for four years, the next handing-over coming about eight years later. Among the Masai, a complete 'age' lasted for about twenty-four years:

Year 1-3	Preliminaries for 'right-hand' set to be circumcised.	
Year 4-6	Circumcision of 'right-hand'.	
Year 7	'Right-hand' form warrior companies.	Preliminaries for 'left-hand' set to be circumcised.
Year 9	'Right-hand' become Senior Warriors.	Circumcision of 'left-hand'.
Year 14		'Left-hand' form warrior companies.
Year 16	Senior 'right-hand' marry.	'Left-hand' become Senior Warriors.
Year 19		Senior 'left-hand' marry.
Year 24	End of fighting life of both 'right-hand' and 'left-hand' sets.	

ABBREVIATIONS[1]

P.C.	Provincial Commissioner (in charge of one of the six Provinces: Nyanza, Central, Rift Valley, Coast, Masai, N.F.P.; he is responsible to the Governor).
D.C.	District Commissioner (in charge of one of the districts which make up a Province; he is responsible to the P.C.).
D.O.	District Officer (deals with minor affairs of the district, responsible to the D.C. Chiefs and headmen work under him.)
C.N.C.	Chief Native Commissioner—now called Minister of African Affairs.
N.F.D.	Northern Frontier District, including sub-districts of Isiolo, Marsabit, Garissa, Mandera, Moyale, Wajir—each having a D.C. or D.O. H.Q. is Isiolo. When Turkana was added, the area became too large for a district and was gazetted as N.F.P.
N.F.P.	Northern Frontier Province.
C.M.S.	Church Missionary Society.

1. The abbreviations here listed apply to the period before Kenya became independent

BIBLIOGRAPHY

BUTT, A. J. 1952. *The Nilotes of the Anglo-Egyptian Sudan and Uganda.* Ethnographic Survey of Africa, London. [For the Luo.]

CAGNOLO, C. 1933. *The Akikuyu: their customs, traditions and folklore.* Nyeri, 1933.

CHAMPION, A. M. 1912. The Atharaka. *J. Roy. Anthrop. Inst.*, XLII, pp. 68-90.

CHAMPION, A. M. 1966. *The Agiryama of Kenya.* ed. by John Middleton. Roy. Anthrop. Inst.

FOSBROOKE, H. A. 1948. An Administrative Survey of the Masai Social System. *Tanganyika Notes & Records*, XXVI, pp. 1-50.

GULLIVER, PAMELA and P. H. 1953. *The Central Nilo-Hamites.* Ethnographic Survey of Africa, London. [For the Turkana.]

GULLIVER, P. H. 1955. *The Family Herds.* London.

HAMILTON, R. A. (ed.) 1955. *History and Archaeology in Africa: report of a conference held in July 1953.* School of Oriental and African Studies, London.

HOLLIS, A. C. [Sir Claud] 1905. *The Masai: their language and folklore.* Oxford.

HOLLIS, A. C. [Sir Claud] 1909. *The Nandi: their language and folk-lore.* Oxford.

HUNTINGFORD, G. W. B 1953. *The Southern Nilo-Hamites.* Ethnographic Survey of Africa, London. [For Nandi group, Dorobo, Suk, Masai.]

HUNTINGFORD, G. W. B. 1953. *The Nandi of Kenya.* London.

HUNTINGFORD, G. W. B. 1951. The Social Institutions of the Dorobo. *Anthropos*, XLVI, pp. 1-48.

LEWIS, I. M. 1955. *Peoples of the Horn of Africa: Somali, Afar, and Saho.* Ethnographic Survey of Africa, London.

LEWIS, I. M. 1961. *A pastoral democracy.* Oxford. [The Somali.]

LINDBLOM, [K.] G. 1920. *The Akamba in British East Africa.* Uppsala.

MERKER, M. 1910. *Die Masai.* Berlin.

MIDDLETON, JOHN 1953. *The Kikuyu and Kamba of Kenya.* Ethnographic Survey of Africa, London.

PERISTIANY, J. G. 1939. *The Social Organization of the Kipsigis.* London.

PRINS, A. H. J. 1952. *The Coastal Tribes of the North-eastern Bantu.* Ethnographic Survey of Africa, London.

PRINS, A. H. J. 1961. *The Swahili-speaking peoples of Zanzibar and the East African coast.* Ethnographic Survey of Africa, London.

PRINS, A. H. J. 1963. The Didemic Diarchic Boni. *J. Roy. Anthrop. Inst.*, XCIII, pp. 174-85.

ROUTLEDGE, W. S. and K. 1910. *With a prehistoric people: the Akikuyu of British East Africa.* London.

SANDFORD, G. R. 1919. *An Administrative and Political History of the Masai Reserve.* London.

SPENCER, PAUL 1965. *The Samburu.* London.

THOMSON, J. 1885. *Through Masai Land.* ed. 2. London.

WAGNER, G. 1949. *The Bantu of North Kavirondo.* vol. I. London.

ACKNOWLEDGEMENTS

I wish to thank all those who so generously helped me during the years in which I was making this record, by facilitating my journeys and by helping me to find models. A list of names would include a great many members of the Administration and a great many Headmen, and would be too long to reproduce here, but I would like all to know that I remember them.

I am grateful to The Trustees of the Coryndon, now the National, Museum for allowing me to reproduce paintings in their possession.

I also wish to thank Miss Bulley who kindly made a donation for the specific purpose of enabling me to have more color reproductions in this book than we had planned, without raising its price.

I want too to acknowledge the help I have received from Helen Wolff and Marjorie Villiers in sorting out the great mass of notes which I took during the years in which I was painting the people of Kenya. And finally to record that it was thanks to George, my husband, allowing me to join his safaris and persuading people to sit for me that I was able to paint the tribesmen of the Northern Frontier Province.

INDEX

Figures printed in bold type refer to black and white illustrations, roman numbers to colour plates